JEWS MUST LIVE

AN ACCOUNT OF THE PERSECUTION OF THE WORLD BY ISRAEL ON ALL THE FRONTIERS OF CIVILIZATION

By Samuel Roth

Illustrated by John Conrad

Ostara Publications

Jews Must Live: An Accout of the Persecution of the World by Israel on all the Frontiers of Civilization

By Samuel Roth

Ilustrated by John Conrad

First published 1934

by the Golden Hind Press

This edition 2013

Ostara Publications

http://ostarapublications.com

Contents

"To The First Generation of Jews that will learn how to pronounce my name correctly."

Illustrations

ABOUT THE AUTHOR

About the author: Polish-born Jew Samuel Roth (1893–1974) emigrated to America with his family at the age of four. By the 1920s he was an established poet, with his work published in some major literary outlets.

At the same time, he began publishing erotica, most famously a pirated version of D.H. Lawrence's *Lady Chatterley's Lover*, which, although tame by present-day standards, landed Roth in jail on pornography charges.

Later, he began publishing real pornography and was repeatedly arrested and jailed, eventually serving around nine years behind bars all told.

His last great court case, which took place in 1957 (Roth v. United States, 354 U.S. 476), redefined the Constitutional test for determining what constitutes obscene material unprotected by the First Amendment and became a template for the liberalizing First Amendment decisions of the 1960s.

Jews Must Live

I PROLOGUE—THE GENESIS OF JEW-HATRED

DEAR HERBERT:-

I want you to learn of these things out of the overflowing of my pen, and know my feelings as if you had heard my own voice uttering them. I would not want the tongues of others, strangers or pretenders to my friendship, to touch this story with the sour whimsy of gossip. In any other voice but my own it must sound incredible and ugly that I should have taken this attitude towards our people. But it is not incredible because, as you see by my vouching for it, it is true. And nothing can be entirely without beauty that has lived so close to the fire which consumes.

How shall I get you to understand what an agony of spirit is involved in the launching of this work? It was easy enough to write, I assure you. What I have set down here I had to or go out of my mind. It struck me like a tidal wave; and before I could make any effort to direct it, it bad made an avenue of progress out of every vein and artery of my body, it was riding every one of my living senses: everything I had ever seen, felt, heard and learnt was being welded into artillery and commandeered into action in this new battle of my blood.

Writing the book was really something of an organic necessity. But to give it to the printer, read proofs, arrange pages, and ultimately sign to it my tortured name, that is a metamorphosis I am still agonizing through.

People will say to you: It is obvious that Roth is deplorably blinded by what has happened to him. He apparently got mixed up with a set of ruthless Jews. They fleeced him. And be is ungallantly throwing the onus on the whole Jewish people. Which is unjust and unfair. If it were not for what the Jews did to me, it is possible that I might never have come to this pass, for they lifted me bodily out of the set life of a Jew of forty and carried me here on their own shoulders. Does this impair my case against them? I do not think so. How, I ask you, have messages like this been brought to the world before?

How have people been awakened before, to those strange and terrible visions which have catapulted mankind into what it describes itself today? Would my plea seem more authentic if I presented it in the guise of a series of statistical studies proving what a hideous swamp the Jews have made of Western Civilization? Would it better establish my sincerity if, like one of the minor prophets in Israel, I began my vision with the words *And the Lord appeared to me and said?*

Is there any need to tell you what a lovely, fearful and proud thing my Jewishness has been to me all my life? I remember that when you first wandered into my bookshop on West Eighth Street you sported a silver cross ornament, so far had you strayed from the fenced consciousness of being a Jew. I made no effort, then, to learn how it had come about. I judge now that you must have been born into a particularly ugly corner of Jewish life, and that the cross you wore was merely the symbol of the flash of fancy with which you raised yourself, by your bootstraps one might say, out of a contemptible environment.

My enthusiasm served as a book-chain to drag you back. Yes, I could almost see you change, as day by day you listened to me speak Yiddish and beard me discuss Jewish things. One day the cross disappeared entirely, and you began to speak Yiddish yourself, not badly.

You were present on numerous occasions when I made myself the defender of our national integrity, as when I ordered a celebrated English poet out of my shop because he admitted that he was a contributor to G. K. Chesterton's anti-Semitic weekly.

We lived those days in what the Jews call mockingly the *Olem Hatoi*, the world of illusion, as distinguished from the *Olem Hazai*, the real world, of which they speak with awe and reverence. We looked upon ourselves as free Jews, princes of the world's most precious blood, descendants of the warrior-man Bar Cochba, and of the warrior-princes the Maccabees. For enchantment we had only to sound the names Abraham, Isaac and Moses. For assurance: were we not an active and mighty factor in the upbuilding of America? And for reassurance: were not the deserts of Arabia blossoming under our patient labors of rehabilitation of forty years?

As Jews we were the living embodiment of the vision incarnate. Everything said against us was so much evil slander inspired by envy, disappointment, and an unreasoning hatred-Jew-hatred. Jew-hatred differed from every other hatred in the world because it was altogether inspired by lies. About that there could possibly be no question.

In that spirit I wrote and published two books: *Europe* (Liveright, 1919) and *Now and Forever* (McBride, 1925). Europe was a sort of uncouth epic in free verse in which I attacked Europe for the outrages she had wantonly practised on the Jews during the Great War.

"The face of Israel will shine with power when Europe will be a name difficult to remember," was one of the taunts in it that particularly pleased Israel Zangwill, for he frequently quoted it. *Now and Forever* continued in prose my reprisals against the gentiles, by means of an imaginary conversation on an unimaginable variety of Jewish problems between myself and Zangwill who contributed a characteristic preface.

If I remember correctly you did not like either of these books because, you argued, it should be possible for a man to remain a Jew without developing a serious case of high blood pressure.

But even in the blindness of my racial self-love I was observing things. In *Now and Forever* I pried a surgical knife into the anatomy of the God of Israel. I noticed the earthiness and unloveliness of Jewish women. I pricked the bubble of the theory that Jesus was a man of peace.

I regretted that the Zionists bad not had the fundamental decency to remain faithful—in spite of alluring British promises-to their prewar pledges to Turkey.

And I suggested that I would probably live to see Jews roasted alive on Fifth Avenue. My book was none the less a passionate defense of the Jews against their enemies. Yet, under the heading "A Playboy Prophet in Israel," a man named Franklin Gordon, reviewing my book in *The American Hebrew* of July 10, 1925, wrote:

"What is the significance of this book, its salient characteristic? Perhaps its absolute freedom from cant, its plain speaking. So outspoken is Mr. Roth in voicing his sentiments that that one may question the advisability of having a book like his promiscuously circulated. So much of it is open to misconstruction; so many pages in it could be lifted to serve as material for anti-Jewish propaganda..!

I remember that this paragraph perplexed me a little amused me a great deal more. How could I take seriously the possibility that I might be instrumental in adding to the already overcrowded armory of the enemies of my people? Apparently I had pointed out serious blemishes in our poor defenses. But did even the most fanatic of Jews claim that we were a nation without faults? In their times, did not the Prophets report the blemished of Israel from the housetops? So, secure in my illusions, I rested till the early months of 1933, the year of calamity...

It is one of the felicities of my life that accident, or it may possibly be fate, always dramatizes my misfortunes by setting them up, as they occur, on a promontory. When news of the Nazi warfare against the Jews of Germany blazed out on the front pages of the American press, my own business affairs have just been swallowed in the waves of catastrophe. An employee of mine, a Jew whom I had discharged for dishonesty, had devised a scheme for stealing my publishing business from me. With the help of several of my creditors, all Jews, a happy conspiracy was hatched. The available stock of my publishing firm, over fifty thousand books, well worth thirty thousand dollars, were sold by means of a fraudulent marshall's levy to satisfy a dishonest judgment of some four hundred dollars. I shall go into the details of the sale later—as an illustration of the working of the Jewish lawyer in America—but for the present let it be sufficient for you to know that by that one stroke in the dark, for no inking was given to me either of the judgment or the sale, my estate, worth easily a hundred thousand dollars, built up out of the hard work and consuming enthusiasm of fifteen years, became valueless.

Almost the same day, as it usually happens in my life, the dreadful news from Germany broke. Adolf Hitler, having become Chancellor of the Third Reid in spite of what had appeared to be insurmountable obstacles, was invoking all the powers of his new office against his political rivals, but especially against all of the Jews of the realm. A general boycott had been proclaimed against Jewish business men and Jewish professionals. Jewish lawyers were being ousted from German courts, Jewish doctors from German hospitals, and Nazi troops were stationed in front of Jewish stores to warn Germans against patronizing Jew-owned shops.

Did you ever read Ovrohom Raisin's story of the little ghetto boy who set down in his notebook the Jewish Almanac's figure of the world-population of the Jews, and, as they were reported in the press, subtracted from it the number of Jews killed in the Russian pogroms? As a Jew you know how true a picture of a Jewish child this is. Jewish children are brought up to take to heart all the difficulties of their people, as if what is happening to *Kol Yisroel*[1] is the business of *Ben Yisroel*.[2] They get to feel that way whether they are brought up to it or not.

I was only ten years old when the Kishenev pogrom broke out in 1904. But on account of it I could not eat or sleep well for a month. I knew no one in Kishenev. Like millions of others I had never heard of the place before reports of the massacre emblazoned its name on my revolving mind. It was as if people very close and dear to me had been assaulted. Fifteen years later I was on an Eighth Street crosstown car when a newspaper, opened in a seat opposite me, headlined the news that General Denikin was marching through South Russia at the bead of a vast army bearing on a multitude of banners the slogan: "*Kill the Jews and Save Russia*". Tears gathered in my eyes. I got out at the next corner and wandered about the docks of Manhattan in a daze till past midnight.

And so, in the midst of the news of the misfortune that had befallen the Jews of Germany, I wandered down Broadway, my own plight almost completely forgotten, when I remembered that the Harlans, friends of ours, were coming to the house for dinner. I must get home a little earlier, I thought. But time had already passed me and left me far behind. When I reached home the Harlans were in my library. Cocktails were being served; mine was already set aside for me.

"Still worrying about your business?" asked Mrs. Harlan.

---

[1] *The whole people.*

[2] *A son of the people.*

It was not my business but rather the loss of it that was worrying me, I was about to reply when, suddenly, the peculiarity of my position flashed on me unpleasingly. The Harlans were gentiles. Moreover they had never tried to hide their dislike of Jews as a people. In this tragic moment of my people's disillusionment was I not giving comfort to the enemy? I consider it cowardly and dishonest to entertain such thoughts in secret, so I proceeded to explain myself to the Harlans. A few days ago, I said to them, German Jews and German Gentiles were meeting in a cordial fellowship, such as we are meeting in here tonight. Today, thousands of German Jews are knocking in vain on the doors of erstwhile friends, German Gentiles, for sympathy. Suppose, as appears to me entirely possible, what is happening in Germany today should break out in America tomorrow? I wonder if I might not find myself coming to you to ask you to harbor my children from the violence of the mob, even as Jews are doing in Germany today, only to hear you say, as many an honest German burgher is saying today to a suppliant Jewish neighbor: "*I cannot do what you ask of me. It is against law and order.*"

Mrs. Harlan, whose first novel I had just published, undertook to answer my question. "We do not like Jews, as you know," she said. "But we do like you, and we are particularly fond of your children. If in the fury of mob psychology we should so far forget ourselves as to forget in our anger against your race our affection for you and your children, I suggest that our loss will be even greater than yours."

I felt both mollified and rebuked, and for a while the subject was dropped. After dinner, we played, as usual, two hours of Pope Joan. The game over, Mrs. Harlan leaned back and said: "I should think, after what you've gone through in the last few days, that you'd become something of an anti-Semite yourself."

I looked up with surprise. "Why?"

"If you could forget," she mused, "a lot of what you must have learned in Hebrew school just long enough to get a glimpse of what the Jews are doing to you, you wouldn't have to ask why."

"I see your point," I said. "But how can I let the thought of a few dishonest Jews blur for me the vision of a whole people?"

"But you really m your mind a vision of the whole people?" she pursued. "You have a vision, of course. But it is not a vision which came to you out of the experience of your life. It was imposed on you, like any other form of patriotism when you were too young to examine anything critically. It was grafted into your blood by the rabbis, in the spirit of *my country, right or wrong.*

"You have probably, all your life, suffered experiences such as these at the hands of the Jews you dealt with. But have you allowed your vision of a whole people to be modified ever so slightly? It just simply hasn't occured to you that the living people has to back the living vision, Your vision, believe me, is one thing. What the Jews are in reality is something entirely different."

Such an argument in my own house! I would never have thought it possible. For the moment I was even too stupefied to protest.

"I have heard you talk of your princely Jewish blood," continued Mrs. Harlan. "You may have something of a mystic strain in you yourself. But look at the Jews you associate with. We ate and drank with them at your table. We have been meeting them in your house during the past year. Didn't they continue to come here days after they had secretly sold you out? Are we to accept them as specimens of your princes of the Jews' blood? In the course of our own lives, my husband and I have met many Jews, for how is one to avoid them in New York? But even knowing Jews as genuine as you and your wife has not helped to modify our impression that Jews are a nation of leeches crowding the sensitive arteries of mankind. Take what is happening in Germany."

"Blind race hatred?" I interrupted.

"Conducted by eighty-five million people? Do you believe a whole civilized nation would stand aside, witness what Hitler is doing to the Jews without a protest, unless there were real abuses on t e part of the Jews which justified what is happening?"

I could not permit such an argument to remain unanswered. I told the Harlans vehemently and sincerely that it is wrong to blame a whole people for the malpractises of a few of its members. "You are wrong," I averred, "and so is Hitler's Germany. Germany's Jews have enriched Germany far beyond her capacity for gratitude. Are not Germany's foremost living scientists, doctors and lawyers Jews? We are not mad enough to expect gratitude. But we do ask for a little reasonableness. As for my own difficulties, I added, I don't think I can conscientiously blame the people who cheated me, as Jews. It is so easy to cheat me, the temptation would be too overwhelming even for a society of saints."

The Harlans smiled and tactfully changed the subject of the conversation. I don't think they had the faintest notion of what they had accomplished. For they had opened in me the locked gate of an emotion that must have been pounding away at my heart for a long time. It dawned on me suddenly, blindingly that all the evils of my life had been perpetrated by Jews.

How powerfully woven about me had been my racial illusion that even a suspicion of this had never occurred to me before? The scroll of my life spread itself out before me, and reading it in the glare of a new, savage light, it became a terrible testimony against my people.

The hostility of my parents towards me, reaching back deep into my childhood. My father's fraudulent piety and his impatience with my mother which virtually killed her. The ease with which Frank had sold me out to my detractors.

The Jews whose machinations had three times sent me to prison. The conscienceless lying of that clique of Jewish journalists which built up about my name the libel that I was unfair to the authors of the books I published. And a thousand minor incidents too petty to mention.

I had never stretched out a hand to help a Jew or a Jewess without having had it bitten. I had never entrusted a Jew with a secret which he did not instantly sell cheap to my enemies. It wasn't as if I didn't understand such things. I had myself needed help so many times in my life, and I had always been so grateful for crumbs tossed in my direction. What was wrong with the people who accepted help from me? Was it only an accident that they were Jews?

Please believe me. I tried desperately to put aside this new, this terrible vision of mine. But the Jews themselves would not let me. Day by day, with cruel merciless claws, they dug into my flesh and tore aside the last shreds of the veils of illusion. With the subtle scheming and heartless seizing which is the whole of the Jew's fearful leverage in trade, they drove me from law office to law office and from court to court, until I found myself, before I properly realized it, in the court of bankruptcy. It became so that I could not see a Jew approaching me without my heart rising up within me to mutter: "There goes another Jew-robber, stalking his prey."

And in the meantime, the ages-old Jewish clamor grew noisier and noisier: *Help or we will be exterminated.* The Jewish population of Germany was crying out, just as the Jews of Russia, Poland, France and Roumania had called out before, within my own lifetime. The appeal to me was just as personal as it had been in the days of my illusion: that is a habit one never outlives. But I could no longer make the same response. I found myself in the towering seat of judgment. I felt, in that dizzy position, as helpless as the crew of a ship described in Barbellion's celebrated *Journal.* This crew had become so beloused that they were unable to steer the ship, and so helplessly floated out on it into a stretch of ocean where they died of starvation. On every side I was being eaten alive by Jews. And yet I had to make some answer to that cry. The realization of what that answer must be at first horrified me....

For weeks I went about in a daze. Better, I vowed to myself a thousand times, be quiet, say nothing. But how could I keep quiet? In the name of what should I say nothing? After a lifetime of honest thinking was I to hold back because I could not reconcile myself with an old and apparently unsound tradition? I must give utterance to my feelings or forever after remain in a foul and oppressive darkness. One night, after spending the whole day wandering down the long span of Manhattan, I felt that I could not return home and since my feet would not sustain my wandering any longer, I betook myself to one of those cheap lodging houses on the Bowery where for a quarter they let you have a bed in a dormitory containing about thirty beds.

Old, unshaven, windbitten faces, without a trace of hope or cunning, floated by me as I undressed. And I realized with a warming of my heart why I had come there. It was not the sort of place where one was likely to find a Jew... None of those shrewd robber faces would appear to molest me. ... At last I would be able to sleep: My eyes closed with almost no effort. I slid into a light comforting slumber. . . And then a face an old familiar tortured face, floated into the subconscious area of 'my mind. Maybe I could keep the Jews out of a temporary shelter. But how was I to keep them out of my dreams? The face spoke to me wearily, soothingly: Why have you permitted yourself to get into such a fever? Do you think you are by any chance the first Jew to have been robbed by Jews? See what they did to me. Jews have always been like that. Jews always will be like that. It is not worth bothering about."

"I know," I replied. "But what do you want with me?"

"You seem angry. That is strange. You've spoken and written about me a score of times. But I cannot remember that you were ever angry with me."

"You're a Jew," I said. "And I came here to get away from Jews. What do you want with me?"

"I want to beg a consideration of you. Get out of the habit of talking and writing about my love of Jews. I know you mean well. But do you realize how you mock me when you do that? I remember gladly a warm corner in the synagogue where I first learnt my Hebrew alphabet. But what did I know then about Jews that my love should be remembered, set apart, and singled out for praise? Look at me. I live eternally in a sea of crooked noses, foul teeth, and cruel jibes which you describe as Calvary. Is it just to me that you should go on talking of my love of Jews?"

"I didn't know," I said.

"There is much more you are yet to learn. But don't be afraid. What you are now learning is to be hated, not feared." And the face and the voice vanished.

I lay back on that shallow cot, my eyes fixed on the ashen shadows moving along the old wall before me. "I may not have been the first Jew wronged by Jews," I vowed to myself. "But I will be the first Jew to arise and tell the truth about them." From that point on I slept peacefully.

Somewhere in the Bible I must have read the line *I will utterly destroy this people, saith the Lord God*. Was it Jehovah speaking to Moses about the people he had just led out of Egypt? Whoever wrote that line had it in his heart about the Jews as I have it in my heart today. Disraeli set the Jewish fashion of saying that every country has the sort of Jews it deserves. It may also be true that the Jews have only the sorts of enemies they deserve, too.

And suppose I wanted to keep this terrible secret of mine? Where, supposing I had the strength to bear such a burden, would I hide it? On my back? The Jews themselves would pursue me through the streets, as the children pursued Elijah, and call hunchback after me. In my heart? They would be sure to spy the swelling, mistake the bulk for bidden treasure, and I would find myself engaged in constantly tearing their filthy fingers out of my bosom. At home? I have growing children there. I would as soon think of keeping sticks of dynamite loose about my house...

"But you're a Jew, our brother!" I hear a million little oilemhazainikis cry.

Very well. I have always accepted this responsibility solemnly. I shall not fail you this time, I promise. I will make myself worthy of the honor.

Sarah at the Tent Door

II THE JEW-HATRED OF *GENESIS*

The scrolls unroll before me. "*In the beginning God created the heavens and the earth. And the earth was unformed and void, and darkness was on the face of the deep.*" The very first words I ever read. They are still the most beautiful words I know. "*Baaraishes buroo Elohim as hashamayimm ve-hu-uretz. Ve-hu-urtez hoysu sehoi uvohoi, vechoischach aal penai tehoim.*" That is how the words actually sounded. I read on through the unfolding scrolls, from the first word to the last, and the ancient wonder stirs into music for me again. Good, deep, true lovely old, book. It tells a straightforward honest story. None of the illusions, following which I almost broke my neck, are here. Only the rabbis lied to me.

The first time I heard the words of the poet-author of *Genesis* it was from the mouth of my father, and I revered him as if he were himself their author. My father's father was a great man in the country in which I was born: I heard him recite Hebrew words one Yom Kippur night, and he wavered like a great god with wings between the two tall taper lights on each side of the Ark of the Covenant. My father had three brothers, each as tall and as stalwart as himself: occasionally Hebrew words would emanate from them, and they appeared to grow into godhood in front of my eyes.

They are all dead now except one. I realized long before they died that they were not gods. My father's father, his father before him, and all the Jewish fathers yielding all the way back to Abraham the father of them all—they were all Jews, far, far from gods.

No one knew this better than that wise poet-author of *Genesis*—now that I have learned how to read him correctly. "*And there was a famine in the land,*" he relates, "*and Abram went down into Egypt to sojourn there: for the famine was sore in the, land. And it came to pass when he was come near to enter into Egypt that he said unto Sarah, his wife: Behold now, I know that thou art a fair woman to look upon. And it will come to pass when the Egyptian will see thee, that they will say:*

'This is his wife,' and they will kill me, but thee they will keep alive. Say, I pray thee, thou art my sister; that it may be well with me for thy sake, and that my soul may live because of thee. And it came to pass, that, when Abram was come into Egypt, the Egyptians beheld the woman that she was very fair. And the princes of Pharaoh saw her, and praised her to Pharaoh; and the woman was taken into Pharaoh's house. And he dealt well with Abram for her sake; and he had sheep, and oxen, and he-asses, and men-servants and maid-servants, and she-asses and camels.

And the Lord plagued Pharaoh and his house with great plagues because of Sarai Abram's wife. And Pharaoh called Abram and said: 'What is this that thou hast done unto me? Why didst thou not tell me that she was thy wife? Why saidst thou, She is my sister? so that I took her to be my wife,· now therefor behold thy wife, take her, and go thy way.' And Pharaoh gave men charge concerning him; and they brought him on the way, and his wife, and all that they had. (13) And Abram went up out of Egypt, he, and his wife and all that he had, and Lot with him, into the South. And Abram was very rich in cattle, in silver, and in gold."[3]

Apparently these words describe one of the very early stages in the career of this nomad chieftain to whom the blood of our race rolls back. By the evidence of the little (practically nothing outside of his wife's beauty) he brought along with him to Egypt Abraham was rich only in his dreams of the future.

Else—supposing as we have no right to, that he had a strength such as is not represented by worldly goods—why should he have been afraid of Pharaoh? But there can be no misunderstanding the nature of this little jaunt of Abraham's. It was only one of several such raids told with cynical politeness as to detail by the author of *Genesis*. There probably were more raids which it was pointless to record. One thing is certain: those visits were not motivated by friendliness.

According to the most reliable historians of that period the nomads wandered through many countries, sometimes by pre-arrangement with those countries, but more frequently in the spirit

---

[3] *All Biblical quotations in this book are from the Jewish Publication Society translation, accepted by the Jews as the most faithful to the original Hebrew, obtainable in English.*

of sheer invasion. The historian of the *Encyclopaedia Brittanica* says: "In times of draught and food-shortage such nomads as these ... were compelled to raid their agricultural, settled neighbors."

But in that first recorded trip to Egypt, Abraham, of whom the ancient historian Nicolaus of Damascus wrote that he "*came with an army out of the land above Babylon*" and "*reigned at Damascus*," was not yet strong enough to enrich himself by violence. There are, however, more ways than one of making conquest. The one chosen by Abraham, and resulting in his being laden by Pharaoh with presents for the favors of his beautiful wife, has become a very popular occupation.

Apparently, also, few of the tricks in the game as it is played today were unknown to Abraham. How else are we to understand these words in *Genesis*: "*The Lord plagued Pharaoh and his house with great plagues because of Sarai Abram's wife.*"

I cannot accept the popular anti-Semitic interpretation that Abraham and his wife suffered of a venereal disease. On the contrary I do not think anything physical is implied here at all. Whenever he means to convey the idea of a physical ailment the poet of *Genesis* is always at great pains to name it. Here he merely says that the Lord plagued Pharaoh and his house. Is it too rash to assume that this plague sounds a little more like blackmail than syphillis? Or why, if this is not true, is the poet at pains to explain that when Abraham returned with his family out of Egypt he "*was very rich in cattle, in silver, and in gold.*"

That Abraham, having discovered this new racket, decided to practise it further, becomes apparent when he repeats the adventure in a similar manner before the king of another people. "*And Abraham journeyed from thence toward the land of the South and dwelt between Kadesh and Gerar. And Abraham said of Sarah and his wife: 'She is my sister.'*[4] *And Abimelech King of Gerar sent, and took Sarah. But God came to Abimelech in a dream of the night, and said to him: 'Behold, thou shalt die, because of the woman that thou hast taken; for she is a man's wife.' Now Abimelech had not come near her; and he said: 'Lord, wilt thou slay even a righteous nation? Said he not himself unto*

---

[4] *Even the bare pretense that this is done for fear of his life is abandoned in the telling of the second adventure.*

me : she is my sister? and she, even herself said: He is my brother. In the simplicity of my heart and the innocency of my hands have I done this.' And God said unto him in the dream: 'Yea, I know that in the simplicity of thy heart hast thou done this, and also witheld thee from sinning against Me.

Therefore suffered I thee not to touch her. Now therefore restore the man's wife; for he is a prophet, and he shall pray for thee, and thou shalt live; and if thou restore her not, know that thou shalt surely die, thou, and all that are thine.' And Abimelech rose early in the morning, and called all his servants, and told them all these things in their ears; and the men were sore afraid.

Then Abimelech called Abraham, and said unto him: 'What hast thou done unto us? and wherein have I sinned against thee, that thou hast brought on me and on my kingdom a great sin? Thou hast done deeds unto me that ought not to be done.' And Abimelech said unto Abraham: 'What sawest thou that thou hast done this thing?'

And Abraham said: 'Because I thought: Surely the fear of God is not in this place: and they will slay me for my wife's sake. And moreover, she is indeed my sister, the daughter of my father, but not the daughter of my mother; and so she became my wife. And it came to pass when God caused me to wander from my father's house, that I said unto her: 'This is thy kindness which thou shalt show unto me; at every place whither we shall come, say of me: he is my brother.' And Abimelech took sheep, and oxen, and men-servants and women-servants, and gave them unto Abraham, and restored him Sarah his wife.

And Abimelech said : 'Behold , my land is before thee: dwell where it pleaseth thee.' And unto Sarah he said: 'Behold I have given thy brother a thousand pieces of silver; behold , it is for thee a covering of the eyes[5] to all who are with thee; and before all men thou art righted.' "

Abraham became a really rich man. There was too much for him to lose now if having tried this little game, it should happen to fail. Besides, having had the greater means, there were other grander schemes to work.

The story of Abraham becomes eloquent with intrigues and alliances between himself and other desert bandits and—God. He solemnly announces his allegiance to a new Deity, and, probably to

---

[5] 'Covering of the eyes' the oriental expression for 'hushmoney.'

economize on the expensive materials which went into the making of idols, and to save himself the trouble of having to cart them about with him in the desert, he invented God's incorporeality. This carried him far into the esteem of his gaping contemporaries. Only one thing seemed to trouble him: the lack of a son to inherit the spoils and found a new nation in his name, as he had promised himself in his dreams.

Genesis reports that Abraham was not really very particular. Finding himself too old to beget children of his own, Abraham was quite content to let Ishmael, a son by his wife's servant Hagar, to be his heir. If the passion of the narrative here is to be trusted, Abraham was more than ordinarily fond of Ishmael. But Sarah had never forgiven Hagar for laughing at her, and as she hated Hagar she loathed Hagar's offspring.

No under no circumstances was that obnoxious handmaiden of hers to fall heir to the name and riches of Abraham. Rather, since Abraham was too old for the hope of a child by him, would it be a son of her own by the seed of another man which might fructify within her.[6] Nothing is clearer in the book of *Genesis* than that Sarah was a shrew, and that Abraham was a henpecked husband.

The stream of the narrative in *Genesis* is often turbulent and unclear because it is really two narratives blended into one, with .spots where the process of blending was not so successfully accomplished. But the unfolding of the strange circumstances leading to the birth of Isaac is not the result of this difficulty. It must have been told quite honestly by the author (or authors) of *Genesis;* but it was obviously tampered with by those Hebrew scholars in Alexandria who committed most of the mischief in Biblical exegesis. Here is the passage as it is given to us today:

"And the Lord appeared unto him (Abraham) by the terebinths of Mamre, as he sat in the tent door in the heat of the day; and lifted his eyes and looked; and lo, three men stood over against him; and when he saw them, he ran to meet them from the tent door, and bowed down to the earth, and said: 'My LORD, if now I have found favor in thy sight, pass not away, I pray thee, from thy servant. Let now a little water be fetched, and wash your feet and recline yourself under the

---

[6] *A barren woman is a firm believer in her husband's barrenness.*

17

tree. And I will fetch a morsel of bread, and stay ye your heart; after that ye shall pass on, foreasmuch as ye are come to your servant.' And they said: 'So do as thou hast aid.' And Abraham hastened into the tent unto Sarah, and said: Make ready quickly three measures of fine meal knead it and make cakes.'

And Abraham ran unto the herd, and fetched a calf tender and good, and gave it unto the servant; and he hastened to dress it. And he took curd, and milk, and the calf which he had dressed and set it before them and he stood by them under the tree, and they did eat. And they said unto him: 'Where is Sarah thy wife?' And he said: 'Behold, in the tent.'

And he said: 'I will certainly return to thee when the season cometh round, and lo Sarah thy wife shall have a son.' And Sarah heard in the tent door which was behind him. Now Abraham and Sarah were old, and well stricken in age, it had ceased to be with Sarah after the manner of women. And Sarah laughed within herself, saying: 'After I have waxed old shall I have pleasure,[7] my lord being old also?'

And the Lord said unto Abraham: 'Wherefore did Sarah laugh, saying: Shall I of a surety bear a child, who am old? Is anything too hard for the Lord? At the set time I will return unto thee, when the season cometh round, and Sarah shall have a son.' Then Sarah denied, saying: 'I laughed not,' for she was afraid. And He said: 'Nay but thou didst laugh.'"

Until the very last bantering words it is wildly possible that a story as gravely beautiful, as poetically sincere as *Genesis* might have confused humanity and divinity so badly. But would even the most rabid apologist for Abraham and our national pride insist that the Lord carried on such petty and utterly useless banter with the woman Sarah?

Notice that three people appear before Abraham. Three people are fed by him, and fed "to stay the heart," an expression that would never have occurred to the original author if he tried to convey the impression that Abraham knew he was entertaining the Lord himself. But Abraham, you will notice, carries on his conversation with only one. The expurgators of the Bible who here did their best

---

[7] *The issue is whether Abraham shall have an heir. But notice what the old bitch is thinking about.*

to veil the clear sense of the narrative, would have you believe that the trio consisted of God and two of his angels.

Nothing concerning their nature is said or hinted in the first part of the narrative here quoted. But in the next part, when, their leader having remained behind to converse with Abraham, the two are described entering the city of Sodom, the Alexandria meddlers seem to have made up their' minds, and those who are described as men in Chapter 18 are definitely referred to as angels in Chapter 19. This inconsistency is made plausible by the fact that the Hebrew word *maluchim* means both angels and messengers.

Now to any intelligent unprejudiced reader it should become obvious from the fact that Abraham greets three visitors and holds conversation with only one, that the one was some important local chieftain, on his way to prosecute an important business and that the two who accompanied him were his bodyguards. To prove that these two were servants and not angels, it is only necessary to prove that their master was a man, and not God.

The Hebrew text, so inexpertly tampered with, proves this conclusively. The word Lord is written in two ways in Hebrew. When intended to denote the Deity it is spelled Yahweh, and pronounced Adenoi. But when the word is intended to denote a human master the word Adenoi is spelled as it is pronounced. In that part of the narrative where I reproduced the word LORD in capitals, the expurgators of Genesis—who faltered so frequently in their mystifications—spelled the word Adenoi, as appertaining to a man.

Instead of being, what it has been made to appear, a meeting between Abraham and God, the incident is merely that of a meeting between Abraham and one of his more powerful neighbor chieftains.

His message to Abraham is in effect:

Obviously, Abraham, you are not a man to trifle with. One capable of inventing your particular monstrosity of a god, should be consulted on all important desert matters. Well, I don't like the behavior of the people in Sodom. I understand the lovemaking of man and woman because it is sweet and fruitful.

But what comes of the love of man and man and woman and woman? Certainly nothing that can be seen by the naked eye. And what a terrible example for our children. And what of the future of the race?

Their destruction which is certain should be hastened. Towards that end I have sent my messengers ahead for a view of their fortifications. Then we'll knock hell out of them.

So much for our moral chieftain's message. He began by accepting Abraham's hospitality, and, with the insolence of the just, ended by proposing to provide him with an heir.[8]

It is to be presumed from the context that the beauty of Sarah was as well-known as Abraham's unfortunate lack of an heir; so that when this chieftain saw the aged desert beauty winking at him from behind the doorway it was only natural for him to become licentiously interested.

But are you not going a bit too far from the accepted reading of the story, I can hear the reader ask.

In proof of my belief that the incident as I quote it from the Old Testament has been tampered with[9] and that the story is really as I am setting it forth, I offer the corroboration of Philo Judaeaus, the greatest Hebrew scholar of all time. Philo, who lived about 10 B C., must have had available the unaltered text of Genesis.[10]

Here is his version of the matter:

---

[8] *The reader might object that Abraham could hardly believe that a son would be his, if he were born of another man's seed. A modern Abraham might not. But the ancient Hebrews had a peculiar attitude in such matters. I refer you to verse 6, chapter 38 of Genesis: "And Judah took a wife for Er his firstborn, and her name was Tamar. And Er Judah's firstborn, was wicked in the sight of the Lord: and the Lord slew him. And Judah said unto Onan: 'Go in unto thy brother's wife, and perform the duty of a husband's brother unto her, and raise up seed unto thy brother.'" But how, it may be asked, could the chieftain so glibly promise that the issue would be a boy, and not a girl? The Arabians had a conceit about such matters, and thought they knew by position in love how to predetermine the sex of a child. Besides, an enamored man tries to be not accurate but persuasive.*

[9] *The prevailing edition of* Genesis *has the Lord saying to Abraham that his seed would be a stranger in a land not theirs and be afflicted for 400 years. In the version of* Genesis *available to Philo the text read 40 years. Here, too, you see the hand of the expurgator attempting to connect this prophesy with the Jews' eventual sojourn in Egypt.*

[10] *A similar accusation is made in the Koran. Several instances of vital falsification are cited. But the Koran is a very poor critic of almost everything else,· and so I hesitate to cite it even where it is correct.*

"And when those persons, having been entertained in his house, address their entertainer in an affectionate manner, it is again one of them who promises that he will himself be present, and will bestow on him a seed of a child of his own, speaking in the following words: 'I will return again and visit thee again, according to the time of life, and Sarah thy wife shall have a son.'"

Apparently the Old Testament's tamperers cut down his lordship's proposed two visits to one, for it is only too obvious from the original, as quoted by Philo, that the first visit, "according to the time of life," was for the sowing of the seed, and the second, that he might see the seed in flower.

But Abraham lived to bitterly regret this bargain. The account Genesis gives us of Isaac, his indolence, his lack of pride and venturesomeness, makes him a pale ragged figure beside that of the flaming Ishmael. The more Abraham looked at Isaac, the son of a stranger by his wife, the more he loved Ishmael, sprung from his own loins.

He grew to hate Isaac with a terrible hatred, and it seems altogether likely to me that Abraham would have thought of the sacrifice of Isaac even without divine intervention.

If Isaac died, Abraham decided, he would never again let Sarah inveigle him into such an arrangement. And, whether Sarah liked it or not, Ishmael would inherit everything.

If my suggestion that Abraham really took Isaac into the wilderness, when Sarah happened not to be aware, with the object of murdering him, is not true, why was Abraham so secretive about his operations! It could not be that he was performing a religious rite. All other religious rites Abraham performed within sight of all his family and servants.

The carelessness of our Hebrew fathers with regard to the chastity of their wives passes on in the same deliberate tradition, to Isaac. When, like his father, Isaac fell upon evil days, he wandered out with his family into the land of the Philistines, the people ruled by Abimelech whose affair with Isaac's mother had been so costly to the tribal treasury.

"And," records Genesis, *"Isaac dwelt in Gerar. And the men, of the place asked him of his wife, and he said: 'She is my sister; for he feared*

to say: 'My wife, lest the men of the place should kill me for Rebekah, because she is fair to look upon.' And it came to pass when he had been there a long time that Abimelech king of the Philistines looked out at a window and saw and behold, Isaac was sporting with Rebekah his wife.

And Abimelech called Isaac and said: "Behold of a surety she is thy wife, and how saidst thou: she is my sister?" And Isaac said unto him: 'Because I said: Lest I die because of her.' And Abimelech said: 'What is this thou hast on; unto us? One of the people might easily have lain with thy wife,[11] and thou wouldst have brought guiltiness upon us.' And Abimelech charged all the people saying: 'He that toucheth this man or his wife shall surely be put to death.'

And Isaac sowed in that land, and found in the same year a hundredfold; and the Lord blessed him. And the man waxed great, and grew more and more until he grew very great. And he had possessions of herds, and a great household; and the Philistines envied him."

It must have been this propensity to trade the favors of their women for gold that caused the Jews to be held in such abhorrence by the ancient world.

How deep-stung was this hatred of Jews in olden times is testified to eloquently by the author of *Genesis* in his description of the feast set for Joseph for his brethren:

"And Joseph made haste; for his heart yearned towards his brother; and he sought where to weep; and he entered into his chamber and he wept there. And he washed his face, and came out; and he refrained him self, and said: 'Set on bread.' And they set on for him by himself, for them by themselves; because the Egyptians might not eat bread with the Hebrews; for that is an abomination for the Egyptians."

That is all. The subject matter is never again broached either in *Genesis* or in the rest of the Old Testament. Why did not the author of Genesis, who had such a deep respect for Egypt, make some effort to explain Egypt's contempt for the Jews?

He might at least have tried to explain why the Egyptians at that table, all inferior to Joseph in rank, would have felt it an abomination to eat with him? His complete indifference to the matter is a more terrible accusation against the Jews than any to be found in the works

---

[11] *What a compliment this is to Rebekah's virtue!*

of Livy and Apion. But might there not have been some explanation which was torn out of its context by the great expurgators?

The portrait of the third of the great founders of our blood is done in even more lurid colors. Jacob did not stop after stealing his brother Esau's birthright: *"And it came to pass,"* runs the story, *"that when Isaac was old, and his eyes were dim, so that he could not see, he called Esau his elder son, and said unto him: 'My son;' and he said unto him: 'Here am I.' And he said: 'Behold, now, I am old, I know not the day of my death. Now therefore take, I pray thee, thy weapons, thy quiver and thy bow, and go out to the field, and take me venison; and make me savoury food, such as I love, and bring it to me, that I may eat; that my soul may bless me before I die.'*

And Rebekah heard when Isaac spoke to Esau his son. And Esau went to the field to hunt for venison, and to bring it. And Rebekah spoke unto Jacob her son, saying: 'behold, I heard thy father speak unto Esau thy brother, saying: Bring me venison, and make me savoury food, that I may eat, and bless thee before the Lord before my death. Now therefore, my son, hearken to my voice according to that which I command thee. Go now to the flock, and fetch me from thence two good kids of the goats; and I will make them savoury food for thy father, that he may eat, so that he may bless thee before his death.'

And Jacob said to Rebekah his mother: 'Behold, Esau my brother is a hairy man, and I am a smooth man. My father peradventure will feel me, and I shall seem to him as a mocker; and I shall bring a curse upon me and not a blessing.'

And his mother said unto him: 'Upon me be thy curse, my son only hearken to my voice, and go fetch me them.' And he went, and fetched, and brought them to his mother; and his mother made savoury food, such as his father loved.

And Rebekah took the choicest garments of Esau her eldest son, which were with her in the house, and put them upon Jacob the younger son.

And she put the skins of the kids of the goats upon his hands, and upon the smooth of his neck, And she gave the savoury food and the bread, which she had prepared, into the hand of her son Jacob. And he came unto his father and said 'My father;' and he said : 'Here am I, who art thou, my son?' And Jacob said unto his father: 'I am Esau thy firstborn; I have done according as thou hast badest me. Arise, I pray thee, sit and eat of my venison, that thy soul may bless me.' And Isaac said unto his son: 'How is it that thou hast found it so quickly, my son?' And he said: 'Because the Lord thy God sent me good speed.'

And Isaac said unto Jacob: 'Come near I pray thee, that I may feel thee, my son, whether thou be my very son Esau or not.'

And Jacob went near unto Issac his father; and he felt him, and said: 'The voice is the voice of Jacob but the hands are the hands of Esau.' And he discerned him not because his hands were hairy, as his brother Esau's hands, so he blessed him...

And it came to pass, as soon as Isaac had made an end of blessing Jacob, and Jacob was yet scarce gone out from the presence of Isaac his father, that Esau his brother came in from the hunting.

And he also made savoury food, and brought it unto his father; and he said unto his father: 'Let my father arise and eat of his son's venison, that thy soul may bless me.' And Isaac his father said unto him: 'Who art thou?' And he said: 'I am thy son, thy firstborn Esau.'

And Isaac trembled very exceedingly, and said: 'Who, then, is he that hath taken venison, and brought it me, and I have eaten of all before thou camest, and have blessed him? Yea, and he shall be blessed.' When Esau heard the words of his father he cried with an exceeding great and bitter cry. . . '

When the children, in the old little synagogue where I learnt my Hebrew letters, came to this portion of the Law, the rabbi would add: "And the cry which Esau uttered was so terrible that the fiery Gehannah itself opened before him."

The rabbi must have added this to frighten us, to give us an inkling of what a monster out of Hell the man Esau was, so as to make us loathe the hairy man.

Instead, a thrill of sympathy shot through me for the cheated Esau. In my heart, I must have loved him more than I loved Jacob.

Only one thing relieves the portrait of Jacob, this man of monstrous cunning and endless guile: his love for Rachel. The appearance of Rachel introduces a new element into the story of the Hebrew race. Unlike the wives of Abraham and Isaac, shrews of the shrillest, order Rachel was beautiful and gentle.

One can almost see her softening influence on the character of her husband who combined business subtlety with a fierce determination to rise even above the birthright he had purchased. The delicate fingers of Rachel soften some of the hard lines in the portrait of Jacob.

Pursuit of a Murderous Instinct

III IS MONOTHEISM A PURELY JEWISH CONCEPTION?

What have we thus far?

The portraits of three subtle barbarians. Our forefathers, yes, but barbarians. Shrewd, careful, sinister, adventurous, bargain-driving, wily men—but barbarians just the same. It is not mentioned by the author of *Genesis* whether they could read or write. And so steeped are their portraits in the very blackest colors of barbarism that to suppose them to have been literate is the very wildest flight of fancy. There they are: three old barbarians. As I look upon them I wonder how their names could have inspired the world with such awe; I wonder which of the three I dislike the least. A conclusion not difficult to reach. Much can be forgiven Abraham for his power as a warrior. Much more will be conceded to Jacob for his tenderness for the woman Rachel. But what shall redeem for us the centuries of fantastic devotion which we heaped upon the lazy, stupid swaggering figure of Isaac?

But you are forgetting something, I can almost hear the rabbis object. You have not only Abraham, Isaac and Jacob. You have also Monotheism.

Ah, Monotheism! I had almost forgotten it!

I do not think the average scholar will attach much value to my opinion on the importance to civilization of the monotheistic conception of the universe. Philosophers, ethical philosophers in particular, usually rate it—the conception, of course,--very highly. But these same kindly people invariably conceive of human history in terms of a cycle of progress, which is only one of the many ways in which they give expression to their delightful naiveté. As for me, the word progress itself has always appeared as a sort of inverted mirage. Nevertheless I know that the world in which we live is devoted to the idea of progress, so much so that it has made of the theory of evolution—that scientific development of the idea of progress which the late Jacques Loeb riddled so devastatingly—a sort of modern religion.

This same world holds in a towering esteem the monotheistic conception of the universe. So that at the basis of every reputable historian's work is the undisputed hypothesis that it is one of the three essential pillars of European civilization. Rome, he would solemnly have you believe, gave the world its laws. Athens, its arts. Jerusalem, monotheism.

It is clear that these historians build not out of what they know but of what they have been told. It is an exercise in mortification to observe them at their work. They go to the library for the bare facts and no-one can find fault with the ardor with which they pursue their studies. But when it comes to reaching the very simplest conclusion—which alone could justify their labors—they go for it to their church.

First observation: God has never offered himself in the same form to two races. To one race he has appeared in the form of the stump of a tree. To another as the sun; to still another as the moon. Dependmg on the nature of the recipient of the vision, God has appeared as a bull, a cow, a tiger, a donkey, a creature with two heads, one a lion, the other a dog; to another race, with an instinctive reluctance to bother with expensive images, he appeared totally invisible.

Second observation: The meaning of God has never been the same to two races of mankind. To one race he would appear as the creator of a universe the gradual dissolution of which was to him a matter of amused indifference. To another he was a vengeful demon who was continually stayed from destroying it, only by the most lavish sacrifices offered up to him by men. Man, like God, creates in his own image. And Zeus is as peculiar to the Romans as Jupiter is to the Greeks.

Now nothing has a more obvious stamp of truth than the assertion that everything in an organic universe goes back to one primal seed out of which all the known forms of life sprouted and developed. Once you have conceded this singular genesis, it is almost gratifying to personify it and endow this personality with the charm power and humour of an omnipotent creator. And yet, except to be used by one class of people as a symbol by which to dominate another of what use to mankind is this fictitious centralized deity?

Someone should make a creditable beginning of the denial of monotheism before the imagination of the race is completely destroyed by it. As a matter of fact, life does manifest itself to our senses in many different forms. The best we can see for the beginning of any form of life is some accident in space to which it might be traced by a wisdom as yet unknown to us. Why, therefore, should we confine all of the phenomena of life to one major accident! Why could there not have been many accidents, quite unrelated to one another? But, to return to the original question, why cannot the historians go for their conclusions to the facts which they investigate so zealously?

If the footnotes with which these historians strew the margins of their texts tell an honest story, they do a great deal of varied reading and research. Yet you do not have to go very far into historic origins to recognize that every ancient literature embodies, in one form or another, the monotheistic idea. Indeed, many works based on it antedate the writings of Deutor-lssaiah (in whom the Jewish conception reaches a measure of clearness and sincerity) by a thousand years and more. Zarathustra who lived some time in 800 B.C., and might almost be said to have been a contemporary of lssaiah's, certainly expressed the same idea in much loftier if less passionate imagistic speech.

Why, then, is Jerusalem credited with monotheism? Party because, while the disciples of Zarathustra tended to their homefires in India and Arabia, the Jews, through Mohammed and Jesus, shot the idea of one God to the north and the south of the Mediterranean. But chiefly because the Jews themselves, Torah in hand, and the cry *Hear O Israel, the Lord our God, the Lord is One* on their lips, insinuated Monotheism into every nook and cranny of the earth. True or not, the belief that monotheism sprang forth from the racial genius of the Jews has become so common that even the official enemies of the Jews—and some of them, such as G. K. Chesterton and Hillaire Belloc, should know better,—do not trouble to deny it. Their attitude seems to be that it would be much simpler to deny altogether the value of monotheism and create a better repute for the virtues of paganism, than to try to wrest this brass laurel from the crown of Israel.

There have been, as a matter of fact, two dissenting voices, voices ventured forward so meekly, that they have scarcely been heard· the voice of Ernest Renan, who spent a lifetime on Semitic studies only to discover when he was too old to tum to anything else, that the whole matter (learning and people) were exceedingly distasteful to him; and the voice of William Robertson Smith, a Scottish theologian whose only radical departure from custom was to occasionally drop the William from his name.

Renan cautiously propounded the theory that monotheism was really an instinct, and that a semitic one; therefore the universal belief that it was inimical to the Hebrew race should be modified. Smith, who probably never gained access to the writings of his delicate French contemporary, brings his even more dilatory argument to a head with the suggestion that "what is often described as a natural tendency of semitic religion toward ethical monotheism is in main nothing more than a consequence of the alliance of religion and monarchy."

Of the Jews themselves, however, the attitude of Rabbi David Phillipson is typically cocksure: "The Hebrews alone of all semitic peoples reached the stage of pure monotheism through the teachings of their prophets; however, it required centuries of development before every trace of idolatry disappeared even from among them, and before they stood forth as 'a unique people on earth,' worshippers of the God, and Him alone."

We must, however, get ourselves a more impartial definition of monotheism than the pronouncement of this pompous rabbi. We find one in the essays of Dr. George Galloway who describes monotheism as "the ripest expression of the religious consciousness. It rests on the conviction that the ethical and religious values must have a sufficient ground and, this is the one God on whom all existence and value depend."

A good definition this. Probably as good a one as will ever be offered. I had this definition in mind while going through the Old Testament again. During a rather careful rereading in which it became increasingly clear to me that I was the book's first intelligent reader in two thousand years[12]—I find that, with the exception of the first cloven chapters of Genesis, which might or might not have been written by a Jew, there is not much more than an occasional hint of the monotheistic idea to be found in this whole structure of Judges, Kings and Prophets. The conception of God in the first eleven chapters of Genesis is singularly lofty.[13] After that, it becomes the portrait of an ordinary tribal god; except that in none of the chronicles of tribal gods that have come within my reading range, have I encountered a tribal god as cruel, jealous, lustful, mean, lying, cheating and treacherous as that great little guinea pig the God of Israel.

The very opening words of the twelfth chapter of Genesis begin to set the character of the God of Israel: *"Now the Lord said unto Abram: 'Get thee out of thy country, and from thy kindred, and from thy father's house, unto the land that I will show thee. And I will make thee a great nation, and I will bless thee and make thy name great; and be thou a blessing. And I will bless them that bless thee, and him that curseth thee will I curse, and in thee shall all the families of the earth be blessed."*

To be a true and just God, in accordance with the monotheistic ideal, God would have to be aloof from all men. So it is a bit surprising that his first human announcement should be that he has made an alliance with a man. More regrettably, no reason is assigned for his selection of Abraham for such an important business: it seems an affair like love at first sight, where the object has as yet to prove worthiness. But there is here one touch of true monotheism; for, be God's reasons for choosing Abraham sufficient or not, He does promise that "in thee shall all the families of the earth be blessed."

---

[12] *It would here be to the point to remind the reader that for nearly three hundred years millions of intelligent people read and recited the most famous of Shakespeare's sonnets in the belief that they were addressed to a woman. The discovery that they were writ ten to a man—and could not possibly have been inspired by a woman—was not made till the very end of the nineteenth century.*

[13] *This is the only drawback to the theory that Genesis is really two narratives blended into one. How can two men of such imaginativeness have written at the same time and in the same country?*

The promise continues in the fourteenth verse of the next chapter: *"And the Lord said unto Abram, after that Lot was separated from him: 'Lift up now thine eyes, and look from the place where thou art northward and southward and eastward and westward; for all the land which thou seest, to thee will I give it and to thy seed forever. And I will make thy seed as the dust of the earth; so that if a man can number the dust of the earth, then shall thy seed also be numbered. Arise, walk thou through the land in the length of it and in the breadth of it; for unto thee will I give it."*

It is only natural, if God has chosen to work his wonders for the rest of the world through Israel, that the latter should be endowed with some fertile territory to develop in. But in the opening of the fifteenth chapter the operations of the Lord become definitely suspicious: *"After these things the word of the Lord came unto Abram in a vision, saying: 'Fear not, Abram, I am thy shield, thy reward shall be exceeding great.'"*

If Israel is to become a blessing for the nations what evils would there be to shield Israel from? And why this offer of an excessive reward as if it were not a reward but a bribe? What are Israel's labors to consist of? In return for what particular favors to the Lord are such lavish favors being offered?

The Lord's frankness to his dearly beloved chosen ones increases. In the opening words of the fifteenth chapter we get a rather definite intimation of what the Lord expects of his people Israel. *"And he said unto Abram: 'Know of a surety that thy seed shall be a stranger in a land that is not theirs, and shall serve them; and they shall afflict them four hundred years; and also that nation whom they shall serve, will I judge; and afterward shall they come out with great substance.'"*

Can the last words of this momentous passage mean what they appear to tell on the surface? Is God really promising Abraham that some day the nation to develop out of his seed will be permitted by the Lord to loot a nation that is not their own?

If there is any doubt that the meaning is precisely what appears on the surface of God's words it is dispelled by verse nineteen of the third chapter of Exodus: *"And I know that the King of Egypt will not give you leave to go,"* God says to Moses, *"except by a mighty hand. And I will put forth My hand, and smite Egypt with all My wonders which I will do in the midst thereof. And after that he; will let you go. And I will give this people favor in the eyes of the Egyptians. And it shall come to pass that, when ye go, ye shall not go empty; but every woman will ask of her neighbor, and of her that sojourneth in her house, jewels of silver, and jewels of gold; and raiment; and ye shall put them upon your sons, and upon your daughters; and ye shall spoil the Egyptians!"*

When an English novelist, Charles Dickens, portrayed in a great novel, *Oliver Twist*, a Jew named Fagin, instructing little English boys in the art of pocket-kerchief snatching, a howl of protest went up from universal Jewry that resounded through every corner of the civilized world.

Dickens was excoriated as a liar and a Jew-hater. The book, one of the most beautiful in all literature, was declared to be a nasty deliberatively venomous slander of a noble, long suffering race. Bt when it is our own sacred book of record, instructing our children in the very lowest possible way to rob their neighbors it is to be regarded as sacred scripture and unimpeachable evidence of the nobility of our racial character.

But you do not have to wait till Exodus to discover the true character of the God of Israel, to realize what a palpable sham and hollow pretense is this promise of his, through the goodness of Israel to bless the families of the earth. In his first and only interview with Isaac the second of that great thievish triumvirate,[14] he betrays what is his real attitude towards the rest of the nations:

"And Isaac went unto Abimelech king of the Philistines unto Gerar. And the Lord appeared unto him and said: 'Go not down into Egypt; dwell in the land which I shall tell thee of. Sojourn in this land and I will be with thee, and will bless thee; for unto thee, and unto thy seed, I will give all these lands, and I will establish the oath which I swore unto Abraham, thy father."

This land in which the blessers of the world were to develop their peculiar talents was to be taken away, stolen outright, not in the name of any political or commercial treaty, but in the name of a mysterious arrangement with the divinity, from the people who had cultivated it and who were still in peaceful possession of it.

[14] *God, it would seem, had no better opinion of Isaac than did his father Abraham. For, having once addressed him, he never troubled himself with Isaac again.*

"But," I can hear a pompous rabbinical voice intervening, "these Canaanites were just so many pagans, and unworthy of a land as fruitful as Palestine."

The Old Testament here is a deadly witness against the integrity of the God of Israel, and especially against the cynical Jewish claim that the best proof of Israel's superiority over the rest of the nations of the earth is in Israel's survival. Yes, Israel did eventually conquer all of Canaan and put most of its inhabitants to the sword. But compare the Hebrews described thus far, with the people ruled by Abimelech, King of the Philistines. How pure and beautiful they appear to be, compared with the Jews, especially in that marvelous line spoken by Abimelech, after he had caught Isaac disporting himself in public with the woman he had pretended was his sister. Instead of just kicking Isaac out of his domain as he might very well have done without any difficulty, he turned to him and said: *What is this that thou hast done unto us? One of my people might easily have lain with thy wife, and thou wouldst have brought guiltiness upon us.* If there is a nobler, more moral speech in the literature of the world I have not come across it. It certainly shows that these Canaanites were more sensitive to fine moral values than even the most loquacious of the Hebrew prophets. If the Jews survived, as they did, a people so much nobler than themselves, what is there left to say for the virtues of mere survival?

The only Jewish effort to explain away this horrible enigma was made in his vast history of the Jews by Professor Heinrich Graetz. Graetz tried, in a half-hearted round-about way, to develop a rationale for the Jewish claim to the lands of the Canaanite nations. "These claims," he wrote, "derived further strength from the tradition left by the patriarchs to their descendents as a sacred bequest, that the Deity, whom they had been the first to recognize, bad repeatedly and indubitably, though only in visions, promised them this land as their possession, not merely for the sake of showing them favor, but as the means for attaining a higher degree of culture. This culture would frequently consist in Abraham's doctrine of a purer belief in the One God, whose nature differed essentially from that of the gods whom the various nations represented in the shape of idols and by means of other senseless conceptions. The higher recognition of the

Deity was designed to lead Abraham's posterity to the practise of justice towards all men, in contradiction to the injustice universally prevailing in those days."

This is a very remarkable paragraph. If I had it in my power, I would post it on the door of every synagogue in the world. For it embodies in a few innocently meant words almost every form and species of our peculiar Jewish hypocrisy.

To begin with (1.), there is the remarkable assertion (put forth so brazenly that, offhand, no one would think of disputing it) that the Jews were the first people in the world to conceive of the idea of a One God Universe. When you remember that this was an illiterate and unlettered people born into a world already vastly enriched by every species of literature, that their first exercise in writing was in Chaldean (the Yiddish of their time), with centuries to elapse before they would develop their own language, the conceit is too pitiable even to laugh at.

2. That the conception of the One God as a God of Justice and mercy was an innovation that was not only Jewish but would have been impossible of conception except by Jews. This of a people born in bastardy, weaned on pillage, and brought to the estate of a nation in a state of such constant butchery that the average life of their kings on a throne was something like two and a half years.

3. That religious belief is the very highest form of culture, that there cannot be any culture outside of faith and prayer.

4. That for the expression of a profoundly divine idea, gossip is more effective than the art of sculpture. The Old Testament itself is replete with expressions of contempt for images, those painted as well as those molded out of wet clay. It would have been a relief to find in a people, deprived of the privilege of sharing so much loveliness, at least a sincere expression of regret. But no, Jews must take pride in their aesthetic castration as far forward as the end of the nineteenth century.

5. That the covenant between Abraham and God was an unselfish one, aimed at the enrichment not of Israel but of the world of na tions about him.

And lastly (6.), that before the appearance of the Jews, the world was a den of vice and iniquity. Abraham, Graetz would have you believe, caught the first human glimpse of God, and with the opening of his eyes let the first ray of good dawn on an unborn moral world. What Graetz and the rest of the Jewish apologists today call the Jews' very own peculiar monotheism (without a murmur of protest from a stupified world), began life two thousand years ago as a simple but totally incredible explanation of the unwarranted stealing of a peaceful country by a horde of savages.

The explanation of seizure by divine inspiration was not a new one to the world. It had already grown old with mankind when it was put forth. But once offered, the credulity with which it has been met is truly amazing.

Never before had national thieving been brought to such a high estate and rendered so precious in the annals of man.

I believe I have shown how little there was in the history of the Jews before Moses to justify the world's even entertaining the idea of their divine choice as the chosen people of God. What do we find after the advent of Moses?

In one Midianite camp alone, the Lord God supervised the captrue of six hundred and seventy-five thousand sheep, seventy-two thousand oxen, sixty-one thousand asses, and thirty-two thousand virgins. All the men, and all the wives, and all the male children were massacred; the girls and the booty were divided between the Jews and their Lord God.

In Jericho, at the instigation of Joshua, who was impatient with details, the Lord of Israel placed an anathema over the whole population. He massacred them all, Virgins and asses alike, and spared only the harlot Rahab for sheltering the Jewish spies who had reached there in advance of this sacred expedition.

A whole tribe, or almost all of it, was slaughtered in civil war at one time, without anyone raising a finger to stop it.

Twenty six nations in all were conquered by this great and just Lord God. For one of them, Amalak, whose sin was that they had the insolence to dispute the Jews invasion of Canaan by way of their own territory, God conceived such a deadly hatred of that be ordered the wholesale destruction of the nation, men, women, children and cattle, that even their remembrance might fade out under the heavens.

All this towards what end! That the Jews might be able to besnot the plains of Canaan with a national life that has not a single artistic grace to relieve its monotonous and fearful ugliness.

You have here a portrait not only of the God of Israel but of his chosen people as well. Man, like God, creates in his own image.

UNCLE MOSES: *Just a fencing bout . . .*
UNCLE SAM: *Fencing bout hell. This is a fight to a finish.*

IV JEW-HATRED AS A NATURAL INSTINCT

But what sort of speech is this for a Jew, you are probably asking yourself, by this time? I can see the question half-glimmering in your eyes. My answer must be steel set in granite. The dew of compassion has entirely dried up in my bowels.

I am myself a Jew, I know it. But I am a Jew who has been brought to the point where he so loathes his people that he thinks in terms of their destruction. No, it has not escaped me that the destruction of Israel would mean my own end, too. I would not want to survive in a world without Jews.

Yet, by God, I don't know how I shall ever again contentedly live with them: I pray for my own effacement as fervently as I pray for theirs. This is a work of terror, and I am trying to make a terribly good job of it. I have taken out the old Jewish carcass to expose it in the sun. I shall rub it till every sore on it shines like a planet of light.

I know how well the Jews have earned the hatred which is in my heart towards them. I do not doubt that they have earned in equally good measure the hatred which the nations entertained towards them since records of such international courtesies have been made.

Anti-semitism is the natural effect of a social cause. I cannot understand why such a deep mystery is made of this simple cause.

The causes of anti-semitism lie in the very deepest recesses of human nature. They are like pebbles at the bottom of a very deep stream. But the waters of the stream are clear and I have no difficulty making them out.

The first cause of Jew-hatred goes back to the nature of Jewish leadership, a black veil on the conscience of the race. The second goes back to the nature of the people itself, and it is an evil no less foul. The first appears to be an evil without a remedy. But the second does not seem to me impossible to deal with.

Beginning with the Lord God of Israel himself , it was the successive leaders of Israel who one by one foregathered and guided the tragic career of the Jews—tragic to the Jews and no less tragic to the neighbouring nations who have suffered them. But we must have been a pretty horrible people to start with. Our major vice of old as of today, is parasitism. We are a people of vultures living on the labor and the good nature of the rest of the world.

But, despite our faults, we would never have done so much dam age to the world if it had not been for our genius for evil leadership. Granted our parasitism. But Parasitism is a virtue as well as an evil. Certain germ-parasites are essential to the steady flow of blood through the arteries of an organic body. Certain social parasites, by the same dispensation, are important to the functioning of the blood of the body politic. The shame of Israel comes not of our being the bankers and the old clothesmen of the world. It comes, rather, of the stupendous hypocrisy and cruelty imposed on us by our fatal leadership, and by us on the rest of the world.

The whole career of Jewry divides itself for me into three distinctive and significant parts. The first was the period of the patriarchs when the Jews were numerically so inferior to the nations about them that they practically never went out to war against them but depended, for looting them, on the success of such little games as palming off wives as sisters and buying birthrights.

The second period was the long national rest in Goshen, and the subsequent flight from Egypt, during which the Jews discovered, to their own amazement that they had grown into a population of more than two million people. They were now so superior numerically to the little tribes and kingdoms of Arabia, who stood in the way of their march on Canaan, that it was practically no effort to slaughter them. And so they did. This second period lasted about two centuries to the anguish of a bleeding peninsula.

The inevitable followed, and that brings us into the third major division of Jewish history. The wrath of the larger nations to the north and the west of Judaea was aroused against the usurpers. One by one they swooped down on the Jews. The tide of conquest turned; it was now the Jews who were slaughtered and taken into captivity almost at will. At one time nearly three quarters of the whole Jewish nation was seized and carried into a captivity from which it was never returned. It took a little time for this "stiff-necked people," as the prophets called them, to realize that once more it was they who were numerically inferior to their enemies. The realization sank in slowly but surely.

Wisdom pointed out a reversal of national policy. The time when they could destroy their neighbor-nations by violence being definitely at an end, did they give up the national ghost? Ah, no. For the first of all Jewish creeds is that Jews must live. It does not matter how, by what or to what end? Jews must live. And so a return was made to the ancient policy of conquest by the more peaceful and delicate methods of cheating, lying and pimping.

See the Jews swinging forth triumphantly out of the haphazard crossing through the Red Sea. Behind them their old neighbors the Egyptians are drowning in the waves loosed by the all-just Lord God of Israel. There is a theory that the parting of the waters of the Sea, and the closing up of the waters, the first to let the Jews go through, and the second to drown their Egyptian pursuers, were part of a great engineering feat worked out by Moses and his advisors. I don't think it makes any difference by what agency this business was accomplished; the nature of it alone is important to bear in mind. And the triumph of the escaped servants, laden with the loot stolen from their masters.

Moses and his sister Miriam are singing to Israel. They are singing a new song. It is a song of triumph such as the Hebrews have never sung or listened to before. The people join lustily in the renascence of an old passion—the passion to destroy by violence, hitherto unknown to their cringing natures. Every Jewish crisis seems to have had its particular bitch-Jewess. Miriam was the bitch-Jewess of that crisis.

We can safely set our faces away from the beauty and good voice of Miriam. But the figure of Moses, singing to them in a high voice, and at the same time speaking soothingly to them in a deadly undertone, is not one to overlook:

"I will sing to the Lord, for He is highly exalted;
The horse and His rider hath He thrown into the Sea.
The Lord is my strength and song,

And He is become my salvation;
This is my God, and I will glorify Him;
My father's God and I will exalt Him.
The Lord is a man of war.
The Lord is His name."

The Lord is highly exalted. But not because he is the Lord of the Universe. Not because he is the creator of heaven and earth. The Lord has been promoted. He has become a doer of much grander deeds. *"The horse and his rider hath He thrown into the Sea."* The Lord is the hero of Israel's great hour of triumph.

You have heard the voice of Moses singing aloud. Much more terrible is the roll of his voice as he whispers in a soothing undertone: "You are a holy people. A people superior to and set apart from the rest of the peoples of the earth. For the rest of the people worship Idols and Images.

What are idols and images? Things made out of wood, stone and brass. If the idol is of wood, stone will break him. If he is of stone, brass will crumble him into shapelessness. And if the idol be made of brass a metal stronger than brass will be found to shatter him. But what can be found between Heaven and earth to destroy your God? There he is, your Lord God, high in the sky, where no human being can reach him even with the aid of the eye. There is deep wisdom in having a God whom your neighbor cannot possibly reach either to jostle him or to implore his favors. That is your wisdom, my people, that is your strength. It elevates you to a place so much higher than your ignorant neighbors that you really need give them no consideration whatsoever."

With that music in their ears the Jews proceed to annihilate their neighbors. They go about it like a nation of trained butchers. Nowhere in the history of the world, not even in the story of Timur who "built his ghastly tower of eighty thousand human skulls" is found such sweet relish in sheer butchery. But wait. Something happens to relieve the awful tensionn of this ghastly song. Moses has gone up unto the mountain of the Lord to arrange a set of laws for even thieves need a code to go by.

No ordinary Jew is this man Moses. But a mighty big man. A man big enough to go up the whole height of Sinai and get together with the big mogul of the mountain. For forty days they wrestle with the task and during those forty days Moses neither eats, drinks nor sleeps, by way of emulating the big boss who doesn't have to. On the fortieth day the Lord looks up from the tablets of fire, and down the mountains, and turns his dreadful face to Moses in a savage humour.

"Look down, Moses."—

"Yes, Lord." —

"What do you see?"—

"The tops of rocks and trees, singed by your last passage down the slope."—

"Don't you see your precious people, Moses?"—

"No, Lord. You forget that my eyes are only human."—

"Well, if you could see with my eyes, you'd behold those insects of yours dancing around a calf—a golden calf."—

"Ah, the boys are playing again!"—

"They made a personal covenant with me, Moses."—

"Sure they did. I'm your witness. But what's one or more covenants among good fellows!"—

"Moses."—

"Yes, my Lord."—

"Of what use is it, I ask you, to write laws for such people?"—

"Are you asking me? I told you the answer to that one the first time you tried to scare me from behind a burning gooseberry bush."—

"I remember. You were right, too, and I knew it. But I was trying to keep a covenant of my own. This time I am going to destroy them, the whole damn lot of them."—

"You should have done that in the first place. It would have saved plenty of humiliation all around."—

"Well it's not too late to do it now."—

"It may not be too late. But this isn't really the right time for it, Lord."—

"You're trying to dissuade me Moses. You've become fond of the wretched beggars, and you're trying to dissuade me from destroying them. I tell you I'm going to destroy them, and no one is going to stop me."—

"I didn't say you couldn't destroy them, my Lord. I said you shouldn't. And I said that for your sake, not for theirs.

"Remember when you proposed to me the first time to take them out of Egypt? And how set I was against it? I told you the whole story then, Lord. They're a lousy, thieving quarrelsome people, every bit as like their ancestors Abraham, Isaac and Jacob as vermin grown to the stature of men can be.

"I don't know how you happened to get on such intimate terms with the like of Abraham, Isaac and Jacob. But I didn't ask you then. I'm not asking you now. We all make our mistakes. But why bother with their foul offspring, I asked? Well, there was that damned covenant. And you would fulfill it, and you've done everything you could to do so. As usual, I let you have your own way about it.

"You rooted them out of their precious dungheaps in Goshen, even though you had to do it at the expense of all those swell Egyptians, making the green waters of the Nile run red like the nose of Pharaoh after the queen has violently tweaked it for him.

"Has there been one moment since that terrible day you put me at the head of them in which you weren't sorry for having started the whole affair? Believe me, I loathe them the more every day I see them. Nothing would please me better than to see them utterly destroyed, completely wiped out.

"Old as I am, I'd lovingly go back to swineherding whenever you can arrange to let me off. But I must think of you, Lord, your reputation. So thinking, I advise you not to do it. Destroy them by all means. But not now. Let them get into Canaan first.

"You will in that way fulfill your covenant with their vermin-ridden forefathers and save your reputation amongst the nations. Yes, it comes to that. The Egyptians, for instance, think ill enough of you for associating with Jews. If you crush out their loathsome blood here against the desert rocks and sands, what do you think they'll say?

"They'll say that you fooled the Jews out of Egypt just for the pleasure of squeezing the life out of them in the loneliness of the desert."—

The Lord listens, and he softens. Moses is right. It would hurt his reputation abroad if he took it out of the Jews in this out of the way hole. For the time being, he will let them alone. And so he places the golden tablets with his own hands in the arms of Moses and watches ironically the big man's meditative descent down the slope. Moses, lovingly embracing the results of those labors of forty days and forty nights, reaches the foot of the mountain. And now it is his turn to see with naked eyes what the Mogul beheld looking down from his mountain.

And seeing the jubilant Jews making gay circles around the golden calf, and singing obscene songs as they danced, the hunger in his belly gnawed savagely into his heart and anger like a hot brand flamed up in the starved bowels of the man Moses.

Up went the great arms clutching the tablets and with such force did he fling them against the rocks at the bottom of Sinai that no one has been able to find a whole fragment of them since that time.

Forgotten was the sweet wisdom with which he had dissuaded the Lord from destroying the Jews. In the anger engendered in him by the sight of what had so angered the Lord, he gave the most horrible order for slaughter ever given.

Let every man now proceed to kill the man next to him, he cried out, and a hundred and eighty-six thousand Jews had been slain when the anger of Moses had sufficiently subsided for him to countermand the terrible command.[15]

Moses was a big and terrible man. A man whose soul had great spaces in it. Spaces wide enough to contain the leering face of Elohim forty years of patience in Midbur, and the contemplation of a horde of savages who had no stomach for the uncertainties of the pace he set them.

Moses was a man good to look upon, and he must have been beautiful to behold even when, standing at the foot of Sinai, he perceived the Israelites make a thigh-dance around the abomination of gold.

But, in his way, Aaron was a man of a deeper and sweeter understanding than that great brother of his who could not find in his vast heart a little patience for the Jewish weakness for idols—even for one little golden calf.

Aaron understood. And because he felt that the worship of idols was a good thing for the soul of Israel, even the worship of a golden

---

[15] *You will take notice here that I quote the Bible only when I find that I cannot improve on it.*

calf, he countenanced the business of creating it in the absence of Moses.

"See," said the Jews to Aaron, "all the people about us worship idols. There is no way of becoming friendly with the people about us except to get together with them in idol worship. Are we always to do nothing but murder and move on?"

It must have been from words such as these that Aaron understood why the Jews wanted to go back to idol worship. Half of the Old Testament—Genesis, Exodus, Leviticus, Numbers, Deuteronomy (the world's most beautiful farewell oration), Joshua, Judges and Samuel—is a ballad of Israel resting from the labors of following some evil leader to immerse itself in the delights of idolatry.

Read the story for yourself. Moses dies, so the Jews return to idolatry. Joshua, strengthened by the co-operation of Judah, gains dominance over the people, once more the song of the Lord resounds, and more little tribes and nations are hammered into the dust. Joshua dies, and instantly the Jews return to idolatry.

Gideon brings them back to God and slaughter, and so the race continues to run with the judges and prophets of Israel leading them to slaughter and the people making every possible effort to return to idolatry and a peaceful way of living.

The rabbis have, of course, their explanation of this phenomenon. The idea of an immaterial God was too fine to be grasped by an unlettered desert people all by itself. With the help of a leader intoning into their ears they might grasp the idea and hold it. They could be trusted to hold on to the idea only as long as the leader kept his watchful eye on them. Their song master gone, it was only natural that the Jews should slide back into the low state from which they had been uplifted.

But the explanation I am inclined to believe is the one that must have been in the mind of Aaron when he consented to the making of the golden calf. The Jews, however much they may have enjoyed the violence prophecy required of them, had the gregarious instincts of all other human peoples.

They wanted a little companionship, a little conviviality. By imposing on them the idea that they were, by their affinity with the Lord God, too good to associate with the rest of the tribes in Arabia, the Judges and Prophets threw Israel into a fearful loneliness. It might be a very fine thing, thought the Jews, to be a holy people, if you don't happen to be the only holy people. What fun can there possibly be in being God's chosen people, if there is no one you can talk to about it?

All things considered, it is remarkable how the leaders of the Jews continually managed to force them out of the idolatry they so ardently longed for, and which, during the brief spells in which they were permitted to enjoy it unmolested, must have made them feel human again.

A savage, ruthless and invulnerable people were those prophets and judges in Israel. Up to our own time the making of an idol is an abomination in Israel. Intermarrying with the gentiles is successfully forbidden by the rabbis who in our time take the places of the judges and prophets of old, when marrying Jews and Jewesses must be so painful.

With that invisible wall (more formidable than the great Wall of China which can be seen by the naked eye) erected about them, the Jews marched north, east and west. At one time or another they have been in trouble in almost every branch of what is now the civilized world.

England, among the first European countries to be adopted by Jews as their homeland, expelled them bodily and precipitously in the year 1290. Edward I made a great sacrifice when he did that, because the Jews loaned him money at much easier interest than was demanded by the Italian bankers from Lombardy. But that was the way of the Jews. They asked almost nothing for their money from the king of England—so that when the rest of the people complained to him of their heartlessness he would have reason to keep his ears closed to their crying.

But there is just so much of the protesting of even the most slavish populace that a king can ignore with safety. Edward I knew that, and when he realized that the patience of England was at an end, he signed the famous edict.

So grateful to him for that edict was the population of Britain that even the peasants (whom the Jews had never trusted with money) contributed to a popular subscription of money presented to their king which made it unnecessary for him to ever borrow money again. Edward I booting some fourteen thousand Jews across the English channel, set a fashion that was quickly followed by Italy, Spain, Portugal, France and Germany.

The tide of immigration now turned eastward—into Poland, Russia and the other slavonic nations. But as sure as it had followed them everywhere else, Jew-hatred developed in Poland and in Russia. We have witnessed during the latter part of the nineteenth century and during the early years of the twentieth a revival in the east of the virulent anti-semitism of the west.

The hellish tortures of the Inquisition were rivalled by the pogrom and the boycott. France, which dismissed the Jews in the thirteenth century and readmitted them in the fifteenth, burst into the epic of the Dreyfus case just when Russia was multiplying pogroms. Germany, which had never taken decisive action against the Jews, has broken into such anti-semitic activity that she may destroy herself in the agony of it.

In the ensuing chapters of this book I shall take up one by one both the alleged and the real causes of anti-semitism. Here I merely wish to reaffirm the fact that anti-semitism is so instinctive that it may quite simply be called one of the primal instincts of mankind, one of the important instincts by which the race helps to preserve itself against total destruction.

I cannot emphasize the matter too strongly. Anti-semitism is not, as Jews have tried to make the world believe, an active prejudice. It is a deeply hidden instinct with which every man is born. He remains unconscious of it, as of all other instincts of self-preservation, until something happens to awaken it. Just as when something flies in the direction of your eyes, the eyelids close instantly and of their own accord. So swiftly and surely is the instinct of anti-semitism awakened in man.

If it were true, as the Jews claim, that the gentiles lay violent hands on them purely out of prejudice against their religion, out of envy of their superior commercial genius, how would the Jews ever get into a civilized country to begin with?

Have not Jews been admitted from time immemorial, freely, kindly, almost happily by every nation at whose gate they have knocked for admittance? The story of the Jews, as they have themselves written it out, has always gone out ahead of them, to spread through the foreign peoples and evoke in their minds curiosity and pity. Have the Jews ever had to petition a country for admission—the first time?

Read for yourself the story of the progress of Jewry through Europe and America.

Wherever they come they are welcomed, permitted to settle down, and join in the general business of the community. But one by one the industries of the country close to them because of unfair practices—until, it being impossible to longer hold in check the wrath of a betrayed people, there is violence and, inevitably, an ignominious ejection of the whole race from the land.

There is not a single instance when the Jews have not fully deserved the bitter fruit of the fury of their persecutors. Except possibly what is happening in Germany today. But I shall take up this matter in its proper place.

In those European countries where the Jews have not been reduced to the status of a second rate citizenry (like the negroes in the south) the feeling against the Jews is increasing swiftly and heading matters decisively in that direction.

In Roumania and in Austria there is constant street-violence against Jews. In England and in France the influence of the Jews in politics, business and the professions has created an atmosphere so stifling to the natives that a whole press has sprung up in those countries whose sole business is advocating another, but this time permanent expulsion of the Jews.

Speaking of the press, do not think there is a single news paper in Europe which is friendly to the Jews.

Even in America, the most patient of the western nations, things are coming to a head. It is no secret that the immigration restriction laws passed a generation ago were levelled chiefly against the Jews. Industry after industry has taken steps to exclude Jews as employees. The civil population is chafing under the abuses of Jewish doctors and Jewish lawyers.

There is blood in the eye of Uncle Sam as he looks across the ringside at the pudgy, smiling Uncle Moses.

"Just a fencing bout," says Uncle Moses reassuringly.

"Fencing bout hell," growls Uncle Sam. "This is a fight to a finish."

In just such a position a Pharoah in Egypt once reasoned: "Behold the people of the children of Israel are too many and too mighty for us; come let us deal wisely with them lest they multiply, and it come to pass, that when there befalleth us any war, they also join themselves unto our enemies, and fight against us, and get them up out of the land."

It has become the reasoning of every king and congress of every country invaded by the Jewish People. It has never changed because the nature of the Jews has undergone no reasonable change. We are still the seed of Abraham, Isaac and Jacob. We come to the nations pretending to escape persecution, we the most deadly persecutors in all the wretched annals of man.

Apion, in his vicious and lying arguments against the Jews, tried to spread the infamy that the Jews were leprous and instead of running away from Egypt, were really kicked out of it.

Apion was probably as great a liar as any Alexandrian rabbi of his day. There is no reason to believe that the Jews were any less healthy than the other wanderers in the wildernesses of Asia and Africa who had the hygienic sagacity to finecomb their hair at least once every other week. But I remember, in this connection, Franz Oppenheimer's brilliant theory concerning the formation of states.

In the beginning, he argues, there are two kinds of communities from which the state is evolved: the peaceful, unchartered tillers of the soil who may be compared collectively to the passive female organ; and the bands of wandering marauders whose only means of living is to fall on one or more of these peaceful settlements, enslave them and commercialize their talents and labors.

This second type of community he compared to the male. When these two meet, and one penetrates the other, the theory goes on, conception takes place, and there is a blessed event—the birth of a new state.

The Jewish nation certainly constitutes a community such as Franz Oppenheimer designates as the male organ. The organ is constantly at work and may be depended on for services in and out of time. But there is a grave difficulty.

The organ is diseased. The disease is a sort of moral gonorrhea known as Judaism, and seems to be, alas, incurable. The results of such mating, as any good doctor will tell you, are invariably treacherous and unhealthy. If you are in doubt take a look at any Jew-ridden country in Europe. If you need to be further convinced, take a look at what's happening in America.

Always Take!

V LEOLOM TICKACH: ALWAYS TAKE

I was born in (N)ustchar[16] a village on the river Strippa, where Austrian Poland relinquished her nationals to the less tender mercies of the Russian Empire. As well as I can remember, we were one of less than a dozen Jewish families in the environs. Only four of them are completely within my recollection. Lippe Goy was a breeder of pigs. Reb Sholom the lumber merchant had a mortgage on the village church at whose iron door he collected a toll every Sunday morning from the worshippers—to reduce his mortgage.

The Tavias ran the big inn (which had once belonged to my grandfather) at the crossroads leading from (N)ustcha to Pidlipitz; and we operated a new, smaller inn on the hillside leading to the church. I learned to read the Bible when I was barely two years old. I had just passed my third year when my father deposited me in the home of an aunt of mine in Zborow, further down the river, because, he said, there was nothing left that he could teach me.

I knew even in (N)ustcha that the gentiles regarded us with a terrible loathing. But how was it possible for them to love us?

Lippe Goy sold them sick pigs at prices which would have been too much to pay for healthy ones. The Tavias made them drunk at the inn every Saturday night, and robbed them of their week's wages (just as they had robbed my grandfather of the Inn); and Reb Sholom every Sunday morning, including Christmas, sent his wife with the church-key to collect the toll or refuse to open the iron door to the worshippers.

I once heard my father wonder that Reb Sholom's wife who was cross-eyed and bad never been taught how to count beyond ten, should invariably come home from these jaunts with the correct sum.

---

[16] *I had always heard the word pronounced as Nustcha, and so I have spelled it in several books of mine in which I had occasion to refer to the village of my birth. But I have learned, since, that the real spelling of the word is Ustcha.*

My family's position in the village was a trifle better than that of the rest of the Jews. My grandfather and his four sons had made of themselves a sort of local legend. Without ever having been known to lay violent hands on a human being, the old man had established a reputation for great physical strength and courage.[17]

He also had a cunning in dealing with people in matters of business, though he had never been known to employ it dishonestly.[18] All in all, we had never been known to deal evilly by any of the gentiles· and since the Jews had robbed us as well as themselves, the goyim had a sort of softness for us. But that applied only to the older men and women. To the children we were just *zhidas,* like the children of Lippe Goy, Tavia and Reb Sholom; and when I accompanied my sister to the village spring for water they invariably threw stones at us.

My earliest knowledge of the Jewish attitude towards their gentile neighbors came from listening at our Inn to the stories of Jewish travellers (who stopped with us for a drink or a night's lodging) about their business dealings with the goyim. To my innocent brain it appeared that the whole purpose of a Jew in business was to get the best of the goy.

When the goy had been cheated business was good. When the Jew bad just come out even, business was very bad indeed. For the greater the harm he had done in business transaction with a goy, the deeper appeared the narrative delight of the Jew to whom I was listening. I could not help feeling towards the goyim some of the pity

---

[17] *An instance of this. A goy once tried to kiss my young aunt Sarah, behind the bar. She cried out, and my grandfather strode in. "If someone doesn't take out this swine, something terrible will happen," he drawled, and the rest of the goyim almost tore the offender apart in getting him out of the Inn.*

[18] *Instance. While my grandfather was in charge of the building of an important road, a woman in the village was robbed. Certain that it was one of the workingmen, my grandfather called them together during the lunch period, told them of the robbery, and suddenly displayed to them a handful of evenly cut straws. "I am going to give every one of you a straw," he announced, "and the straw of the man who robbed that poor woman will have grown an inch, when I come to take it back." He distributed the straws, gathered them back a minute later, and he recognized the thief because when he came to him he found that he had bitten off a whole inch of the straw.*

I had felt for Esau when he let out that bitter cry on discovering the duplicity of Jacob.[19]

The reader, and especially the incensed Jew, may here get the impression that I am currying favor with the gentile or his religion or both. Nothing can possibly be further from what IS the real state of my mind and my heart. I don't think I ever shared the Jewish contempt for the goyim, which is part and parcel of all Jewish psychology. But for thirty-nine years I have watched the violence of the goyim against a people I loved. The hands they laid on the Jews were lain on me. The bruises which Christendom inflicted on the body of Israel are living bruises on my body. It does not matter that my heart has turned against the Jews.

I am, because of that no more friendly to their tormentors; and I am not the kind of Jew who is ever likely to kiss the rod with which he was once smitten. Luckily for me, it is not necessary, m my country and my age, to make a choice of religion. I, as would have been true in the Middle Ages, I had to make a choice between Judaism and Christianity, I would simply have to cut my throat.

I am trying to tell an honest, unbiased story. That was the state of affairs between the Jews and gentiles (N)ustcha, the village in which I was born. I have no reason to believe that things were any different in any other village in the world at that time.

In Zborow, where my father brought me to continue my Hebrew education, the Jewish religion prevailed, among the Jews, in its most orthodox form. The town was one of the oldest in Poland, its marketplace one of the busiest. To a stranger, come upon this scene of petty and virulent barter, the impression must have been that he was in a Jewish town. Behind the stalls, fiercely vying to outdo one another, brown-bearded, peak-capped men and bewigged, red-shawled women, raged to and fro.

Yet Zborow was not a Jewish town. More than seventy percent of its inhabitants were Slavonic Poles. The Jews formed much less than a third of the population. Why then, you might ask, this decided predominance in the general appearance of things, since even in the matter of property ownership the Jews were in a humble minority?

---

[19] *I knew the goyim of (N)ustcha only by sight, for I never learned to talk a word of Polish.*

The simplest answer is that the appearance of things in this world is usually illusory, and we Jews have always been past-masters in the arts of illusion. We have learned to dominate the landscape of any country by the very singular process of electing ourselves to do all the grouping. More than a century before I was imposed on the scene, the old wooden synagogue that stood in the midst of the marketplace in Zborow had been reared.

It was a very old building; it had already survived four fires and three massacres. Yet there it towered in its agedness as firm and as imposing as any structure in the town. Morning, noon and night, Jews held festive, strangely joyous prayer meetings before the screened Ark of the Covenant in the heart of the synagogue. A Jew prays a little more frequently than a Christian and a little less frequently than a Mussulman.

But the Jewish form of prayer differs both in heart and in outline from any other species of prayer in the world. The difference is the difference between one's approach to God and another. Mohammedans and Christians humble themselves before their deities.

The Christian in church. The Mohammedan wherever he may happen to be when the muezzin announces the hour of prayer. The Jew has everything very carefully arranged. God belongs in the synagogue. He, the Jew, belongs in the marketplace. God has only one business. It is to look after the prosperity of Israel. The Jew walks briskly into his synagogue three times a day, at set hours, to remind God of this important business.

The Jews formed only a fraction of the population of Zborow. But by virtue of their sensitiveness to their inherent worth, they regarded themselves as its natural masters. Concerning their superiority over the rest of the population of the town, there could be no question in their minds. It was all very simple. They were Jews. And the goyims were only goyim. Superiority, come to think of it is not exactly the word with which to explain the precedence which the Jews of Zborow felt over their neighbors.

The numerical superiority of the goyim was an accident unworthy of being given a second thought. Their superiority in legal possession—ah that was the real rub! What the goyim had was only a temporary possession which the stupid law of the gentiles was attempting to make permanent. Were not they, the Jews, God's chosen? Did not God mean in the very beginning that all the good things of the world should belong to his favorites? It was a Jew's business to remember this at all times, especially in his dealings with goyim. It was practically a moral obligation on the part of every conscientious Jew to fool and cheat the goy wherever and whenever possible. The impression this arrangement made on me at that time was that the world had been created by God for the habitation and prosperity of Israel.

The rest of Creation—cows, horses nettles oak-trees dung and goyim—were placed there for our, the Jews', convenience or inconvenience, depending on God's good humor for the time being. Just then, I understood, God's attitude towards his chosen ones was, and for many centuries had been one of stern disapproval. That was the reason why the goyim had everything and we had practically nothing. If we went to synagogue regularly (especially on the sabbaths and Yom Kippur, the Sabbath of Sabbaths) God would eventually relent and let us fool back from the uncouth laps of the goyim all the divine favors which really were intended for us.

The Jews pride themselves on their reluctance to proselytize. They explain that this is a sign not only of religious exclusiveness, but of their good will towards the rest of the religions. It is nothing of the sort. The Jews do not proselytize because they are firmly convinced that they will eventually inherit the earth, and they want as few claimants as possible to this windfall.

I have referred to the "festive, strangely joyous prayer-meetings before the screened Ark of the Covenant." The Jews of Zborow belonged to a sect of mystics, then the most popular in Eastern Europe, known as the Chassidim. The whole philosophy of the chussid (as a chassidic Jew is referred to) was to be happy in adversity because the kingdom of God was terribly near at hand.

The morning, noon and evening rounds at the synagogue were cycles of breathless singing and crazy dancing before the screened Ark of the Covenant. We had a sort of secret understanding with Torah our bride, and God's representative on earth. On holy days we lingered over kissing the Torah, as though we hoped to overhear her reveal the exact day of the confusion of the benighted goyim.

We despised the goy, and we hated his religion. The goy, according to the stories crooned into the ears of the children, wantonly worshipped an unsightly creature called the *yoisel*—and a dozen names too foul for repetition. The *yoisel* had once been a human being and a Jew. But one day he had gone out of his mind and in that pitiably bewildered state announced that he was the Lord God himself.

To prove it, he offered to fly over the populace like an angel. With the help of a page blasphemously torn out of Holy Writ, and placed under his sweating arm the *yoisel* did fly over the multitudes of Jews in the crowded streets of Jerusalem. So impressive a spectacle did he create that even the most pious among the Jews were moved in his direction. But Rabbi Shammai, angered at the foul impudence of this demented creature, and fearful of a possible religious crisis on earth, tore out two leaves from the pages of Holy Writ, and placing them one under each arm flew even higher than the *yoisel* with only one page of Holy Writ for motor power. He flew over the *yoisel* himself and urinated over him. Instantly the power of the *yoisel's* bit of Holy Writ was nullified and the *yoisel* fell to the grounds amidst the jeers and taunts of the true believers in the streets of Jerusalem. This extraordinary caricature of the founder of the opposing religion made possible one of the queerest adventures of my life.

Six years later I was looking through the eyes of a nine year old boy over the early spring harbor of the city of Hamburg. The family was migrating to America, to join my father who had left four years before. Several hundred of us, men, women and children, in ragged clothing were being borne submissively in a small boat towards the ocean liner *Pretoria* which was to carry us across a bleak stretch of water to America—a land of promise that promised different things to so many different people.

The splendid well-dressed people travelling first and second class bad gone out before us. We had caught occasional glimpses of them in the office of the agent and in the lobby of the hotel, during the two days in which we had to wait for the *Pretoria* to steam into the harbor. One by one, as we stepped from the gangplank that had led us into the larger ship, every one of us was handed, gratis, a small booklet with black paper covers.

Whenever my eye falls accidentally on the daily ship-list of the *New York Times,* I look to see if the Pretoria is still afloat. Invariably I find that she is either going to or coming from America. Is it another ship that has inherited the name of that damnable old tub? I cannot believe that a ship plying today a course of trade between Europe and America can contain a den as dark, dismal and lurid with wormy horror, as the hold of the *Pretoria* which enveloped our poor weary bones in 1904. The beds were raised one on top of another, six beds to a row. There was just room enough between a bed and the bed over it for a human being to crawl and stretch out. Two beds were our whole reservation, the fourth and fifth in a row. On the fourth my mother slept with my sister; on the fifth I slept with my younger brother.

The beds were dark, dirty and verminous. Since there was no deck on which third-class passengers could promenade, we were expected to remain where we were placed, and only creep out from our terrible holes for the little food that was served to us in wooden bowls three times a day. It could not have been much worse if we had been prisoners instead of paying passengers. Some kerosene lamps suspended from the ceiling gave forth a white unsteady light. The ventilation was the most elementary possible. And to add to the unpleasantness, the ragged mattresses gave out a queer green odour. I have been in prisons whose fare and general atmosphere were superior to the hold of the *Pretoria*.

Then in that loathesome darkness something really wonderful came to pass.

On the second day of the voyage I opened one of those black booklets and began to read in it. I became interested immediately because it was written in the only language to which I had become accustomed, the language of prophecy. The whole thing concerned a new Jewish prophet. His name was Yehoshea.

Long after all the old prophets of Israel had died out, this Yehoshea a direct descendent of King David, had arisen to bring back to all Jews the promise of eternal life which Jacob had been on the point of communicating on his death bed to his sons when sudden death, alas, paralyzed his tongue. How, when the rabbi recited the tale of that interrupted prophecy, I had grieved that the angel of death had so cruelly cut him off! For, if Jacob had only been able to utter for us those few precious words how much of our pains and difficulties might have been spared us in the thousands of years of our terrible exile! And now I had lived to see the day when the whole people had outlived the catastrophe!

"Listen to this," I cried out to my mother and sister in the lower berth. And I read to them the words of the new prophet in Israel. My mother and sister listened, as did the rest of the miserable residents of that dungeon. How tender those words must have sounded to them in their foul dark beds!

"In that hour came his disciples on Yehoshea, saying: Who, then, is the greatest in the kingdom of heaven? And he called to him a little child, and set him in the midst of them, and said, 'Verily I say unto you, unless ye turn and become as little children, ye shall in nowise enter into the kingdom of heaven.

"Whosoever therefore shall humble himself as this little child, the same is the greatest in the kingdom of heaven. And who so shall receive one such little child in my name receiveth me; but whoso shall cause one of these little ones which believe in me to stumble, it were profitable for him that a great millstone should be hanged about his neck, and that he should be sunk into the depths of the sea."

You can imagine for yourself from what I have already told you of the appearance of the occupants of the hold of the *Pretoria* that there was very little real learning amongst us.

How was I how were they, to recognize in the names of Yehoshea the founder of Christianity whom we knew only by the foulest of names? Was it possible for anyone to recognize in the sweet words in that book (which I was to learn years afterwards was the New Testament) the religion we had been taught to abominate!

Every day I read aloud a new portion of the little book with the black covers. The green sea continued to pound sonorously on the walls of the old ship. We pressed ill fed bellies against the soft dank mattresses that were like so many elevated graves. But every ear was strained intently for the strange music of the new speech. On the eighth day I had finished reciting the whole book.

But I was urged by everyone to begin it all over again from page one. The strangest conversations took place during that time between myself and some of the other passengers. I felt important for had I not discovered this new prophet for my people?

"What did you say was his name?" an old Jew asked from the other end of the line of beds.

"Yehoshea."

"Strange. It sounds like Yeshia. But it is most certainly not Yeshia. I know every word of the prophet Yeshia, and these are not his words."

"Certainly he is not the prophet Yeshia. It says here that Yehoshea is a prophet," I reminded him.

"Maybe so. But we have not been led to expect a new prophet. The only one we expect is the Messiah."

That was true. I remembered it. "Then who can this Yohoshea be?"

The old man slowly shook his head.

The answer came to us suddenly and dramatically. One afternoon, as I was in the midst of one of my recitations from the little book with the black covers, I heard a strange outcry as of someone in great danger. I looked down from the elevation of my bed and saw a man in a silk mantle and a red beard pointing a finger at me and shouting with such fury that his words were incoherent to me. He was obviously not one of us. He was richly garbed, his locks were black and well combed, and he had a paunch.

Word concerning what had been happening amongst us had apparently reached the upper deck of the ship, and there stood the man with the red beard like some avenging angel.

"Don't you realize that he is talking to you!" cried out the old Jew from the other end of the hold.

"I can see. But what does he want!"

By this time the Jew with the red beard had regained clarity of speech. "Give me that heathen scroll!" he thundered, pointing to the little book with the black covers.

I hesitated. After all I didn't know who the man was. And the book was my own property. It had been put into my hand by someone who had said to me with his eyes: This is for you. It is yours to hold and to keep.

"It's the Rav from Pinsk," I heard the voice of the Jew crying to me.

Tremulously I surrendered my precious possession to the avenging angel with outstretched hand below me. The moment his fingers touched it, he began to tear it into pieces. He tore the book first into several parts.

Then he tore ten pages at a time. Then he seized the large pieces of pages and tore them into smaller bits, all the time holding on to all the fragments for fear that some piece of it might remain large enough to make it possible for someone to read it.

When he had satisfied himself that not a decipherable line was left he flung the whole thing in one white shower over the floor of the hold.

He decided, before leaving to take one last parting shot at me.

"You should he laced in cherem!" he thundered. Then, turning to the older people in the cots about me, he continued to pour out the vials of his wrath: "Fools! Oxen! Asses! To be misled by a child! You will all burn for this!"

And so cursing he strode out, climbing the stairs which led out of our hell to the civilized quarters he occupied on one of the upper decks.

So you see, I have been what in my estimation is even worse than a priest or a rabbi. I have been a missionary. But it was not really my fault. It was the fault of the rabbis who so grossly misrepresented Christianity to me.

The Jewish answer to this is that the Jews of Poland are carrying out a policy of retaliation. It is true that the Polish children in the neighboring cloisters were led to believe much more grotesque things about Jews. Without first giving them any idea of historic background Poles teach their children to believe that the Jews killed their Saviour. The children go out into the world with the belief that the very Jews they are about to meet in the streets, in offices, in restaurants, are the killers of Christ.

The result is that when the little *shkutzim* becomes big goyim they look upon the Jews they meet with vague hatred and an eerie suspiciousness. But there is a noteworthy difference in the working out of these two programs of misrepresentation.

All that the priests promote in the Poles is a little occasional violence which the goy permits himself to carry only occasionally to an extreme which hurts. But what of the little Jews who are told that they are the salt of the earth, that what they see before them really belongs to them, and is only to be won away with the superior brain with which God has endowed his chosen ones! Each of them, when he grows up, becomes an agency of cunning to defeat the civil law. The Polish Jew does not remain in Poland. He migrates.

Eventually he finds himself a rich nest in England, in France, in Germany, in America, or in one of the South American countries. To each of the countries of his invasion, the Jew brings the whole bag of commercial tricks and statutory manoeuvers with which he poisons the arteries of the civilized world.

I was a little more than nine years old when I left Poland. I never returned to it. My only other experience with a European Jewry was some six months I spent in London during the winter of 1919–1920. In London I knew only two Jews—as wide apart as the poles of the earth. The first Jew, Israel Zangwill, with whom I had had considerable correspondence while in America, was one of the noblest people it has been my privilege to meet.

He stands in my esteem as a human being next to Theodore Herzl who died the year I came to America. Like Herzl, Zangwill gave his whole life to the Jewish people. Like Herzl, he died of it. The Jews ate up Zangwill alive just as they had eaten up Herzl before him, and every decent Jew who gave them a leadership of pity.

I saw them killing Zangwill here in America with my own eyes. He had come over at the invitation of the Jewish Congress to open up the first session of 1924. In accepting the invitation, Zangwill had made one reservation: he must be permitted to speak without interference.

He would not brook having anyone read and approve his speech in advance of delivery. The famous meeting took place in Carnegie Hall. Evidently Stephen Wise and "the boys" had no idea what Zangwill meant by the liberty to say what was in his mind. Zangwill rose that night and brought that meeting to the front of every newspaper in the world.

He told the Jewish Congress, in effect, that it was a movement of people who preyed on the lamentable condition of international Jewry for only two reasons: the big ones for the publicity, the little ones for the miserable salaries which they dragged down in their various positions. It was the truth and it hurt. "If you are prepared to meet the Jewish problem with the courage and self denying labors it demands, I am here to join you, to work with you, if necessary to die with you. But I can not permit myself to join in a movement whose whole business is the satisfaction of some smaller and larger vanities."

The answer to that was the most ferocious attack I have ever seen directed on one man. Zangwill returned to England a broken man. The last few months of his life he spent in a half insane effort to prove to London audiences that if he was a poor Jew he was at least a very good playwright.

He spent almost every cent he had in the world producing his plays to empty houses in His Majesty's Theatre. He left practically no estate when he died.

The second Jew I met in London was the editor of *The Jewish Chronicle,* a weekly journal, one of the richest in England, which for years had reprinted without permission from me and of course without offering anyone any remuneration, my weekly contributions to the *Hebrew Standard.*

I went to him when my money had given out, I had no job and had no money left for food and shelter.

I did not come to ask him to pay me for work of mine he had already used. I offered to sell him some parts of my new book which I had just finished.

But he would not as much as look at it.

"But you may want to run some of this," I urged.

"In that case," he said, "we will reprint what we want after the book has appeared in America."

"You don't understand," I insisted. "I haven't eaten for nearly two days. I must have some money immediately. I wouldn't come to you I assure you if I did not find myself stranded."

He smiled sourly on me. "I do understand that you need money," he said. "But why should we pay for something we know we will eventually get for nothing?"

I looked at him with dejected stupefaction, and rose to go. He rose too and held out to me a dark, wrinkled hand. I wanted to spit into it, but remembered that he was a very old man. "You're a hell of a Jew" I said wresting my eyes away from that mean hand.

He broke out into an ugly cackle, Jewish grace in London. "I am a good Jew. It is you who are not much of a. Jew. Have you never heard of the saying of our Fathers: *Leolom Tickach*—always take?"

Yes, I had heard of it. But the awfulness of its application in real life, real Jewish life, had never come to me before.

Decorating the Street Corner

VI THE BRINGING-UP OF THE LITTLE JEW

Jews are constantly telling me what a grievous disadvantage they find themselves under in conducting their business because they happen to be Jews. The word "happen" is theirs, not mine. They forget to make a very important distinction, which can only be made if you have been honest enough to observe it.

Being a Jew is a disadvantage only if you are a Jew doing business within the Jewish tradition. But you can be a Jew who conducts his business honestly and decently. I have met one or two such Jews in my life. I have never known them to suffer of racial prejudice.

But most Jews (unless they deal exclusively with their own kind, in which case Heaven help them!) find themselves up against the rock of gentile prejudices even before they have had any dealings at all with the gentile. It certainly cannot be fair, it will be argued, to condemn a man even if he is guilty, before he has had a chance to show his hand.

The answer is that there is no law compelling the gentile to wait till he has been cheated before he steps out of the way of the Jewish trap. The average Jew displays his disposition on his face, the result of his peculiar up bringing on the principle: *Leolom Tickach, always take*. It has brought the old wolf so much into his face the gentile has to be a born ass to let himself be bitten.

About two years ago, Harry Montor of the Seven Arts Syndicate came to ask me for an interview. "There is really only one question I want you to answer," he said. "You've developed quite a publishing business. Have you found being a Jew an obstacle to your career?"

My answer, syndicated as *The Strange Career of Samuel Roth*, was easy to give.

I had not found being a Jew an obstacle to me either in the publishing business or in any branch of the life I had lived. In spite of my naturally indolent attitude towards studies, I was graduated from a gentile grammar school with honors. I obtained entry for my poetry and prose into the best newspapers and magazines, just by submitting my work through the mails. I got a scholarship in Colombia University, not by passing examinations, or exerting influence, but by submitting to the scholarship committee a few immature but ambitious sonnets. I lived in Hartley Hall on the Columbia campus the quietest and most beautiful months of my life. But for America's entering the war, I would still be there.

Yes, the goyim were always generous to me. But, on the other hand, I never tried to fool them or even court their favors. In grammar school, I made no effort to become friendly with my gentile teachers or with the students in my classes who were not Jews. John Erskine and Carl Van Doren, whose gracious interest made possible my Colombia scholarship, knew that they were helping a Jew because it was almost the very first things I told them.

My very first contribution to Columbia Spectator was the review of a Jewish book. It was a very strict principle with me. If I found it at all necessary to deal with a goy, I made certain to warn him in advance that I was a Jew and liable to change shape and eat him at a moment's notice.

Discrimination against Jews at the University was plentiful, of course. But I do not remember that anyone discriminated against Irwin Edman, Frank Tannenbaum or myself. The very contrary to the usual was true, I know, in my case. I was liked rather than avoided for my aggressive Jewishness. After I publicly announced that I would join no fraternity to which Jews were not admitted, I believe I received more pressing invitations to join than many a popular gentile in my class.

I advance the suggestion that it is altogether possible for a Jew to live at peace with the Christian world about him, if he begins by presenting his proper credentials, and does not try to establish with it a basis of equality which does not exist. Being born a Jew is a misfortune, like being born a Pigmy.

I have never known a Pigmy to advance his fortunes in the world by affecting stilts. But a Jew can make a beautiful position in the world for himself merely by being honest.

Israel Zangwill made it a point of honor to impress his nationality on all the people he dealt with, although the overwhelming Jewishness of his physiognomy should have made that unnecessary. He liked to tell how on board the ship, that took him to America the first time, he had the good fortune to become acquainted with an eminent economist who was to occupy the chair in economics at one of the great eastern universities.

The economist labored under the disadvantage of a bad case of spinal curvature, but Zangwill found him one of the pleasantest of companions and the days and nights passed swiftly for both of them because of their numerous animated conversations. When finally the Statue of Liberty was sighted in New York harbor, the economist suggested to Zangwill that they might, if he wished it, continue their lively discussions on shore. "But you understand that I'm a Jew," interposed Zangwill gravely. "Yes," replied the economist, "and you understand, of course, that I'm a hunchback." I do not imply that there is necessarily dishonest in the attitude of a Jew who undertakes a business relationship with a gentile without warning him in advance that he is a Jew.

In most cases when he fails to do this, the Jew is merely exercising his constitutional right as a citizen of a free republic. No one can blame the Jews for being reluctant to give up without a struggle the civil privileges which during the last hundred years they have wrested, by main force of wheedling and wit, from unwilling constitutional governments.

I am, however, advancing the opinion that if we exercise our newly acquired rights more cautiously, our chances will be better not only to keep them but possibly to gain even new ones. The presence in the American constitution of articles granting the Jews equality in the face of the law does not alter the fact that to the average American, a Jew is still a Jew, and subject to great suspicion.

Suppose the American constitution does give us equal rights with Gentile American citizens? Does that alter the fact that every once in a while another great American industry joins in the boycott of Jewish labor? Does our theoretical equality makes it easier for Jewish students to enter American colleges? Constitutional rights that have been granted can also be taken away. The increasing hostility of America to its Jewish citizenry would seem to indicate it as the height of folly for American Jews to rest nonchalantly on their constitutional rights.

During my days as a bookseller on West Eighth Street, I became friendly with a man who employed more than four thousand people. It was known of him also that he did not permit Jews to work in any branch of his business. "Will you tell me why?" I once asked him.

"Just business," he said, "Jews are not dependable, and they are untrustworthy."

"Would that explain their success in business?" I asked.

"I don't know what explains a Jew's success in business," he replied. "But have you ever heard of a Jew who made a success of another man's business?"

I was silent.

He smiled. "When you find such a Jew," he said "send me a wire collect, and I'll begin hiring Jews immediately."

"Have you never employed a Jew, then?"

"Sure, many of them. By accident. They come around to our employment department, give Christian names, and get away with it—until I spot them. At the works they say that I've got an unfailing eye for Jews. They never escape me."

I protested that this seemed both remarkable and unbelievable. I, a Jew, very frequently mistook a Jew for a gentile!

"Being a Jew isn't it enough, Roth. You've got to have a nose for Jews. You've got to be able to smell them out. If I can't spot it in their features, I can find their Jewishness in their conversation."

"What about Jews with Harvard accents?"

"You've got me wrong. I didn't mean their accents at all. Most American Jews talk like Americans, and less with their hands than regular Americans do. I have a more infallible way of recognizing a Jew in my employ. When a Jew talks to his employer he usually looks over his head."

I think I know exactly what this man meant. Isaac looks over the head of his employer to the invisible Lord God of Israel. Since all the wealth before him was really meant for the enrichment of Israel, there must be at hand some nice easy way to get out of the crude hands of the goy in actual possession. He cannot help this dishonest feeling. It is almost as instinctive with him as it is instinctive for the gentile who sees him to pass by him. That's how poor Isaac has been brought up. And what a little Jewish boy has learnt, to quote a contemporary patriotic Jewish drama, he never forgets.

What is this Jewish upbringing! To know it you have to enter and live in, a Jewish home. I only knew one Jewish home intimately, the one in which I was, so to say reared, and so I shall give you some inkling of it. It was typical of all Jewish homes, rich or poor alike.

The Hebrew of the rabbis was all I had been permitted to learn in Poland. My father's respect for what might be learned outside of the Pentateuch being very scan, it was lucky for me that public school attendance in New York City was compulsory. I was enrolled in the public school of my district.

But that did not mean the end of my Hebrew studies. To continue those I was compelled to go to *cheder* (Hebrew school) for two hours after school every afternoon.

My father had to pay so much every week for my Hebrew schooling. What he paid came out of the slender means by which we were fed and clothed. And what poverty we lived in, those days! My father drudged heavily and bitterly for the little money he earned. For some fifteen or eighteen dollars he found once a week in his pay envelope he had to rise four o'clock mornings to go to work, and he stuck to his machine till nearly ten o'clock at night.

The agony his livelihood cost him made a miser out of my father. He could not bear to part with the greenbacks which came to him with so much anguish of body and spirit. But not once did I hear him complain of the cost of my Hebrew education.

It was really heartrending. He grudged my poor mother every penny he allowed her for the bare necessities of life and the rental of the insect-ridden apartment we occupied on Broome Street. If he found in the ice-box, when he came home, apart from what had been left for his supper, a little butter, an egg, or some barley, he quarreled about it interminably with my mother, and was certain to cut down her allowance the following day. Yet when it came to parting with *cheder* money, no questions were asked. Why?

The explanation for this is simple enough. Without the aid of a local police to enforce it, Hebrew education is compulsory among

Jews. To fail to force me to go to *cheder* would have meant complete social ostracism for my father and mother. The Jewish boy must learn enough Hebrew whereby to read his prayer book on Saturday mornings in synagogue, and for the ceremony of *Bar Mitzvah*, his thirteenth birthday, when he is installed as a full-grown member of the Jewish community, with full responsibilities of a citizen. To have failed in this important preparation is, in Jewish life, an act of high treason to the Jewish nation. That is how it happened that, against my own wishes I spent the precious hours after school, learning Hebrew.[20]

If you stop an American Jew and ask him why he plagues his children with Hebrew studies (after the already exhausting sessions of the public schools) he will give you one of two reasons. He will either plead that he is giving his son the religious education he needs to complete his equipment for a successful career, or that he thinks it is important to supplement the cultural training his son is acquiring in the public school with the cultural Jewish training that is traditionally just as important to his son.

The first answer is given by the simple ignorant Jew, the sort of Jew my own father was. The answer is sincere and honest enough, for it was transmitted to him by a hundred thoughtless generations. But fundamentally it is untrue. The amount of Hebrew a child needs to know for purely religious purposes, he learns in two years, before he is six years old, before he is required to begin his secular education. And religion is not taught in the Hebrew schools.

Hebrew instructors are not religious and do not bother to teach religion. I was a *cheder* student when a child, and I was never taught religion. When I grew older I held a position with the Bureau of Jewish Education maintained by funds publicly collected from the Jewish community of New York. I do not think I violate any confidences when I assert that neither its chief executive nor any one of his dozen department heads were believers in the Jewish religion.

The cultural reason sounds more plausible but has even less foundation in fact. If the Hebrew schools foster Jewish culture, where

---

[20] *When I became a Zionist in 1912, I had forgotten the little Hebrew I had learnt; but, having resumed Hebrew studies of my own free will, I found them delightful and instructive.*

is this culture? Now culture is either creative or absorptive. Creative Jewish culture we have not in America even in its lowest form. As for absorptive culture—which consists of the contemplation of culture created by others, and so transmitted through time and space—there is almost none of that in America either. What have we of Jewish culture in America, really?

The national anthem, a few field songs from Palestine, and some anemic modern adaptations of themes from the Old Testament. The few serious Hebrew works imported into the United States from Europe and Asia Minor are for the absorption of the few European Jews who have made of America a sort of haven of despair in their old age.

The cultural argument is the rankest sort of pretence. Do the thousands of French families in the United States compel their children to study French after school so as to preserve with them the inheritance of French culture? Or is there any reason to believe that the French think any less of their culture than the Jews think of theirs? How many German schools do the fifteen million Germans in the United States maintain to help their children keep the inheritance of German culture?

The preservation of Jewish religion and culture are merely excuses for something else, a smoke-screen. What the Jew really wants and expects to achieve through the instrumentality of the Hebrew school is to cultivate in his son the sharp awareness that he is a Jew and that as a racial Jew—apart from all the other races—he is waging an old war against his neighbors.

The young Jew must learn to remember that before anything else he is a Jew, that, before any other allegiance, comes his allegiance to the Jewish People. He may be a good American if it is good business to be a good American. He may even pose as a good Chinaman. But no obligation he contracts with a non-Jew is to be considered valid if it violates the interests of this most important obligation of his.

The first thing the young Jew learns is that he is a Jew. The second thing he learns is that being a Jew makes him different from the members of all the other peoples on the face of the earth. Sanctity, because of the ever presence of the synagogue as a background is inevitably part of his impression of his function as a Jew. If the family in the midst of which he is reared has shed all of its religious feathers, then a sense of superiority takes the place of the feeling of sanctity. The third thing he learns is that, as a member of a nation of priests, it is his business to make for himself a high place in the world, some position from which he will be able to compel the world to pay him tribute.

Most desirable for the young Jew, he is told impressively, is it, for him to become a member of one of the professions—to become a doctor, a lawyer, an engineer, even a salesman or an agent. To be compelled to go to work, to do manual labor for one's livelihood, is the very worse state the young Jew can fall to, something to make him really ashamed and humiliated.

This attitude of the Jews towards manual labor is historic. The Jewish apologists have a neat explanation for it. In most of the countries of the Diaspora the Jews were not permitted to own land or to work on it. Nor were they permitted to work for Christians. And since Jewish merchants could give employment only to a fraction of the great numbers of young Jews, the rest had to turn for careers to salesmanship, money-lending and the other promoting aspects of trade.

This does not explain why Jews have never, like other peoples, gone into a wilderness and built up a land of their own. Nor why in England, in the thirteenth century, under Edward I, they did not take advantage of the offer by which Edward promised to give them the very opportunities Jews had been crying for, for centuries.

After imprisoning the whole Jewish population in his domain for criminal usury and debasing the coin of the realm, Edward, before releasing them, put into effect two new sets of laws: the first made it illegal for a Jew in England to lend money at interest. The second repealed all the standing laws which kept Jews from the normal pursuits of the kingdom.

Under these new statutes Jews could even lease land for a period of fifteen years and work it. Edward advanced this as a test of the Jew's sincerity when he claimed that all he wanted was an opportunity to work like other people. If they proved their fitness to live like other people, the inference was that Edward would let them buy land outright and admit them to the higher privileges of citizenship. Did the Jews take advantage of Edward's decree? This way. To get around the laws against usury they invented such new methods of skinning the peasants and the nobles that the outcry against them became greater than ever, and Edward had to expel them to avert a civil war. It was not recorded that one Jew took advantage of the new right to till the soil.

During the Napoleonic era there was a rabbi in Metz, Aaron Worms by name, who felt deeply the shame of the traditional Jewish attitude towards manual labor. He took the trouble to publicly rebuke the people for it, and, as an example, apprenticed his son Eijah to an artisan. But it was a vain gesture, as has been the effort of every Jew of integrity to civilize his people.

For his pains, there were Jews in Europe who called him an apostate—and worse. The Jew's feeling of superiority to manual labor has become second nature with him. It has been inborn and inbred in him as carefully and painstakingly as the virtues of a life of useful labor are inbred in the lives of the children of the rest of the nations.

The Jewish boy's progress through school is observed with the most hawk-like watchfulness. Does he show himself argumentative? Deep of voice? Cunning of device? It is immediately taken for granted that the Law is his natural, God-given profession. Plans are made to finance his way through the best possible law-school. There may not be money for other things in the house or with which to pay legitimate debts.

But there will be money, and plenty of it, forthcoming for Willie's tuition and upkeep in law school. Aptness in science, on the other hand, marks Izzie for the medical profession. It is not, of course, as simple to make a doctor as it is to make a lawyer, for at least three times as much time and money is required. To make a doctor out of Izzie, practically the whole family is set to work; it is sometimes even necessary to marry him off in advance so as to get him the help-in-advance of a goodly dowry. A facility with figures, in the same manner, points to a career in engineering and accountancy. Every promise is noted and capitalized.

Now there would not be so much harm in the Jews taking in such immense droves to the practice of the cardinal professions if they approached them in the proper spirit. But the Jew does not, cannot, turn to the law with anything like reverence for the profession or for its splendid traditions. Willie sets his jaw grimly to the task of competing with several thousands of other Willies for the few scraps of pickings in law lying about loose, and Izzie's attitude towards medicine is not much more cheerful or respectful. The attitude of a young Jew towards his profession is really like that of a gangster towards a new racket. The real end is the amount of money it is likely to yield him in exchange for the smallest investment of labor and enthusiasm. But more of this when we take up the Jews as doctors and as lawyers.

Does poor Simon bring home bad marks from school? He is continually warned, by parents and neighbors, that unless he shows decided improvement he will without doubt forfeit the support of his family in the direction of a career. It is pointed out, with the most painful emphasis, that unless he picks up in his studies, he will sink into the horrible ignominy of having to work for his livelihood. So deeply is it impressed on the growing Jew that to have to work with his hands is the most awful humiliation of life, that, no matter what becomes of him, he inwardly determines that he will not submit to work.

The easiest business for the young Jew not apt enough to enter one of the major professions, is selling newspapers. Almost all the news stands in America are owned by Jews. The news stand, however, is only a stepping stone. Once he has saved up a few hundred or a few thousand dollars, the Jew sells his news stand (to some other Jew beginning a similar career) and buys into a business where the chances of monetary profits are greater. He takes to selling haberdashery, hosiery, and real estate. Businesses in which the margin of profit is limited by established prices do not interest him.

But you must have some money with which to buy even a news stand. The young Jews who have no money at all to start with, and certainly no legitimate positions to fill,[21] take to selling. They sell kitchen utensils from door to door, things which have no standard

---

[21] *There was a time when young Jews in great number took to jobs as street-car conductors. That was before the car companies installed efficient check-up systems for fares collected. Today the only Jews found as conductors in street-cars are Jews who were reared in orphan asylums where the prejudice against real work is not so assiduously cultivated.*

price, "blind articles," they are called, on which the return in profit is from five hundred to a thousand percent. These young Jews have created an amazing variety of things to sell.

There was always a strong streak of perverseness in my nature. After being graduated from Public school, in which I showed no aptness for arguments or science, but did write a history of the world in rhymed couplets, I was expected to at least find a position in an office. I went to work instead, in a smoking-pipe factory where the air was full of an evil-smelling dust, most obnoxious in my division where the stems were cut.

The factory was on Avenue B and Seventeenth Street, the very heart of the East Side, but there was only one other Jew working in that factory, a Galician Jew who was foreman. When he learned that I was not only a Jew but a graduate from public school, he decided that I must be out of my mind.

What becomes of the young Jews who cannot attain to one of the professions, have not the money with which to buy a news stand or the mental resourcefulness to create a selling line? Most of them remain on the street-corners of their neighborhoods and become the petty thieves, hold-up-men, strike-breakers, back-store crap-shooters, street-corner mashers, dope peddlers and dope smugglers, white slave traffickers, kidnappers and petty racketeers of every peaceful community in America.

Certainly Jews are not the only people who become gangsters, to make civilized life on this continent creepy with a thousand species of repellent crime. The Irish, Greek and Italian immigrants contribute their substantial share. There is, however, this difference between their respective contributions. The Irishman, the Italian and the Greek become criminals out of sheer necessity, and remain so only as long as the necessity lasts.

As in every other thing the Jew touches, he immediately conceives of it as a career. The Irish, Italian and Greek gangsters are skin sores on the social body. Eventually, with a little application of remedy, they can be cleared away. The Jewish gangster imbeds himself deeply in the flesh of society. He becomes a permanent if not a fatal tumor.

The Jew's Contribution to American Literature

VII WHAT HAVE THE JEWS CONTRIBUTED TO AMERICAN CULTURE?

The Jews have made a habit of saying, when someone goes to the Bible for criticism of Jewish things, that the Devil is fond of quoting from the Scriptures. I am afraid that, before they are through reading this book, it is not at all unlikely that they will accuse the Devil of having written them.

I call your attention to verses ten and eleven of the sixth chapter of Deuteronomy: *"And it shall be when the Lord thy God shall bring thee into the land which He swore unto thy fathers, to Abraham, to Isaac and to Jacob, to give thee—(there will be) great and goodly cities which thou didst not build, and houses full of good things which thou didst not fill, and cisterns hewn out, which thou didst not hew, vineyards and olive trees, which thou didst not plant, and thou shalt eat and be satisfied."*

The Lord might have added, in the same spirit: "And there shall be paintings and statues for you to appraise, breathe profoundly significant words over, and sell at a goodly price, which thou hast not conceived in thine own heart; poems to recite and put into eloquent anthologies which thou hast not written or encouraged; operas (containing prima donnas ready for seduction) which thou wilt parade pompously through the world's great cities, but which thou hast not taken the trouble to measure out; and the great businesses to inflate which were first conceived in the brains of the goyim, wrought into shape by the sinews of the goyim, but the profits of which shall legitimately be yours. All these and much more shall be thine for the adopting and adapting, that they may shine as a cultural light over thy dark heads, to remain a glory to Israel forever."

The author of Deuteronomy had a real understanding of the profound indolence of the Jewish national attitude towards the real work of the world. He brings it into light in more places than the passage I have singled out for quoting. He says nothing about the Jewish attitude towards the arts, for the very excellent reason that the Jewish arts then, as now, were quite non-existent. I have never paid much attention to the national Jewish reluctance to join in the manual labor of the world, although it has always seemed to me a very grave flaw in our character. But I have been annoyed by our attitude towards the arts, and once, in my book *Now and Forever* I tried to explain it away in the following manner:

"*Zangwill*: You don't seriously mean that you look upon the making of statues and paintings as harmful?

"*Roth*: Only the other day I was explaining this to one of your Georgian poets who was sharing tea with me in a dark corner of the Savoy dining-room. 'How is it,' he asked me, nodding a pig's head, 'that you Jews have contributed nothing to the plastic arts?' I took up the delicate saucer from under my cup and rapped it gently against his bald pate. He looked grieved but I hastened to explain myself. 'If you knew,' I said to him, 'that every time you made such a saucer it would split over your head, would you be anxious to continue producing them?'

"But the making of statues and paintings is harmful to us in yet another way. To survive, we Jews must love nothing better than ourselves.

"This is how the rabbis considered the matter. Once Jews take to the making of images, they would create in shadow and in stone, figures so much more beautiful, and so much more appealing than the figures in their own flesh and blood, that, being a people with a sense of justice, they would learn to prize them more.

"The rabbis feared that the presence within our sight of overwhelmingly beautiful figures sprung out of our foreheads, would degrade for us the people passing before us in the common robes of humanity."[22]

---

[22] *Since writing these lines I have realized the unsoundness of the thought which underlies them. At no time have the goyim held against us the few honest contributions which Jews have made to the arts in Europe. Russia has never thrown at the heads of Jews any of the statues of Antokolsky. Nor has any Englishman tried to stop a Jew's mouth with one of the drawings of Jacob Epstein.*

But no. Jews are not satisfied with understanding their barrenness. On the contrary, they must make it appear that the barrenness is an illusion. The desert is not a desert if it is a Jewish desert, but an orchard chocked with fruit trees. It is not necessary to even respond to the spirit of creation to prove yourself of a creative nature—if you happen to be a Jew. A pose is all the equipment you need. And so it has become an old Jewish habit to assume that the Jew has culturally enriched every country he has favored with his presence and his patronage. This lofty assumption, especially in the field of culture, comes instinctively to a people whose interest goes out to all things the pursuit of which involves the expenditure of a minimum of energy.

Many articles and books have already been written on the subject of how much the Jews have enriched America culturally. Needless to add, Jews authored them. And while it is undoubtedly true that Jews have given themselves over infinitely to the vain-show and inglorious barter which everywhere accompany the development of the arts and the sciences, I cannot find anything of value that they have themselves created in their two hundred and fifty years residence on the American continent.

This is true in science as well as in arts. In science, it is usual for the American Jew to invoke the names of Jacques Loeb in biology and Charles Steinmetz in electricity. But American Jewry's claim to these laurels is very vague. Both Loeb and Steinmetz were born in Germany. They grew up in Germany and developed their insights in German universities and laboratories. Having attained noticeable stature in their own countries, they were invited, as was Albert Einstein later, to make their homes in America. The invitations, even, came not from Jews but from non-Jewish organizations interested in scientific research and in whatever values these men could bring to the promotion of certain vast commercial enterprises. It had nothing to do with culture in the first place.

And, in the second place, if it were a matter of culture, the Jews would certainly have had nothing to do with it. A cultural contact between these two scientists and American Jewry would have been unthinkable and abhorrent to the scientists. At no time while Loeb and Steinmetz lived in America did their lives even faintly touch the life of the Jewish community. If being in America meant anything to Jacques Loeb, it certainly did not crop up in his work which was a magnificent attempt to prove that animal (including human) life is as mechanical as any machine which we ourselves put together out of the raw and crumby materials of a disordered nature. As for Steinmetz, no man of his time worked harder than he to split up the poor electron which has neither race nor sex. It is difficult to imagine even his corpse at a Zionist rally.

In painting, sculpture and music the Jews conjure up a swarm of names. In painting as in sculpture there is not a name I would trouble to remember or repeat.

In music it has become good form to praise the work of George Gershwin. But you have only to sound it next to the name of Edward McDowell to realize its hollowness.

In poetry, what Jewish names can we offer to place next to the names of Edgar Allen Poe, Walt Whitman, Robert Frost or Edwin Arlington Robinson?

The closest Jewish approach to poetry in America was in the work of a woman, Ada Isaacs Menken, a descendant of French Huguenots in New Orleans, who for two years before the appearance of *Leaves of Grass*, published her *Infelcia*, in the same style, poetry both trenchant and lovely.

She married a Jew in Baltimore, and her marriage was short-lived; owing to the untimely death of her husband. But she had become so strangely enamored of Jewish ideas that she continued to regard herself, for the rest of her life, as a guardian of the Jewish People. She began, after her husband's death, to publish a weekly periodical devoted to Jewish news and the discussion of Jewish problems, but found Baltimore too tedious, and moved her operations to Europe and England.

In England she became the center of attraction for English writers and European writers who came to England to visit.[23] When all Jewry was excoriating Charles Dickens for the character of Fagin in *Oliver Twist*, it was she who extracted from him the promise that he would

---

[23] *Swinburne wrote his lustful* Dolores *to her and posed with her in a photograph which the British Museum will let you look at if you can show the librarian a doctor's certificate.*

remunerate the Jews for the damage done them by creating, in another novel, the character of a good Jew.[24] But it should also be noticed that, after her husband, she never again made friends with Jews. She married again three times. Once she descended to the level of taking a prize fighter for a husband. But never another Jew.

Emma Lazarus repeated in English some of the plaintive melodies of Heine. But in her own right she was not a poet worthy of remembrance.

The names of James Oppenheim, Alter Brody, Donald Evans and Joseph Auslander are repeatedly suggested. But they only testify to the Jew's eternal reaching out for honors which are beyond his reach. James Oppenheim's verses reveal the futility of an American Jew trying to climb to the prophetic heights of Issaiah on the ladder of Walt Whitman.

Brody's free verse sketches of the Jewish east side have a thin, shrill lyricism; they no more make poetry than the sketches of Martha Wolffenstein which were written in unpretentious (and therefore more serviceable) prose. Donald Evans did achieve a measure of poetry. But his work, alas, broke down, prematurely, with his brief life. He even achieve an imitator in the untidy verses of Maxwell Bodenheim. But no one will be grateful to him for that. So much for what the Jews have contributed to American poetry.

In the production of prose American Jewry is, if possible, even poorer. I understand that Robert Nathan who composed the novel *Jonah* is a Jew. I know that the author of *Dark Mother*, Waldo Frank, is a Jew. Pearl Buck, after spending twenty years as a Christian missionary to the heathen Chinese, confessed blushingly to being a Galician Jewess. But Nathan's is very insubstantial irony. Frank has begun splendidly some of the worse novels published within the last twenty years.

And Pearl Buck is just readable enough to make an amazing exhibition of a cumbersome sentimental machinery. There is, of course, some merit in every one of these writers, I grant you. But can you make a national feast of such crumbs?

---

[24] *Dickens kept his word. The "character" he eventually produced was good alright, but outside of his name he had no Jewish qualities by which he might be recognized as a Jew.*

I am here reminded forcibly of a very portentous omission. If I did not mention him at all, as I feel I should not, people might conclude that I had either forgotten him or that it would not save my theme to measure his value.

I mean, of course, Ludwig Lewisohn, the author of *Upstream, The Case of Mr. Crump*, and a dozen other books with which he has harassed the press within the last two decades. He has attained no mean measure of popularity as a writer of fiction, and even some stature in the critical esteem of the nations as an artist.

Years ago, I recollect, I picked up a book of pleasing translations By Mr. Lewisohn from modern French poets. I have never been pleased by anything from his pen since. As a writer, he seems to me gross, vulgar and insincere. When *Upstream* appeared, American Jewry made such an issue of it, that nearly fifty thousand copies of it were sold before it was generally realized that it was almost impossible to read the book.

The immense vogue which *Upstream* enjoyed, described two tragic spectacles: a popular book that nobody could read, and a newly discovered writer who had gone lost before you could take a good look at him. Israel which followed it was a hodge-podge of Jewish ideas by a Jew only recently converted to Judaism. *The Island Within* revealed hitherto unsuspected narrative powers.

If Mr. Lewisohn practiced long enough, you feel he might qualify as a contributor the *Saturday Evening Post. The Case of Mr. Crump* was still easy reading. But it saddened hope for Mr. Lewisohn's future as a popular writer.

It was now apparent that Mr. Lewisohn too his practice too seriously. There is scant comfort for American Jewry in the prose of Ludwig Lewisohn.

We have, however, made one contribution to the scene of letters in the United States which it would be vain for us to try to pass over. It has made so deep an impression on the life of the continent that it would be difficult to equal in the literary annals of any other country. It is a contribution no one will dispute with the Jews, because it is such an unpleasant one. I mean the gossip-column as invented by Walter Winchell and developed by Louis Sobol, George Skolsky and a dozen other Jewish journalists throughout the United States.

The Winchell idea was a very simple one. People want news, and the majority of the people have a stomach only for news with a certain amount of spice in it. But there is a limit to the amount of spice to be found in regular news.

Even a newspaper like *The Graphic* (in which Mr. Winchell was permitted to develop his new Journalistic formula) could not stretch interest in the shabbier tragedies of a day beyond a certain point. But Mr. Winchell had made a very interesting discovery.

There was a borderline between vital people and the things they would do or might do that provided a much richer field of contemplation for the reader who wanted more spice than even the spiciest news could offer. To exploit this rich, virgin soil was Mr. Winchell's happy inspiration.

I do not know whether Mr. Winchell approached any other newspaper publishers with this idea. The records have it that he came to Bernard Macfadden, just as Macfadden had announced his intention of starting an afternoon daily tabloid for New York City.

There is certainly no doubt that Mr. Winchell found a natural home in the *Graphic* which was reputed to enjoy a total of nine million dollars' worth of libel suits against it when it discontinued publication.

At any rate, Mr. Macfadden was the only other Jewish newspaper publisher in New York, and it was inconceivable that Mr. Ochs who professes interest only in "news fit to print" would have given him a hearing. The Winchell-Macfadden combination was, in the language of Broadway, "a perfect natural."

"I am offering you," explained Winchell, "a new departure in Journalism, maybe in Literature. Something to give a life to your newspaper that will not be enjoyed by any of the papers competing with you.

"I will explain to you, by example. Here is a morning paper. Do you see this paragraph announcing a birth in the Gould family? Pretty flat, don't you think?

"But suppose you had printed a week ago that one of the Goulds anticipated a blessed event? Wouldn't that have been much more exciting? Here is an item about a divorce in one of New York's most famous theatrical families.

"They'll never let the details ooze out, probably too slimy. So of what interest is the divorce? But what excitement there would have been if a month ago I had printed in my column a hint that the home-fires in a certain theatrical household were beginning to burn low! Get me?

"Where will I get my information? Simple enough. Such stuff drifts in by the carload through the mail and the telephone into every newspaper office. As newspapers are constituted today they cannot use nine tenths of this information. In the first place, it is never authentic enough. In the second place, there is always danger of a libel suit. What is needed to bring this mass of really exciting news into the newspapers?

"A new language. English, yes. But an English with more than one meaning. An English with words of possible three or four different kinds of meanings. An insinuating, clear-hinting, spicy language. And it won't matter whether your information is correct or not. You can practically manufacture your own sensations."

This is what Mr. Winchell proposed to make of a column, the medium which once served Eugene Field and still serves Heywood Broun. What he has done, and how successfully he has done it, are matters of record. His manner and methods were very swiftly aped— by other Jews.

Yes, there are a few gentiles who do gossip-columns, but they are conspicuously unsuccessful. The success of the gossip-columnist depends on his ability to shamelessly stick his nose into the most private affairs of people of importance, and on the reckless courage to give publicity to what he learns, regardless of how devastating its effects may be in the lives of the people reflected on. The work of some of the columnists is occasionally covered with a fine film of blackmail. But that is, after all, within the national tradition.

What then? We have certainly partaken of the lustre of the intellectual life of America. But have we added any rays or radiance to its glitter and charm? It would seem not. But that has not prevented us in fulfillment of all the prophecies, from making a good business of the light we found.

In the matter of poetry, for instance. Not in all their combined lives have Poe, Whitman and Frost earned what a well-known Jewish salesman of jewelry earns every year by gathering together their best work, as well as the best works of dozens of other American poets, into anthologies, where they may shine next to "poems" of his own. The same thing happens in painting, in sculpture, and in music. The Jew comes into the concert hall as if the very life of music depended on him. As a matter of fact he is only there to make a collection.

Do you remember, Herbert, one of those innumerable discussions held one night in my West Eighth Street bookshop on what was wrong with the American novel? Let me recall it to you. John Gould Fletcher, in New York on one of his visits from England, had walked in on us accidentally.

Karl Wisehart was there too: at that time he was toying with at least three potential novels of Negro life in the south. Minna Loy (of the white brow, long gold earrings, and rambling free verse poems in *The Little Review*) was smoking comfortably and studying the sounds of our voices. I believe we had also with us that Jewish writer of gypsy stories whose name it is always good taste not to remember.

I don't know how it happened, but the talk had fallen on poor Washington Irving, and someone said what a pity it was that he took such pains with a landscape to which he seemed to have not the faintest human attachment.

Fletcher observed, further, that Herman Melville's persistent preoccupation with foreign scenes made it appear that he was, during his whole life in full flight from American things. Someone else—and that might have been you—spoke briefly of the cheerless inventions of James Branch Cabell.

I, it must have been who added that Theodore Dreiser's ox-like nibblings at American life suggested the enthusiasm of a man feeding on a diet of sand.

And I think it was Karl who pronounced the inevitable conclusion which we all accepted without further argument. American literature suffered because of the absence in America of a real love for the American scene.

"What else is there to writing?" cried Karl. "What is the whole magic of a Tolstoy, a Flaubert, a Dickens, or a Hawthorne? Every page of Tolstoy reflects as in a mirror Tolstoy's love of the Russian land and everything that flowers and crawls on it.

The prose of Flaubert is a reproduction, in the most exquisite miniature, of the flora and fauna of France. So anxious was Flaubert to give his writing the natural scenes of the soil of France, that he winnowed out of it even the shadow of an intellectual life.

Dickens, like Fielding before him, had only the most perfunctory interest in natural landscape, but there was not a department of human life on the British Isles that was safe from his prying and tender eyes.

And had not New England been morally as well as physically frozen, Hawthorne might have been easier to take to one's heart. Since Hawthorne, for all American writers have cared about, we might as well have given our country back to the Indians."

Karl exaggerated, of course, as people usually do in such discussions. But in the main I think he was correct that night. The arts spring forth only out of the love of man for the life in which he is rooted, from his attachment to that part of the earth which he has made his home.

It is a man's performance of the double function of taking root and making a real marriage with his country which constitutes culture and civilization.

The offspring of such a marriage are good books, paintings and statues—jewels which the earth yields up only to the most persistent and energetic of her wooers.

What a sorry spectacle the Jew makes on this continent which he pretends to have enriched! Not only does he fail to contribute any glamour to the scene.

He does not even contribute man-power. He does not dig wells, plough fields, forge skyscrapers, lay bricks, cut out trenches, spin wheels, bake dough, fell trees, pack tin cans, sweep streets, heave coal, fire furnaces, weave cloth, dig subways, raise ramparts, wall floods, rivet bridges, hinge gates, or fight fires.

Even at a time like this, when more man-power is offered this country than it can; alas, utilize, it cannot be disputed that quite as important as the vision of an artist who swings a nation from goal to goal, is the man-power with which the vision is reached and passed on the way to the next. Towards the man-power of America Jewry contributes only that which it catches in its own sweatshops, as in so many rat-traps—set by itself. It seems to be part of the Jew's unwritten code that he should never work. Unless something happens to change his vision, I venture to add that he never will, either.

The Shadow Over Main Street

VIII THE JEW IN BUSINESS

Since, therefore, he neither creates nor labors, how then, you will ask, does the Jew subsist in America?

I find in the March 11, 1865 issue of *Notes and Queries*, an English weekly of very high character, the following letter signed by W. J. Charlton: "Are there any Jews who, answering to what we call 'artisans,' work as such in any of our large manufacturing towns, or in any of our cotton mills? I know there are Jews who keep shops but are there any who work as do our carpenters and laborers? Are there, in fact, any class of Jews answering to our class of artisans? I should feel much obliged by this information."

If you will take the trouble to look through *Notes and Queries* for that year, and for five years after that, you will find plenty of scholarly, impartial correspondence by Jewish rabbis and Jewish journalists on a vast variety of Jewish matters, but no answer whatever to W. J. Charlton's momentous question, a question that has been asked in every civilized country that has offered the Jews freedom of movement, and has always been received with the same frozen silence.

It is my honest belief that nothing the Jew does in America is essential to its welfare. On the contrary, a great deal of what the American Jew does is subversive of America's best interests. Like his creature Jehovah, a teacher he never tires of imitating, the Jew in America is forever engaged in the fascinating pursuit of creating everything he needs out of nothing—his modest opinion of the gentile world about him.

"Alas, we have become a nation of *luft-menschen*[25] moaned the great J. L. Peretz, in the midst of the teeming life of Russian Jewry about him, who were doing in his day in Odessa what the Jews are doing in our day in New York. "We must begin to build," he cried

---

[25] *[Air-people] People who live without visible means of support.*

out warningly. "We must make—out of fools, wise people; out of fanatics, men of sense; out of idlers, workers; useful decent workmen who labor for their own livelihood and thereby increase the wealth of society."

These words were written more than thirty years ago. When Peretz died in 1917 he had not lived to see any substantial improvement in the status of his people, either from within or from without. Without, nations were still enacting civil and political restrictions against Jews. Within, the Jews themselves were not at all chastened: they were still a nation of sinisterly busy idlers.

What is this Jewish business of creating everything out of nothing? It is very fascinating, I assure you. The whole thing may perhaps be expressed in one magical word. But since it is a word to which you have in the course of your life attributed other meanings, I better warn you not to jump at conclusions too quickly. The word is *merchandising*. You will not understand what I mean till I show you how it works out.

John Hanly & Son are running a successful furniture business in Battle Creek, Michigan. John Hanly, who is the senior member today, was the Son of a generation ago. But the business is not only very old. It is very good. They have seven solid busy outlets in the seven biggest cities east of the Mississippi. It would seem that there is not very much left for them to wish for by way of business. John Hanly, Sr., thinks so. John Hanly, Jr., thinks so. And even you might think so. But Mr. Isadore Cohen does not think so.

Mr. Isadore Cohen has just made a big clean-up in the fur business in New York. It will probably be at least three years before anyone else can earn a nickel in the fur business, so effectively has Mr. Cohen cleaned it up and out.

Mr. Cohen realizes this and has turned to other fields for new conquests. He has noticed the advertisements of John Hanly & Son.

He has even passed through two or three of their bright stores. In the back of his mind Mr. Cohen has made the following note concerning John Hanly & Son: *Good furniture makers, but like all goyim, too damned conservative.* The whole thing recurs to his mind now. He calls up Mr. Hanly, Sr., establishes an appointment with him, and something like the following conversation takes place:

Mr. Cohen: I believe you sell about half a million dollars' worth of furniture a year, Mr. Hanly?

Mr. Hanly: You are correctly informed Mr. Cohen.

Mr. Cohen: Well, how would you like to treble your business in six months' time?

Mr. Hanly: Very much. What's your plan?

(He knows in advance that the Jew has a plan. Every Jew he has ever met has had some kind of plan by which he made money, without hazarding anything like a real investment. And if you can make money just out of a plan, what couldn't you make out of a whole furniture factory?)

Mr. Cohen: I will explain my plan to you by example. There is in the eastern window of your factory building a magnificent dining-room suite, probably the most elegant manufactured for general consumption in America. Approximately how many sets of it do you dispose of in a month?

Mr. Hanly: I would say about sixty. Around Christmas the figure might be doubled.

Mr. Cohen: Would you say that within the class of people for whom this suite was built only sixty people a month are tempted to buy it?

Mr. Hanly: But you forget that it sells for twelve hundred and fifty dollars a suite. Many more are probably tempted. But only those who can afford to spend twelve hundred and fifty dollars, actually get it.

Mr. Cohen: You mean only those who can spare so much out of their savings can get it—for your terms are cash with delivery.

Mr. Hanly: I guess that's about right.

Mr. Cohen: Would you say that a man who earns five thousand dollars a year can afford such a suite?

Mr. Hanly: Certainly. He makes such a purchase only once in a lifetime.

Mr. Cohen: But most people who earn five thousand dollars a year do not put much into savings accounts. Did that ever occur to you? They like to spend their money lavishly, and they do—on everything except your furniture. In entertainment, for instance. The average man pays a dollar a seat in the theatre, but your five thousand a year man pays at least four, and often as much as ten. In clothing. The average man pays thirty dollars for a suit of clothes, but the five thousand a year man pays a hundred. In furniture. There are companies which soak him twice as much as the prices you ask for things worth not half of the things you manufacture—why? You know the answer. He is not compelled to go to his slender savings. Your five thousand a year man has good taste, and he would infinitely prefer buying your suite to the things he is compelled to get from the installment houses. But you don't let him.

Mr. Hanly: Suppose the five thousand a year man loses his job?

Mr. Cohen: If he hasn't paid for his merchandise, and cannot go on paying it, we take it back from him.

Mr. Hanly: That would never do. To dispose of it, I'd have to go into the second-hand furniture business.

Mr. Cohen: Certainly not, sir. You would have nothing to do with that. I have in mind a man who will buy from you every installment contract you make. You will have none of the trouble of collecting or retrenching on your contract. You will be paid by this man the full amount of the purchase the day after the contract is signed and delivered.

Mr. Hanly: But to produce so much more furniture will require a much larger factory than the one we have. More machinery and more money with which to buy materials and build.

Mr. Cohen: You have nothing to worry about. I know the very man who will supply you with the capital you need at moderate interest.

Mr. Hanly: But such a new system of doing business will require a radically different organization: new methods, new people.

Mr. Cohen: Didn't I tell you that you have nothing to worry about? I'll supply you with the men, the money and the new organization. And you will retain a controlling interest in the business.

What is the result?

Hanly succumbs to the plan. Cohen gets the run of the plant. Israel Isaacs, a friend of Cohen's, agrees to buy all of the new Hanly installment contracts at a discount of fifteen percent for cash, which Hanly adds on to the bills of his customers. Another of Cohen's associates (the same fellows who helped him make that killing in the fur business in New York) Rueben Samuels, lends Hanly the half a million dollars he needs for the expansion of the business along the new lines. Before the Hanlys can realize what has happened, everything about them, in stores and factories, has been so completely changed that it is practically not the same organization. All of their old employees have been discharged. The new faces about them are long and dark, and burn about the eyes with a strange lustful fire.

"It's beginning to look as if we're running a Yiddish colony," complains John Hanly, Jr., dryly.

"What's the use of crying?" says John Hanly, Sr. "They get the business—and isn't that the real important thing?"

"I wonder," says John Hanly, Jr.

The Jews get the business, alright. There is no disputing that. At the end of the first year, Cohen's brightest conjectures have been surpassed. The reorganized firm of John Hanly & Son has sold nearly two million dollars' worth of furniture. But for the first time in many years it is in financial difficulties.

For there is a grave difference between the book profits of a business and its net profits. The one thing Hanley had not taken into reckoning was the interest on that half a million dollars advanced to him by Rueben Samuels for the expansion of the business. With the bonus, that alone comes to forty-five thousand dollars. A lot of money.

There is more trouble with Israel Isaacs. Mr. Hanly, Sr., discovers that he had made no arrangement with Mr. Isaacs as to what was to be done with reclaimed furniture.

When a purchaser of a Hanly suite of furniture defaults in his payments, Mr. Isaacs has a novel way of collecting. He seizes the furniture, sells it to himself (through a dummy) for a trifling sum, and then sues the purchaser and collects from him the full balance through the courts.

How does he collect? Mr. Isaacs has established such an influence in the courts that you would think, watching how his accounts are called in and threatened, that the district attorney's office is really only a collecting agency functioning solely for the benefit of Mr. Isaacs. Having bought back the furniture at a price much less than it costs the Hanly company to manufacture, Mr. Isaacs can afford to sell it to the public at about half of what the Hanly stores ask for the same set. The Isaacs Furniture Company opens its doors to the general public, and it isn't long before a rumor spreads that the furniture at the

Isaacs Company is not really second-hand. It is just a way the Hanly Company has devised of selling its surplus of expensive furniture.

Isaacs sales rise. Hanly sales rise, too—but the prices fall. At the end of the second year of the business of the new organization there are not even book profits. There certainly is no money for the interest on Rueben Samuel's loan. And here a real crisis arises. Mr. Samuels will not accept the interest alone, even if the company can raise it. He wants the whole principle because he has another enterprise in mind. He must have all the money or else.—Or else what? You've guessed it. Within six weeks another important change takes place in the personnel of John Hanly & Son.

The business remains the same. The name remains the same. But when the legal clouds have rolled away, it is discovered that the new president of John Hanly & Son is Mr. Isadore Cohen. The new treasurer is Mr. Rueben Samuels. The new secretary is Mr. Israel Isaacs.

What has become of John Hanly, Sr., and John Hanly, Jr.? They are lucky if they have been permitted to retain clerkships in their own business.

America is full of businesses bearing old Christian names, but which are really owned by Jews. Most of them have been acquired in the manner I have just described, the way the Jew creates something out of nothing.

The charge is frequently brought against the Jew that he is in financial control of everything on the American continent. It is a compliment he hardly deserves, and it is very easy to prove that there is absolutely no truth in the charge. One has only to make a cursory survey of the big banks of the country to arrive at the realization that far from being in control of the nation's finances the Jews are themselves underlings on Wall Street.

What people do not realize is that the underlings of Wall Street are the lions of Main Street.

High finance—in America or elsewhere—the Jews most certainly do not control. The management of the moneys, the life blood of a nation comes under the heading of statesmanship, which the Jews— as in Disraeli and Garibaldi—have occasionally produced for the goyim, but never for themselves.

But what need has the Jew for high finance? Does he not exercise a control he could not possible wield from a seat as lofty as Wall Street? Financial mastery he has. But it is a subterranean one. It is a mastery he enjoys much more, precisely because it comes to him more naturally. The Jew better than anyone else in the world knows how to dispossess the poor and the members of the middle class. To fit this case, the old P. T. Barnum adage needs only a little changing. A gentile enters business every minute, with two Jews waiting to take him out of it.

"What difference does it make that the sun shines, if there is still a Czar in Russia?" sang Lermontov.

So might an American merchant ask: "Of what use is it that J. P. Morgan is king of Wall Street, if when I need money, I have to come to Levy?"

Levy, Levy, Levy. A familiar name. Let's get a little closer to him.

Mr. Levy's office is not on Wall Street, it is on any one of several hundred Main Streets in the United States. Very close to the railway station. Whether this is designed so that he may be in a conspicuous place or to keep him where he can make his escape at a moment's notice, I do not know. Whatever the reason is, one thing I am quite sure of, Mr. Levy is playing safe.

Mr. Levy's methods are very much like the methods of Mr. Rueben Samuels. But there is just enough difference between them to make a sketch of it interesting.

The case in point is that of Mr. Levy's dealings with Mr. Frederic Linton.

Mr. Linton works a farm twelve miles from a railway station on Main Street. Nr. Linton is a pretty shrewd business man even if his business does happen to be farming. For a long time he has managed to extract from his sixty acres just a little more than a good livelihood. Witness the fact that he has a son at Yale and a daughter at Vassar. It takes a little money to manage that.

But no one is proof against an occasional attack of bad times. Suddenly, almost without a warning sign, Linton discovers himself alarmingly short of cash. It's purely a problem in economic policy. If he does not immediately make certain important repairs in his house, barn and machinery, he will eventually run into much graver trouble with them. His balance at the bank has been, of late, so meager that he is almost ashamed of making his slender deposits. As for asking for a loan. Nevertheless he hardens himself to the task and seeks out the manager of the bank.

The banker listens to Linton's recital of his needs attentively and sympathetically, although it is a story he has had to listen to many times. But in the end he has to shake his head. He would like to make the loan, he tells Linton.

He has no doubt that it is a very safe loan to make. But he cannot. There are orders from high up which he does not dare to disregard. The new bank safety, he has been sternly warned, lies in greater restriction in the making of loans.

Since he is already in town, Linton decides to try his luck with some of his friends. Old friends like Eddie Howe and George Brent. He begins by telling them about his visit to the bank. They are sympathetic. But they have been caught quite as badly as he. . . .

"Tell you what," says Eddie Howe. "There's always one man in town who has ready cash to spare. Why don't you try to see Jake Levy?"

"But doesn't he drive a rather shrewd bargain?" objected Linton.

"Sure," agrees Howe. "But when you get down to doing business with Levy it means that you practically have no other choice."

Linton had almost decided to let the repairs go hang when a whim changed his mind. Wonder what sort of man this Levy might be. What sort of security could he ask for that the bank knew nothing about?

The first thing Mr. Linton notices is a sign in Levy's window: MONEY LOANED AT LEGAL INTEREST

Funny, thinks Linton. Like a man hanging out a sign to inform people that he is not a criminal; something queer about it; too damned much legality. Besides, there is a rate of legal interest, and it is six percent. Yet one heard of people paying this Levy the most exorbitant interest for comparatively small loans. . . .

The second surprise is Mr. Levy himself. Mr. Levy is nothing like Linton has pictured to himself. Mr. Levy is tall, clean-shaven and bears himself supply, almost graciously. The sort of man one might find in the best clubs, Mr. Linton was thinking when Mr. Levy reached out his hand and greeted him by name. Then Mr. Linton got the uncomfortable feeling that he had been under the surveillance of those shrewd gray eyes for a long time.

"Twelve hundred dollars," muses Mr. Levy. "And how much time do you want in which to pay it back?"

Mr. Linton thinks. "Four months would be plenty of time," he says.

"You're counting on a good market," observes Mr. Levy.

"Have you any reason to believe that it won't be?"

"No Mr. Linton. But it's good business, in such matters, to count on a poor market. Besides, I will charge you for eight months the same rate it would cost you for four. It's a minimum I've set myself, and you may as well get the benefit of the additional time."

So far everything sounds lovely. A little too lovely. Mr. Linton knows that there must be something else. Something hidden. "And the rate of interest?" he asks.

"The legal rate—six percent."

"Very well, then, will you take my note?"

"Certainly." And here Mr. Levy makes a slight, significant pause. The surprise is coming, Linton says to himself. "There is another condition I have not mentioned, Mr. Linton. We charge a service fee of ten percent on the face of the note."

Mr. Linton is taken by surprise, in spite of himself. "Service fee? What for?"

"Technically, Mr. Linton, it is for bookkeeping, billing, etc. Actually it's for making a loan which the bank considers unsound. You have been to your bank, have you not, Mr. Linton?"

"Yes. But damn it all, you wouldn't make this loan to me if you were not certain of your ability to collect it?"

"The service charge is essential and unavoidable," says Mr. Levy with cold finality.

Mr. Linton takes the twelve crisp, brand new one hundred dollar bills and signs for Mr. Levy a note for thirteen hundred and ninety two dollars.

A week before the note falls due at Linton's bank, Linton receives the following note from Levy. Its surface considerateness puzzles him.

"I am taking the liberty of calling your attention to your note to the amount of $1200.00, which falls due in another week, because it is just possible that you may not be in a position to meet it in full. You are at liberty, should you find it necessary, to arrange for renewal. Please come to see me at your earliest convenience."

Linton wonders how Levy could have guessed that he was unprepared to meet the note. Again he gets that creepy feeling that he is being secretly watched. But there is no alternative. He must see Levy and arrange a renewal.

"This time," says Mr. Levy, "I shall ask you to give me two notes: one payable in ninety days to the amount of twelve hundred dollars, the other for the balance of four hundred twenty-eight dollars and sixty-four cents, due ninety days after that."

Linton feels that he is slowly getting into some kind of trap. But it is too late to retreat. He cannot help himself. To pay the note in full now would leave him without the cash needed for his children's tuition at school for the following year. He signs the notes.

Before the due date of the first note, the one for twelve hundred dollars, there is this time no advance letter from Levy suggesting a renewal. So Linton goes, uninvited, to Levy's house. But as usual, when Levy has determined on a course of action, he is not to be swerved. "That note for twelve hundred dollars must be met, Mr. Linton. I make it an unbreakable rule never to let my cash stay out more than eleven months."

"But in another three months you will have got more than four hundred dollars for your loan. That's nearly forty percent interest. Surely you can afford to be a little more lenient."

Mr. Levy now rises gravely in his chair. All his elegance has been strained to a fine vanishing point. "I am sorry, Mr. Linton," he says with suppressed excitement, "but I will have to judge for myself how lenient I can afford to be. If your money is not in the bank to meet my note I will have to protest."

The twelve hundred dollar note is duly met, without protest. To accomplish this, Linton has to sell some of the machinery he has had mended, and some cattle he can spare just a little, and ninety days later when the second note, the one for four hundred and twenty-eight dollars and sixty-four cents comes due, there is absolutely no way he can raise the money.

He even tries the bank.

Once more the manager of the bank listens to him. This time with more care than sympathy. "I wish I could help you, Mr. Linton," he says, in conclusion. "Unfortunately you have made yourself quite helpless. There is no way in which a decent banking institution could remedy your difficulties."

And once more we find Linton pleading with Levy.

"Renew," says Levy. "But how can you expect it of me? You've sold pretty nearly everything salable on your land. In a forced sale, what you have left will hardly bring back the amount of this note."

"But you don't understand, Mr. Levy, that I want to pay you back? Why talk of a forced sale?"

Mr. Levy looks across the littered table with tremendous earnestness. "Because there will be a marshall's sale if you do not meet this note, Mr. Linton."

The note is not met. Judgment is entered. A marshall appears on the property and levies on it full. The sale takes place. And Mr. Linton's poor sixty acres from which he had derived such a proud livelihood go—do you know to whom? You've already guessed it. To Mr. Levy.

A disillusioned man, Mr. Linton hunts up Mr. Levy in his house several hours after the sale. "This is going to be terrible news to my children at school," he explains in the flat even tones of a man whom you cannot possibly punish anymore. "Can you try to arrange to give me some time in which to adjust my affairs so that I will be able to break it to them gently?"

Here the inborn messianic qualities of the man Levy rise to stupendous heights. He places both hands on the shoulders of Linton. "But you don't have to leave at all if you don't want to," he says soothingly. "Why can't you and your wife remain on the farm and continue to run it as if it were your own? You can move into the smaller house, and when your children come back from college they can help you run things. You don't mind occupying the smaller house, will you? I have some relations in mind for the bigger one. And they will work along with you gladly, happily to make things hum on the farm. What do you say?"

If Mr. Linton had thought before that he had been reduced to the final stage of humiliation he now knew that he had been mistaken.

All the ruthless scheming of the Jew, all his apparent unaccountable hardness, had been directed towards this one terrible point. There were some people of his, Jews, who needed a place in the sun—and Levy had supplied it to them out of his, Linton's, life. Levy might have made more money on him by continuing the loan, but that was not really what Levy had been after.

Someone had to be dispossessed that his relations might have a home. Linton realized with a sinking heart that he really had no chance. His whole life had been lost the moment he crossed Levy's threshold. He had been dealing not with a man but with a whole people.

There is nothing for Mr. Linton to do, however, but to accept.

Mr. Levy shakes both his hands vigorously. The man is almost warm again. "I knew you'd be a sport," he cries. "And I'm sure you'll be very comfortable."

Maybe. But the likelihood is that poor Linton will never again be comfortable till they stretch him out in a good strong pine box, out of reach of the swarm of Levys that have been loosed on the farm, to direct him, his wife and his children. What Linton will never understand, even if he lives to be eighty, is how a loan of twelve hundred dollars at legal interest can have made such a difference in his fortunes.

* * *

Linton and Hanly belong to the more substantial part of society. The damage done there is deadly, to be sure. But the Lintons and the Hanlys have some hope.

Under the title *Bootlegging Blood Money*, Isaac Don Levine gives an account of the workings of the Loan Shark among the poor masses of America. He cites the case of a man in Dallas, Texas, who paid $640 over a period of four years on a loan of $20, and still owes the principal. Another of a young clerk who paid ten dollars a month over a period of two years on a fifty dollar loan, and has not yet got rid of the loan shark. A woman who paid $194 in interest on an original loan of $5 and did not complain to the police until the usurer threatened to seize her furniture. Also the case of a youth of nineteen who "enmeshed by a loan shark before he had reached the age for making a legal contract, paid $148 on a $5 debt to an automobile finance company, which was able to extort 1000% interest from the victim with the aid of a justice of the peace and two constables."

Most dramatic and noteworthy, however, is the case of David Law, a Tampa negro who borrowed $5 from a loan shark company, and was so hounded by the usurers that he killed one and dangerously wounded another and—in Florida where negro lynchings are still plentiful—was freed on the plea of the prosecuting attorney who held that, under the circumstances, the negro was fully justified in the shooting.

What measures cannot be justified against people who, for the advance of a small sum of money, tie up salaries, practice black-mail, sell-out and ruin estates, and even prey on the slender incomes of helpless war veterans!

* * *

We see the Jew, then, in business, as promoter, money-lender, salesman par excellence, the author and chief instigator of a system of credit by which a nation-wide usury rises like a Golem with a million hands on a million throats, to choke the honor and the freedom-of-movement of a hard-working people.

These Levys who make money simply by lending it shrewdly at tremendous heart-eating interest, it is not in their miserable souls to bring anything into existence, nor is it in their hearts to sustain the life of those bright beautiful things which have been brought into the world of life by others. They know only the great bargain by means of which they make themselves the masters of the things manlier men than themselves have dreamed out.

Kol Nidre!

IX JUDAISM IS NOT A MISFORTUNE TO THE JEWS ALONE

"Judaism is not a religion, but a misfortune," said Heine in one of his bitter moments. He was thinking of his own unhappiness. No one has as yet calculated the extent of its misfortune to the rest of the world.

The defender of religion (and because they are usually people to whom it is a source of livelihood, they are not the very nicest people to get into an argument with) insist that religion is absolutely essential to the well-being of society. Let religion be taken out of every day life, say these spiritual prodigies, and with it will go every sense of what is right and what is wrong: before you know it, the world would find itself in a state of moral if not actual anarchy.

I am quite certain that religion is not essential to the welfare of society and that it brings into every community it pierces, much more harm than good. And I am fully in accord with Edward Gibbon who hated Judaism and Christianity alike and, years after the publication of *The Decline and Fall of the Roman Empire*, confessed that his examinations of the Old and New Testaments might have been in error; but so absolute was his feeling of the completeness of his case against them, he had not felt it necessary to go through them with the care he had bestowed on other works of antiquity.

I happen to like reading the Old Testament purely for the reading pleasure it gives me. But if that sort of writing does not give you satisfaction, reading almost anything else will be better for you.

Gibbon accuses Christianity on inheriting from Judaism religious intolerance along with the rest of the religion. One of Gibbon's most vigorous opponents,[26] Abbate Nicola Spedalieri, a catholic scholar of charm and distinction, replied that Christian intolerance was not

---

[26] *A horde of critics and disparagers of Gibbon sprang up right after the publication of the first volume of his famous work.*

derived from the Jews: it sprang from the overwhelming zeal of a fresh young people for a new beloved religion.

Spedalieri was too engrossed in the studies of his religion to realize that religious intolerance was practically unknown in the world before the appearance of Judaism. The very genesis of the Jewish People is in religious intolerance. They have lived by it. And it seems to me to be a neat bit of historic justice that they will eventually themselves be destroyed by it.

Search painstakingly through the best extant accounts of the ancient world. Go carefully through all the learned studies of primitive peoples, from Taylor to Frazer. Can you find even a trace of a proselytizing religion?[27]

Strictly speaking, of course, Judaism never was, and is not even today, a proselytizing religion. But Judaism was the first religion in the world which divided everything into those things which are right and those things which are wrong.

And that started all the mischief. As long as religions were content with inventing idols in their own images, or in the images of their great teachers, or in the images of birds and beasts whom they either loved, or hated, or in images of the sun, the moon or some great boar, religion was simply the modest means by which the peoples of the earth paid tribute to the mysteriousness of their origin and destiny.

But the moment one people decided that its own conception of these mysteries was right, and the inspirations of all the other peoples wrong, thereby creating an aristocracy of the emotions, the pot of religion overboiled and scalded a whole world. It was this conviction, that it was right and that all the other people in the world were wrong, that Christianity inherited in full from Judaism. Once it found itself filled with the fury of intolerance, Christianity not only attacked the pagan world but its Jewish teachers as well.

I am not prepared to speak for any religion but the religion I was born into and which has followed me about for forty years like an evil shadow. I have no hesitation in declaring that if the Jew's sole chance of survival lies in the preservation of his religion, it is time for

---

[27] *The expulsion of the Jews by Tiberius is the very first sign of religious intolerance in international affairs. The second was the persecution of the Christians.*

him to throw his cards on the table and call it quits. Judaism is today the only bar between the Jews and the world they love and would like to share with their neighbors.

Every synagogue we Jews build in Christian countries is a finger of scorn we point at our hosts, a sore finger we stick in their eyes, like the leering of a senile old woman who does all sorts of foul mischief before you, and feels safe in the knowledge that you will not lay hands on her to remove her, for fear of contamination. It is as we said to the gentiles:

"There is a right and there is a wrong. The right is to be found only behind the doors of our synagogues, and there only. Everything in your churches is spurious, as you should know of your own accord, for your very first churches were built by apostate Jews who knew only how to pervert the true religion which is ours."

By publishing the Ten Commandments among the nations, the Jew gave birth to religious intolerance. By building synagogues in Christian countries they continue to keep it alive, and their own consequent destruction by it becomes daily more imminent. Why, I would like to know, is a synagogue more in place in a Christian country than were the altars of Baal in Palestine when the prophets pronounced them to be an unbearable abomination?

Suppose the Turks began coming to America in great numbers, built mosques in our market places, and began to prostrate themselves several times a day on Broadway, on Grand Street, or on Main Street, depending on where they happened to be the moment the muezzin called them to prayer? Would not Jew join gentile enthusiastically in trying to suppress them? Why is a synagogue different from a mosque or a Buddhist temple?

Jews like to advance the thesis that you cannot, dare not, do violence to Judaism because it is the perfect religion, and probably the highest standard of wisdom and ethics developed by the human race. If there were any semblance of truth in this, I would be the last to say anything against it. Mankind has developed little enough of wisdom and perfection: certainly we should not destroy what little we have of it.

But it is not true that Judaism is perfect in any respect. The observances of the Jewish religion are as varied, as different in assembled virtues, and as full of crudities as any religion I have ever read about. Certainly no other religion in the world has offered the world a spectacle as contradictory, as malicious, as full of the spirit of unreasonableness as the Jewish recital of the prayer *Kol Nidre* during Yom Kippur. I suggest that if we are going to start tearing down this great fortress of Jewish religious prejudice and intolerance, *Kol Nidre* is perhaps the best starting point.

Kol Nidre has been a point of sore controversy for the Jewish People throughout the Middle Ages. I do not like to be the first to raise the hydra-head of this monster on the American continent. But I cannot afford to pass by anything which may help me make my point.

Kol Nidre! What the sound of that word means to a Jew from the first time he heard it in the white twilight of a tall-candled synagogue on the eve of Yom Kippur, and on through the wilderness of ghetto years, only a Jew can understand! The most intimate memories of childhood, youth and manhood, twine themselves about that tune, and he hangs upon it, as upon the branches of a tree, the choicest of his emotions, till to threaten sacrilege against *Kol Nidre* would seem to threaten life itself.

Yet what is *Kol Nidre* actually? I reproduce here an authorized translation from the regular prayer-book issued by the *Hebrew Publishing Company*:

"All vows, obligations, oaths or anathemas, pledges of all names, which we shall have vowed, sworn, devoted or bound ourselves to, from this day of atonement (whose arrival we hope for in happiness) to the next, we repent, aforehand, of them all, they shall be deemed absolved, forgiven, annulled, void and made of no effect; they shall not be binding nor have any power; the vows shall not be reckoned vows, the obligations shall not be reckoned obligatory, nor the oaths considered oaths.

"And it shall be forgiven to the whole congregation of Israel, and to the stranger who sojourneth amongst them; for all the people act ignorantly."

And is that, you ask, all of *Kol Nidre?* That is all there is to *Kol Nidre*, I must answer. In reciting it the Jew solemnly swears before his Lord God that he has only one fealty, loyalty or obligation, and that is to Him, the Lord God. No matter what business he may undertake to promote with his neighbor, be it material or moral, he wants the Lord God to understand in advance that there will be one implicit condition (a condition, however, he does not undertake to explain before entering into an argument): the execution of it must be favorable to Him, the Lord God, or it will be considered by the Jew void, of no account, utterly useless, as if it had never been mentioned, as if nothing relating to it had ever been negotiated.

When the meaning of Kol Nidre became known during the Dark Ages, a cry of rage broke from the throats of the goyim. "In that case," they cried, "a Jew may enter into any arrangement with us, with a light heart. Does his enterprise prosper? Then he abides by the agreement.

If not, he can always denounce the whole affair by remembering that in the moment of *Kol Nidre*, the most sacred of all moments in the Jew's life, he had practically, fully and without equivocation negated it."

And so it came about that the eve of Yom Kippur became, for the gentiles throughout Europe, a time for protest against Jewish knavery. Usually the gentiles living near a Jewish community would announce the coming of Yom Kippur by displaying posters everywhere reading:

"BEWARE: THE DAY IS AT HAND WHEN THE JEW RENOUNCES AS INSINCERE ANY DEALINGS HE MAY HAVE WITH YOU DURING THE COMING YEAR. BEWARE!"

In many communities legislators considered it necessary to have a special form of oath administered to Jews—an oath intended to negate the oath of *Kol Nidre*.

This oath was known as the Jew's Oath. There were judges who absolutely refused to take any supplementary oath from a Jew, as totally insincere and untrustworthy, and they based their objections chiefly on *Kol Nidre*.

The origin of this most extraordinary (as well as un-wisest) of all Jewish prayers is hidden in the mists of the Dark Ages. No one knows how it came into existence, in the first place.

No one has any idea how it became so vital a part of the synagogue service. It is only fair to add that, in spite of the general acceptance which *Kol Nidre* has enjoyed since its inception, there has never been a time when there was not a really strong and honest opposition to it among Jews. One of the six Gaonim of the two Babylonian Academies, for instance, five placed themselves unalterably against admitting it into the program of prayer for Yom Kippur.

How did it happen, then, that, despite the anger of the gentile world which considered the prayer a gross and insulting breach of faith with it, and against the advice of the wisest and most pious among the priests of Israel, *Kol Nidre* was not only adopted into the Prayer Book but achieved such distinction in the Jewish mind that it can be associated in the minds of the people in holiness only with the Ten Commandments?

Usually, as I have already pointed out, the evils of Israel are the evils of leadership. *Kol Nidre* does not follow the rule, for if it were a matter of following the advice of leaders, *Kol Nidre* would have been dropped out of Jewish life long ago.

The retention and magnification of *Kol Nidre* in the grand order of the synagogue is a characteristic bit of Jewish mob obstinacy—in this case an obstinacy entirely without justification in reason or in history.

Its authorship has never been imputed to a vital personality, nor is its origin associated with important events in the history of the people. The text has never even been regarded as sacred, for there are two different versions, one in Aramaic, the other in Hebrew, which differ in several important details.

The accepted current version has an important alteration made in it by Rashi's son-in-law, Meir ben Samuel, who changed the original phrase "from the last Day of Atonement to this one" to "from this Day of Atonement to the next one."

As if, morally, it makes any difference whether you welch on an arrangement already made or on one you might make at a later date!

The members of the two Academies in Babylon only began the long but unsuccessful campaign of opposition to *Kol Nidre*, when Juda ben Brazillaia, Spanish author of the twelfth century, declared himself against *Kol Nidre* because, he claimed, the ignorant Jews took it too literally, and so were the cause of endless embarrassment for the more enlightened of the people.

A rabbinical conference held in Brunswick in 1844 decided unanimously that the formula was not essential to the general concept of Judaism, and should be suppressed if possible. On the other hand, *Kol Nidre* has not been without its champions. The defenses have been many and varied, and they have all agreed on one point: the vows referred to in *Kol Nidre* are exclusively religious.

The Saadya Gaon, for instance, maintained that *Kol Nidre* was introduced only for the whole community, and most certainly was not meant to have any application to the life of the individual Jew. In other words, his argument boils down to this: the Jewish community could enter into arrangements it had no intention of keeping, but the individual member of the community might not!

A more subtle argument—I have not been able to trace to anyone in particular—claimed that "the dispensation of vows in *Kol Nidre* refers only to those which an individual voluntarily assumed for himself alone and in which no other persons or their interests were involved."

But the height of interpretative shrewdness is reached in the explanation of Rabbi Isaiah of Trani.

"Since the Jews come to the synagogue on Yom Kippur to ask forgiveness for *all* their sins, it is important that they clear themselves of all vows which they might carry out during the following year."

Obviously dishonest seems to me, also, the specious argument that the views referred to in *Kol Nidre* are exclusively religious.

If the author of *Kol Nidre* had meant that, he would have begun the prayer with the simple words "All vows unto Thee O Lord made": he would not have taken the trouble to mention "obligations and pledges of all names."

Nor am I more impressed with the explanation that the prayer is intended to apply to the congregation as a whole and not to any individual member of it. This would make the whole business appear both stupid and useless.

For the congregation never conducts any business for itself with other congregations or communities; what need would there be for such tremendous emphasis on nothing?

And what are those (vows) which an individual voluntarily assumed for himself alone, and in which no other persons or their interests are involved? In our own life, they would approximate New Year's resolutions, and the like.

Besides, whereas it is possible to talk of obligations as being intended entirely for one's own self, it is difficult to conceive of pledges which do not involve other people.

I cannot see any more sense or sincerity in the argument that *Kol Nidre* was introduced into the prayers of Yom Kippur, and placed at the head of all of them, so as to facilitate the Lord's forgiveness of the sins of the Jew by the Jews voluntarily abjuring all business arrangements they might make during the following year. It does not improve the stature of the Jew as a human being. It makes of Israel's Lord God an even more odorous demon than he shows himself in the book of Exodus.

The only reasonable theory is the one recently introduced by Dr. Joshua S. Bloch. *Kol Nidre*, he says, originated during the Visigoth persecution of the Jews in the seventh century. The Visigoths forced Jews to forswear Judaism with the most fearful oaths and anathemas. The converts had to solemnly declare that they believed in the Trinity, and that Jesus was the Redeemer promised to Israel by their prophets.

They promised also to make of themselves spies amongst the unconverted Jews, to report to their rulers any scheme the Jews might concoct against their enemies, and also to report, if they discovered it, if any Jewish converts to Christianity practice in secret their own religion, or any part of it.

They were, moreover, forced to vow, never again to intermarry with their own people. The penalty for disobedience was death by stoning.

As, it is needless to add, the forced converts to Christianity invariably remained at heart true to their religion, when Yom Kippur came they found many ways of secretly celebrating it. In this they were troubled by one thing.

They were breaking the vows that had been forced on them by their oppressors. As a means to counteracting this shadow on their consciences, *Kol Nidre* was introduced at the very opening of the prayers of repentance before the ordeal of Yom Kippur might be said to have properly begun.

Through it the Jews begged to be abjured of all vows they had made or would make.

112

But what about the appearance of *Kol Nidre* in the prayers of communities who were not troubled by the Visigoths or any other enemy with the Visigothic tactics?

Dr. Bloch explains that in one form or another this form of persecution was handed on to all Jewish communities, for under their Byzantine rulers, and still later as Marranos in Spain, the Jews suffered of similar vows made to their conquerors.

The chief objection to this theory is that the Jews in Spain did not know Hebrew well enough to introduce the *Kol Nidre* into their liturgy, for its inner meaning. Besides, the Jews of Spain and the Jews of Babylon were in constant communication. How did the Babylonian Jews fail to explain the meaning of *Kol Nidre* to the Jews of Spain, unless, as it seems very likely, no such explanation existed amongst them?

All Jews concede that the real reason for the persistence of *Kol Nidre* in the Jewish ritual is the painful sweetness and haunting tearfulness of the melody. It came into our life a dybbuk, an evil spirit, but it has arrested our ears with the plaintive chanting of an angel suffering.

The musical motive of *Kol Nidre* was not new. It was old and essentially Jewish. From the song of Moses and Miriam, through the songs of Deborah and Solomon, down to the inspired elegies of David, the theme flowed right into *Kol Nidre* where it reached a high tide of beauty and ecstasy. *Kol Nidre* has dug a trench for itself deep in the heart of the Jewish People.

It seems as if to try to undermine it is to undermine the life of the whole people. But, if we must continue to sing it in order to keep alive, why cannot we discard the awful words, words without melody, beauty or imaginativeness? We must unearth *Kol Nidre* and fling the foul corpse over the rim of the earth, if we are ever to get rid of Judaism.

I have the same objection to Yom Kippur (Day of Forgiveness) that I have to the Catholic institution of Confession. It breeds instability of mind and character.

If a man knows that no matter how badly he behaves a whole year, no matter what crimes or iniquities he commits, a day is sure to come when all his transgressions, civil and criminal alike, will be forgiven him, it is only human that he should be tempted to do rash, violent things to promote his worldly fortunes.

The Jewish Prayer Book lists the following sins specifically, as amongst those which are unconditionally forgiven the Jew on Yom Kippur:

Sins committed with incestuous lewdness;
Oppressing one's neighbor;
Assembling to commit fornication;
Deceitful acknowledgements;
Violence;
Evil imagination;
Denying and lying;
Taking and giving bribes;
Calumny;
Extortion and usury;
Haughtiness;
Shamelessness;
Lawlessness;
Litigiousness;
Treachery to one's neighbor;
Tale-bearing;
False-swearing;
Embezzlement;
Stealing.

The Jews with whom I have discussed this matter, answer my objections to the institution of forgiveness in Judaism by pointing out that the modern nations have all approved of the idea of their own accord by themselves enacting laws which nullify debts after statutory time, and by adopting, in one form or another, a bankruptcy law.

What they fail to observe is that bankruptcy law, even in the United States, where it is most generously worded and applied, clears a man of his obligations only when he has managed to prove beyond a shadow of doubt that he has absolutely no property of his own left outside of the clothes he wears, the bed he sleeps in, and, in some countries, the tools of his profession or occupation. Anything else of value he owns must revert irrevocably to his creditors.

Much as the hopeless debtor comes before the Referee in Bankruptcy, the Jew comes before his Lord God in the Synagogue. "Forgive me for I have stolen," he says.

Does the Lord God reply: "You will be forgiven provided you make a complete restitution to those from whom you have stolen?"

No. He forgives the thief unconditionally, just, I suppose, for the honor of finding himself with him in the same room.

The Jew, then, safe in the knowledge that three hundred and sixty-five days later there will be another equally generous Yom Kippur, sanctifies himself at the end of the holy day and continues to steal as before.

In the three prisons in which I have sojourned as the result of my forced association with Jewish lawyers and Jew-controlled courts, I found the overwhelming number of habitual criminals to be Catholics and Jews.

The Catholic knows that he can clear himself of anything by the simple act of going to Confession. But the Jew goes the Catholic one better.

He denies, by his recital of *Kol Nidre*, even before he undertakes it, any possible responsibility in crime. Can it be doubted what a fearful influence for evil this must exert on his character as a citizen and as a human being?

Kol Nidre must go. After *Kol Nidre*, must go the synagogue. And with the synagogue must go Judaism which has been the cause of untold evil both to the Jew and the world about him.[28]

_____

[28] *How the meddling of religion with life works out is illustrated in the famous case of the Tewkesbury Jew. When I first heard this story it was purely one of a horrible atrocity perpetrated by an arrogant gentile lord on a humble, unresisting Jew. The tale, as the Jew tells it, is just a monstrosity. But in a book published in 1258, and entitled* Chronological Outline of the History of Bristol, *it is related as follows: "A Jew fell into a privy in Tewkesbury on a Saturday, and would not suffer anyone to pull him out, for the reverence he had for his Sabbath; and the next day, being Sunday, Richard de Clare, Earl of Gloucester, would not suffer anyone to pull him out for the reverence he had for his Sabbath. On the morrow morning, being Monday, the Jew was found dead.» There is an even earlier commentary written by a local wit*

Perhaps the best advice given to the Jews by one of the greatest of all modern Jews, Karl Marx, in his review of the Jewish question:

"If the Jew wants to be emancipated from the Christian State, then he must demand that the Christian State abandon its religious prejudice. Is the Jew ready to abandon *his* religious prejudices?

"The Jews waits on a future which has nothing to do with the future of mankind.

"For if the individual, although a Jew, can be politically emancipated and receive civic rights, can he claim and receive the so called rights of man?

"The question is whether the Jew as such, that is the Jew who admits that by his very nature he is compelled to live in everlasting separation from others, is capable of receiving and conceding to others the general rights of man.

"The idea of the rights of man was first discovered in the last century, so far as the Christian world is concerned.

"It is not innate in the individual, it is rather conquered in the struggle with the historical traditions in which the individual has hitherto been brought up.

"Thus the rights of man are not a gift from Nature, not a legacy from past history, but the price of the struggle against the accident of birth and against the privileges which history has bequeathed from generation to generation up to now.

They are the result of education, and can only be possessed by those who have acquired and earned them.

"Can they really be claimed by the Jew? So long as he is a Jew, the limiting quality which makes him a Jew must triumph over the

---

in 1228, *which tells the same story in rhyme:*
"Jew reach thy hand to me; from Draugh I wil thee free.
Our Sabbath I observ; and will here rather sterv.
Then Jew, sans more adoo, then keep our Lord's Day too."
This simple, astounding chronicle should serve as a guide-post to the whole of the religious conflict which shows the Jew creating prejudices which his neighbors follow and eventually curse him with. Is it plausible, unless there were something fundamentally wrong with them at the core, that a people as intelligent as the Jews should not call a halt to such arrant nonsense after two thousand years of catastrophic pursuit of it?

human quality which binds him as a man to other men, and must separate him from the gentiles."

The social emancipation of the Jew is the emancipation of society from Judaism.

"I must eat."

X THE JEW AS A LAWYER

"At the death of Moses," says the author of *The Book of Enoch*, "the sun was eclipsed, and the Written Law lost its splendor. At the hour of King David's death, the light of the Moon diminished and the radiance of the Oral Law was tarnished. The consequence was that discussions and controversies began among the sages so that the joy in the study of the Law has ceased for all future generations."

Nothing seems to me more natural than that Jews should be attracted to the study of Law. But, in view of what they have done with the laws of mankind, no other people would seem to me to be less fit to administer them—for the world and even for themselves. And nothing seems to me so monstrously ironical as the liberalness with which the major peoples of the earth continue to admit Jews to the practice of the two cardinal professions—law and medicine: the one governing the affairs of men, the other guarding them against the evils of their mortal origin.

Consult your average business man in England, in France, in Germany or even in liberal America. Ask him why he invariably refuses to employ a Jew in a position of trust. He will make reply and, out of an old habit, defend himself against your question or rather its implication of bigotry. "It's not race prejudice," he will plead. "I simply feel that the Jew's habit is to mind his own business, which is not always, unfortunately, the business of his employer."

Apparently, it is too much to ask the average business man to let a Jew keep his books, run his factory, sell his wares behind a counter, manipulate his cash-register or receive deposits at a teller's window in a bank. But there is no objection to making him an officer of the court. There is no harm in entrusting the Jew with his life and the health of his family.

This is going to be a book of revelations to many. We live on this continent in a Jew-made civilization. So deeply have our institutions been impressed with the stamp of the Jewish mind and temperament, that I find it necessary (if I am to meet my reader on something like a common ground of understanding) to establish definitions for our most elementary institutions.

There is the Law and its administrator the lawyer. We understand, fairly enough, that the Law is a code by which civilized people conduct their individual affairs in a community, with a maximum of gain for the community and a minimum loss to the individual in it. But what is our conception of the lawyer, the man whom we entrust with the work of administering the code for us?

The American idea of a lawyer is something like this. If you have a contract to make or break, a man to sue or a suit to defend, or if you or someone close to you falls into a legal tangle involving possible loss of property or liberty, you go to a lawyer, a man reputed to have a working knowledge of the laws of your community and country, and bargain out with him the conditions on which he is to defend you or serve your interests. Whether you win or lose will depend, you feel, not so much on whether you are right or wrong, but on what kind of lawyer you retain. From the American point of view, it has become more important, in a legal dispute, to have a good lawyer than to be in the right.

If a Christian in New York City pauses to meditate on the fact that more than half of the four thousand lawyers in their telephone directory are Jews, it is only to reflect that the Jews are certainly smart to have managed it. It does not occur to him to think that there may be, because of that, some fifteen hundred more lawyers in his community than can legitimately make a living, and that the presence of such an over-population of lawyers may have a very serious effect on the practice of the laws in the courts to which he has come for rectification of his affairs. Not infrequently, because he regards the Jew as a particularly astute fellow, the gentile will hire a Jewish lawyer to defend him or to extend his commercial interests—in preference to hiring a gentile lawyer who is likely to be more conservative and less enterprising. In the mind of the average American the spectacle of laws, courts and lawyers is somewhat anarchic, a game of catch-as-catch-can in which the smarter lawyer catches the biggest prizes.

This is the picture, and a very bad one. But how, you will ask, do I, a Jew and a foreigner, take it upon myself to say what is the right attitude towards the law? I happened to have spent the first nine years of my life in a gentile civilization, and I can still remember that the lawyer, or *advocat* as he was there called, was looked upon not as a salesman of legal services but as an officer of the court to whom you were privileged to tell, in perfect security, your side of the story, the difficulty you were in. People paid this *advocat* not for his ability to put a fraudulent contract over on their clients' business associates, but for his shrewdness in interpreting the laws in their favor. The old-world lawyer regards himself primarily as an officer of the court. If the American lawyer realizes that he is an officer of the court, he certainly does not take this phase of his function seriously. This callousness is the result of the practice of the Jewish lawyer who swarms the American courts in such numbers that the average lawyer's office has become about as safe, for the poor layman, as a nest of rattlesnakes.

I began to know Jewish lawyers through Nathan Maggog, a Jewish attorney who lives in Manhattan Island and is privileged to practice law in the courts of the State of New York. Of medium height, distressingly stout, he is habitually mopping his florid face with a handkerchief. He gathers his clientele in the home voting district in which he has successfully brought in a safe majority for his political organization for more than twenty years. I became acquainted with Maggog when he was still a young man, before it ever occurred to him to study the law. He was then about twenty-five years old, maybe thirty; and in return for bringing in the vote, he was content with a job of inspector of weights and measures in the local meat and fish markets. That Maggog collected more fines than did the courts from the merchants whose scales did not pass the test of honesty, goes without saying. But I never knew him to be particularly bright. What put it into his fat head to give up such an easy graft for the dubious laurels of being a lawyer on the east side?

The answer is probably in Maggog's first marriage. He married one of those dark skinny little Jewesses whose eyes shine with the lust of the social climber. She it was who must have nagged the slothful Nathan into taking the night-school course which led to his admittance to the New York Bar. It is also possible that he received some encouragement from local political leaders who are always in need of dependable go-betweens between themselves and criminals in the criminal courts. In that, they have found the Maggogs to be their best servants.

Maggog's practice of law is a very simple one. When a pickpocket in his district gets into serious difficulties with the law, his mother brings a hundred, or two hundred, or a thousand dollars (depending both on the seriousness of the offence, and the pickpocket's wealth) to Maggog's office, and turns the case over to him. The next morning Maggog calls up his district leader, and the district leader looks up the magistrate who is to preside over the hearing on the case. If the magistrate is one who is not friendly to this arrangement, the case is postponed till it comes before one who is.

When the case is finally called, the pickpocket is either fined or dismissed. Or, according to the gravity of the charge, he is given a light sentence. Maggog splits fifty-fifty with the district leader who, in turn, splits fifty-fifty with the higher ups. The Maggogs take naturally to this sort of law-practice; from their aptness in it, I suspect that they invented it.

I myself came to Maggog (years after my first meeting with him) because I was in need of the political influence which is his stock-in-trade. I spent, thereafter, many evenings in his home on the east side, where he conducts his most profitable business. I saw clients come to him from every part of his district—always on petty matters connected with the criminal courts. Mostly, they were the women of the men who had got into some moral difficulty. Often they were women who had themselves fallen into the traps of the law. They came to him not because they respected his knowledge of the law, or because they had been attracted by his ability as a pleader, for he had as little of the one as of the other. They came to him because they knew that he represented an organization which sold influence in the courts like so much meat on the table.

Maggog's attitude towards his clients was quite as cynical as was their attitude towards himself. One night, I remember, a poor bedraggled woman in her early sixties came in and counted out ninety one dollar bills on the table before him "It's all the money I have and am able to borrow," she explained. "But with it you must promise me that you'll do something for my boy."

I don't think I have witnessed in my life many tragedies as poignant as the counting out of that ninety dollars on Maggog's table. Each bill had the appearance of having had a career all its own, as do the bills owned by very poor people who handle them and finger them over and over again before parting with them. Thousands of people, as it seemed to me, must have owned those bills before they reached this poor woman. And she must have obtained them from at least twenty different sources.

Maggog pocketed the money briskly, told her he would do his best for her son and advised her to stop worrying.

When the old woman had curtsied and gone out, Maggog told me the pitiful story. Her son was coming up next morning for sentence. The case against him, grand larceny, was the fourth felony of which he stood convicted. Under the laws of the State of New York, it was mandatory on the part of the judge to send him to jail for the rest of his natural life.

"Well, then, you *can't* do anything for him!" I said.

Maggog shrugged. "Certainly not."

"But that money—what is that for?"

He smiled. "Somebody had to take it. Why not I?"

Leolom Tickach. Always take.

I have chosen Maggog as an example of a Jewish lawyer, for two reasons. In the first place he is the sort of lawyer most prevalent wherever there is a corrupt machine preying on the populace through the courts. In the second place, it was a lawyer of Maggog's type who is responsible for the three convictions I have sustained in the criminal courts of the State of New York. Since you will hear a great deal about this from my enemies, you might as well get the truth from me.

Once before, when I dared expose the life of a very powerful man, the only answer he would give to my charges was that since I had three convictions against me I was not to be believed. Neither he nor his numerous journalistic friends who were paid to defend him against the things he was charged with, undertook to explain how the convictions against me were obtained.

If they did, it would have become apparent that if I am a criminal it is in the same sense in which Cervantes, Bruno, Jesus and many other men of ideals and courage before me became criminals in their days.

Towards the end of 1927, in the midst of the controversy over the publication of *Ulysses* in *Two Worlds Monthly* which I edited and published, and when the finances of my publishing company had fallen so low that it had even lost its bank account, a Jew who will here remain nameless came to me with the following proposition.

He had, he said, three hundred copies of *The Perfumed Garden*, a book on the physiological aspects of love written by the Cheikh Nefzaoui in Arabian about four hundred years ago.

The book had been published at thirty-five dollars a copy. If I sent out a circular on it to the people on my subscription list, I would surely sell them out. And as the price per copy to me would be only two dollars, I stood to make almost ten thousand dollars on the transaction—enough to rehabilitate me financially.

Every publisher with a select list of book buyers receives such propositions. I had received them before and turned them down. And I was not particularly inclined towards this one. I knew the contents of *The Perfumed Garden*, and there was no doubt in my mind as to what would be the attitude of the Post Office towards selling it through the mails.

But I was very badly in need of money, and this bookseller was very persuasive. "You need have absolutely nothing to do with the circularizing end of it," he assured me. "Get yourself a fictitious name at a temporary address. I'll mail out the circulars for you. You will receive the orders and the money, and I will supply you with the books as you need them. If there's any trouble, I'll take the blame."

Within a week, on the complaint of the local vice crusader who received one of the circulars through an agent of his on my list with a Long Island address, I was apprehended by two postal inspectors as I was in the act of receiving returns from the circular. One of the agents opened an envelope and showed me the circular which, up to that time, I had not yet seen.

It was not only an obscene description of The Perfumed Garden, it contained a really obscene drawing that was supposed to be a specimen of a series of such drawings illustrating the book. My bail was set at five thousand dollars. I had barely money to pay a

124

bondsman. As for a lawyer, I remembered a Jewish lawyer I once knew. He was not a particularly good lawyer, but he had a reputation for having political connections.

He would, at any rate, be able to advise me through the first steps of this catastrophe, for I had never before been inside a criminal court. "How much money can you raise?" he asked me abruptly.

I replied that I could raise a hundred dollars; maybe more, later, if I needed it. "Get the hundred first," he said.

A few days later I brought him the money. He pocketed it and looked long and lingeringly at me. "That story of yours about somebody else sending those circulars out for you won't go," he said, "unless you can get the man who did it to come to court and take the blame."

I told him that a course of action along those lines was impossible. The sort of rat who played that kind of trick was not likely to take the blame for it. As a matter of fact, he was already half way across the continent towards California.

"There's only one thing left for you to do, then," he said. "Plead guilty. I think I can arrange for you to get a suspended sentence. Another hundred dollars for the assistant D.A. will probably do that."

"But since I'm not guilty," I suggested, "don't you think I'd do better to take a chance and tell my story to a jury?"

"No," he replied. "You can't afford to take a chance with a jury. If they find you guilty, it might mean prison for a year. If you take a suspended sentence, it will be as if nothing had happened to you."

I believed him, as millions of poor people believe such lawyers and such arguments.

But how was I to know that he advised me to plead guilty because he felt incapable of trying the case himself and he was too greedy to share my fee with someone who might be able to do it? Furthermore.

Instead of letting me believe that a suspended sentence would leave me "as if nothing had happened to me," he should have warned me that it meant the beginning of a criminal record. He should have emphasized to me the grave fact that to have a criminal record would mean that I would never again be able to testify in any suit, civil or criminal, without some shyster like himself rising to nullify my evidence merely by asking me if I had ever sustained a conviction.

Sentence was suspended on me, as promised. But I was also fined five hundred dollars and placed on probation for two years. The fine was most unjust because it was to take me nearly a year to pay it back to the people I borrowed the money from. As for the probation, it was not as good as the intention of the court in imposing it on me.

The probation system is probably alright when the government remains in complete charge of the prisoner. But I walked out of Judge Knox's court straight into a net laid for me by the local vice crusader. I could turn nowhere without being accosted by one of his agents, and a more evil-looking, foul-smelling lot of men I have never encountered in my life. Eventually, within less than a year, they found the Jew to get me with.

The name of this Jew was Henry Klein, a merchant in books, whose hobby was the manufacturing and wholesaling of pornography. As I'm writing this he is serving his third or fourth sentence on Welfare Island. He had always seemed to me an amiable sort of lunatic, and I went out of my way many times to be nice to him.

Only a few days before he sold me out, I had helped substantially to get bail for him on one of the occasions on which he was caught with a car-load of obscene books.

His only business with me was to supply my wife with sets of the English and American classics which she placed on sale in her store. The Book Auction at 28 E. 12th Street.

One morning, in the midst of an advertised book auction, the vice crusader, accompanied by five men from the Vice Squad, came in, closed the doors of the shop, and instituted a search. I happened to be present, to help an unlettered auctioneer in the matter of describing the books put up for sale.

The visit of the vice crusaders was not at all surprising, for I knew well his anxiety to get me into trouble and so make it appear before Judge Knox that I had violated my parole. But I was surprised when he fished a package of obscene photographs and drawings out of the dust-bin in the back of the shop. I was arrested once more, and remanded for trial before the Court of Special Sessions.

On getting out on bail, I investigated the mysterious package in the dust-bin and learned that the day before its discovery by the vice crusader, the Jew Klein had brought it into the shop. He had chosen a time when I was not there, and, leaving it with my wife's secretary, he told her that it was something to be put up for sale. On it being opened by my wife, and its vile contents noted, it had been deposited where it was discovered the next day.

Ordinarily such a package would have been thrown out. But my wife and her secretary had thought it would be kinder to Klein to keep it for him and return it to him. This additional kindness cost me nearly a year of confinement.

This time my Jewish lawyer was certain that I was entirely in the right. All I had to do, he said, was get him two hundred and fifty dollars. A certain political leader of his would fix things up for me, even if he himself did not make such a good impression before the judges.

The trial was the most farcical I have ever witnessed or read about. It was more simple in its comic relief than that case in Victor Hugo's *Notre Dame de Paris* which was argued before a deaf judge. The chief legal point in my case was that I did not even own the store in which the objectionable pictures had been found. To my amazement the District Attorney prosecuting the case, a young perspiring Irishman named Hogan, successfully objected to every effort on the part of my attorney to establish this.

My lawyer was so accustomed to having the results of his court cases dictated by a political boss, that he hadn't the remotest idea on how to present one. In this case he must have decided to pocket all the money, too, for there was no trace of political interference visible.

Without giving the matter a second thought the three presiding justices found me guilty and sentenced me to three months on Welfare Island. Some time afterwards, on the theory that I had violated my parole, I had to serve another four months in U.S. Detention Headquarters.

There you have the whole history of my criminal career. On the strength of this, you will be asked to discredit everything you read in this book. As it is, I cannot ever again appear as an effective witness in behalf of any case in a New York court.

But Maggog, who has been married a second time, to another socially ambitious little Jewess who dangles strange lumps of fat on the most unexpected parts of her legs, arms and head, is trying to raise money enough to buy him a temporary magistracy which will enable him to call himself Judge Maggog for the rest of his life.

One of the minor dangers of taking your legal difficulties to the office of one of the Maggogs, is that if Maggog finds that he cannot make enough money out of handling your case for you, ha has no scruples whatever in trying to make up for it by offering his services to your opponent.

When my business was thrown into bankruptcy one of my creditors induced me to hire the services of a Jewish lawyer friend of his who, he said, would do the whole thing for me for a hundred dollars. A few days after I had given him the money I discovered him working against me with the attorney of the people who had defrauded me. I threatened him with the New York Bar Association.

He laughed. "You can go to them," he said. "But you won't get very far. They know that a lawyer has to make a living somehow."

The Maggogs are the authors of the most evil malpractice of law imposed on the poor of America.

Everyone knows how powerfully organized American courts are against litigation over small amounts—the very amounts which mean everything in the lives of ninety percent of the population of the continent. It has become an accepted article of faith amongst us that legal action is so long-drawn-out and expensive, it does not pay to sue for a small amount or to defend a suit against it.

The Maggogs have found a charmed way out of this difficulty. Bring to a Maggog a case for, say twenty seven dollars. He will not only take it, but I promise you that he will make money on it—practically without leaving his office.

He has a subpoena server ready to swear that he has served the defendant with a summons. This makes it possible for to get judgment, and, if the defendant has property which is not directly under his eyes, he has also a marshal ready to swear that he levied on the property lawfully and sold it out for even less than the small judgment obtained. I have been robbed that way many times—always by Jews. Once, when I had absolute proof that I had not been served, I took the matter to court. I managed to get the judgment so fraudulently obtained set aside. But it cost me nearly three hundred dollars in legal fees.

But this, you may object, is perjury. Surely that's too great a risk to take for twenty seven dollars. Twenty seven dollars may seem like a small sum of money to you, but there is no such thing as a small sum of money to a Maggog. If it's money it's worth lying and fighting for. Besides, it is almost impossible to prove perjury in an American court. The Maggogs have seen to that, too.

The recent Seabury investigation into the magistrate court of the City of New York brought into the limelight the nefarious activities of a group of lawyers and bondsmen who fattened on the poor and the unfortunate of this great city. Nearly all of them were Maggogs.

Divorce, intended by lawmakers to be a healing to the domestic life of mankind, has been made into a racket by the unscrupulous Maggogs. Every once in a while a metropolitan newspaper hints the presence of a "divorce mill." When it is thrown open, at least, a swarm of Maggogs will be found fattening in it.

Bankruptcy, the poor man's refuge from the claws of debt, has been turned by these Maggogs into such a high-handed game that a poor man can no longer afford the relief it offers. Look at any list of lawyers practicing in Bankruptcy Court. Occasionally the Maggogs have changed the spelling of their names, but never their evil natures.

"The Jew can plead equally well for either side, especially for the side which pays best," says Professor Werner Sombart in that strangely powerful work *The Jew in Capitalism*. I had an excellent chance of seeing this in practice.

The lawyer was perhaps the most famous Maggog in the criminal courts of New York. A year ago he was defending a great banker against the charges of a singer of my acquaintance who claimed that, after seducing her with the promise of help in her career, the Jew had sent her on a fake concert tour abroad. When she found herself in Europe without any real engagements she tried to get back to the United States, and managed to do so only with great difficulty because the authorities at Ellis Island had been influenced by the banker against her.

In order to frighten the poor woman into accepting a small settlement (only a fraction of what he was getting from the banker as his fee) he opened his case against her by calling her every conceivable distasteful name before the jury. And only a few weeks ago, this same Maggog was in court trying to get a large settlement for one rich woman from another on the charge that the affections of her husband had been alienated, and he wept within full sight of the court as he brought out the fact that this woman had wantonly pulled out the man's shirt tails in his wife's presence.

But there are so many Maggogs in America they are really not in a position to pick their cases—not even the most famous of them. To meet this situation they have developed a series of very extraordinary methods of making every little case which comes into their offices pay and pay and pay.

Here is an example of how such a matter is handled.

Jake Bernstine, on his way to work slips and falls on the pavement of an apartment house owned by Abe Rubinsack. In the factory the worker next to Bernstine notices the discolored flesh on Bernstine's hand and asks him what happened. Then he tells Bernstine that it might turn out to be a very lucky thing. If he would go to the office of a lawyer by the name of Elias Kone, Kone would charge him nothing and maybe get him fifty dollars for the accident.

Jake Bernstine goes to the office of Elias Kone. There is obviously no retainer in this case, Kone sees that quickly enough. But since there is a landlord in the matter, and what can he lose by it, he takes the case. Just for observation, he says to himself. Fancy his delight on further observation, to find that Rubinsack has retained Nathan Maggog to defend him. Something like the following telephone conversation takes place.

"Hello, That you, Nathan?"

"Oh, hello Elias. How's tricks?"

"Rotten. About that Jake Bernstine case, tell me. What's your client's idea about it?"

"Oh, his idea is to give him twenty five dollars and tell him to forget about it."

"Lucky devil. You always get rich clients."

"Lucky, hell. If that guy has money he's not letting me in on it. "What's your idea?"

"Say, if I told this Bernstine fellow that there's ten or fifteen dollars in it for him he'd be tickled silly and kiss my hand into the bargain. But what's there in it for us for settling it that way?"

"That's right. Go on."

"My idea, Nathan, is that it's in the wrong court. Get me? I'll find some criminal negligence on Rubinsack's part and transfer the case to Magistrate's Court. Then you ask Rubinsack for a hundred and fifty dollars—a hundred dollars for fixing the case so he don't go to jail for criminal negligence, and fifty dollars for Bernstine. Tell him it's an insult to offer a man less than fifty dollars in a criminal court. We give Bernstine ten dollars and make him happy, and we split a hundred and forty dollars between us. What say?"

"OK., Elias. You're smart."

That's one way Elias gets money out of a client. There are a thousand other tricks practiced by him and Maggog, tricks equally conscienceless and devastating. I know one such lawyer, a socialist of long standing. As a boy he got from two to three dollars a day for making soap-box speeches for the Socialist Party. Today he draws a large clientele from the labour unions.

He usually takes cases because, he tells his clients, their grievances appeal to him from the point of view of justice. Not that he hopes to make money by them.

But at every little stage in the progress of a suit, this socialist calls in his client and makes a touch for a small sum of money—five or ten dollars, sometimes, if his client is destitute, as little as fifty cents.

"But I told you I had no money," whines the client.

"I must eat, too, mustn't I?" replies the socialist lawyer.

He has very little knowledge of the law, as he has proved to my complete satisfaction. His knowledge of court procedure is almost nil, too. His court room voice and manner made raucous and vulgar by his years of practice as a soap-box orator, are so exasperating that no judge can listen to him with any degree of patience. But you have no idea what wonders that little argument "I must eat" accomplishes for him.

What can a poor man say to it except to take out whatever change he has in his pocket and offer it to him?

By dragging out his cases, therefore, this socialist lawyer gets more out of a client than if he'd have been able to tax him with a big retainer, to begin with. In unguarded moments he confesses to a substantial bank account.

I knew this socialist lawyer, too, before he began to practice law. We were boyhood friends. When my business affairs ran well I would give him a small case and pay him liberally for his services. He happened to be present in my office during certain business transactions involving the stealing of my business from me, and so, in one of the minor litigations connected with the case, I needed him as a witness. When I came to him and broached the matter he did not mince words.

"I know all about it," he said to me. "The other side came to me last week and offered me twenty-five dollars if I would promise not to testify against them."

"Did you accept?" I asked.

"Well, no, I wanted to hear what you'd have to say."

"Is this a hint for me to make an offer?"

"No. But you still owe me thirty-nine dollars from the last case. I've got to eat, and the only way I can eat is to get money out of my clients. I'll testify if you'll pay me what you owe me."

"I'm in rather narrow straights financially," I told him. "But if that's your condition I'll fulfill it. I might subpoena you, of course."

"Sure. But how do you know what my testimony would then be?"

"And if I pay up the thirty-nine dollars?"

"I'll tell exactly what happened."

That was all I wanted to know, I told him. I got the money for him in a few days, and when the matter came up in court he testified. He told the truth strictly—only that he left out just enough of it to lose the case for me. Do you think he earned that other twenty-five dollars too, or not?

It must have been the Maggogs and Kones of his town Mandeville had in mind when he wrote in his *Fable of the Bees*, the following lines:

"The lawyers, of whose art the basis
Was raising up feuds and splitting cases,
Opposed all registers, that cheats
Might make more work with dipt estates;
As't were unlawful that one's own
Without a lawsuit should be unknown!
They put off hearings willfully,

To finger the refreshing fee;
And to defend a wicked cause
Examined and survey'd the laws
As burglars shops and houses do,
To see where best they may break through."

When I tell the story of the looting of my publishing business, I shall give a further account of my adventures among the Maggogs. But is it really necessary to expand the evidence? Has not every reader, in some folder of his own, memoirs of the sharp practice of this wily people? Why, I ask again, if they cannot be trusted with the most menial sort of jobs, is it lightly taken for granted that they can be trusted with the administration of the laws?

Has anyone reckoned out what financial havoc is caused yearly in our society by the letting loose of this swarm of vultures on a defenseless people? When you accuse them of the damage they do not deny it. They merely whine: "It's the only kind of work they let us do," and point to certain portraits of well-known Jews in the legal profession, as a justification.

The question is: Are a dozen Brandeises and Cardozas—granting that there are so many—sufficient compensation for the looting of a continent?

"I get my money first."

XI THE JEW AS A PHYSICIAN

The chief difference between the Jews and the other peoples seems to be this. Other peoples learn from experience. The Jews do not.

Take the Mohammedans, for instance. In Spain, during the first half of the Middle Ages, they experienced two centuries of two religions, the Christian faith and their own, trying to live side by side on one broad, fruitful, not too densely inhabited peninsula. But they found out one thing to be quite inevitable: there was no let-up of trouble continually brewing—and breaking.

Eventually at the end of a series of wars, in which Mohammedans were dislodged, one at a time, out of every one of their fortresses and mosques, they found themselves of necessity in the position of a conquered people. On the Spanish peninsula, at any rate. Did they insist on remaining in Spain and live in sufferance under their Christian masters?

No. Among other things, they took a hint from the fact that, as quickly as they could manage it, the Christians converted their mosques into churches.

The Mohammedans, therefore, moved south and made themselves permanent masters of their own domains.

Ah, but where have the Jews to retreat to? I can almost hear the Jewish apologist putting it. He knows the answer as well as I do, but he never fails to ask the question.

There have always been on this planet, as there are even today, great stretches of un-owned, undeveloped, and cultivatable land where the Jew—if he really thinks his Judaism is too precious a gift to lose—can establish and develop his own civilization, where to build a synagogue will not amount to thumbing his nose at his neighbor and master.

Why have Jews never tried this? Why, when England offered them uninhabited country in West Africa, did they turn it down? We come back once more to the Jew's reluctance to work and build. The Jew must have cities already built for him. The Jew must have vineyards already planted and ready for him to steal nourishment from.

Wherever the Jew went, into Christian country or Mohammedan, after he had been driven from Palestine like a wild beast by the Roman legions, his presence, because it was a taunting contradiction of the prevailing religious hope of the country he invaded, was bitterly resented.

He was fought wherever he settle down, with every available weapon except the sword which the Jew would not pick up once it has been shattered out of his hand to the ground. If a man will not fight against you, there is only one other way of getting the better of him—and that is to talk against him.

A popular superstition was created that the whole business of the Jew in wandering about from land to land and from city to city, was the destruction of his enemy religions.

Popular superstition in Europe has had the Jew poisoning wells and using the blood of Christian children to leaven his Passover bread. And yet—in the face of such monstrous accusations—he has dared to be, within the recollection of Europe, its most persistent physician. The Arabs took to medicine quite as naturally as did the Jews.

For several centuries Arab physicians, who not only healed but actually contributed to the science of medicine, were even more numerous in Europe than Jew physicians.

But the Arabs sensed the feeling of resentment. Gradually fewer and fewer of them continued to practice in the west, until a time came when there was not an Arabian physician left north of the Mediterranean.

The Jews, against whom the feeling of resentment was much keener, merely continued to disregard it, and even took the places of the vacating Arab scientists.

The Church of Rome helped the Jews in medicine as it had helped them in money-lending.

She not only forbade Christians from lending money at interest, she also forbade them the study of the science of healing. Christianity, declared the Church, is the only true science of healing—antedating Mrs. Mary Baker Eddy by more than fifteen hundred years.

The Church denounced Christian doctors as heretics who pretended to accomplish cures which were entirely her own province.

The attitude of the Church towards medicine may have been a great opportunity which the Jewish People let go a-glimmering. Who knows what peace they might not have established with their manorial masters if the Jews, instead of giving honest unselfish medical service, had not improved, as usual, on the opportunities to gain their own ends.

The stern fact is that they practiced medicine, as they practiced money-lending, entirely for personal gain, and without contributing to the advancement of the science itself.

In medicine, as in law and in the major arts, the Jews are at best absorptive. At their next best they are interpretive. They are almost never creative.

I have before me a specimen, Berachya's Hebrew rendering of an ancient Anglo-Latin classic, Adelard of Bath's *Queastiones Naturales* of which the only printed edition is the Latin of 1480.

This curious scientific work, available since the middle of the twelfth century in manuscript form under the title *De eodum et diverso*, is in the form of a dialogue between Adelard and his favorite nephew, and cover almost every phase of mediaeval man's knowledge of nature and his own body—a knowledge that would seem to have been wider and deeper than modern science is willing to grant it. Adelard's work asks and gives answers to seventy-two questions.

The Hebrew author Berachya's (which should be called an adaptation rather than a translation) reproduces only sixty-two— only those susceptible of some slovenly moral modification, and what profound changes our Jewish philosopher institutes!

Adelard's Chapter XIII, for instance, makes answer to the question: *Do Animals Have Intelligence?* Adelard grants it to them on the simple premise that "just as there cannot be sense except in relation to an animated body, so they cannot exist without a mind. There are several sorts of movement, some specially referable to the body, others more particular to the mind.

For as a result of the fire in them, bodies can move upwards, as a result of the earth in them, downwards; as a result of the air and water, to the right and to the left, backwards and forwards; while orbicular motion is referable in the first place to the mind only. Since then this movement occurs in animals, it follows also that they have minds."

Berachya (who calls his work Uncle and Nephew, *Dodi Venechbi*) ignores this brilliant physical explanation entirely. In chapter XIX of his work, he asks the same question and assumes Adelard's explanation without as much as taking the trouble to repeat it.

But he does summon forth pious definitions of *ruach* (spirit) *nefesh* (flesh), and *neshama* (soul), to prove that whereas the first two may be granted the lower brutes, the third is peculiar only to created man.

Berachya contrives, in other words, to becloud the clear physical issue by moralizing it. He pursues this stupid game throughout the entire work.

Medicine developed slowly and painfully through the centuries. As knowledge and skill increased, the practitioners of the profession profited. Jewish physicians continued to enjoy the profits of the science of medicine without making any valuable contribution of their own until the middle of the nineteenth century, and then they made their contributions only in one country, Germany, the only country in the modern world which the Jews embraced sincerely, enthusiastically and creatively as though it were really their own. In America and in England, especially in America, Jews contrive to make of medicine a means of increasing their own wealth, without making any return to the science or the profession.

The Jews do become shrewd practitioners and occasionally, very able surgeons. But they do not approach their calling in the spirit of the Hippocratic oath.

They make out of the human body a contrivance for raising money very much as the Jewish lawyers described in the previous chapter manipulate the affairs of their neighbors to their own financial aggrandizement.

The strange part of it, the part which seems to me so incredibly idiotic, is, I repeat, that they are permitted to continue to operate on the public body without prejudice by the very people who are reluctant to entrust them, in their business, with the very simplest responsibilities!

* * *

A Jewish physician whom I have known for many years recently paused with his son before my table in *Cafe Royal*.

The son having recently been graduated from college, I enquired of the father, whom we shall call Dr. Grubnyak, what plans he was making for his prodigy.

"Medical school, if possible," was the reply.

"But why *if possible*?"

"The usual restrictions."

"Nonsense. Your son is an excellent student. I think you can depend on him to pass almost any test."

"Almost any test but one. Religion."

"Oh, well. You passed by this restriction. And so, I suppose, will your son."

The doctor shook his head. "The restrictions are much harder today than they were in my time."

One need but glance at a list of the physicians in any classified directory in the United States to realize that the restrictions against admitting Jews to the study of medicine cannot possibly be hard enough.

Nearly one out of every two physicians turns out to be a Jew. Aside from the fact that it is wrong for people to be allowed to capitalize on something with the creation of which they have so little to do, thus making them the benefactors of a labor in which they do not participate, there is a really grave consideration that cannot be overlooked.

The Grubnyaks do not make good physicians. Grubnyak in medicine like Maggog in law, is a dangerous racketeer. Not quite as bad. But pretty nearly so.

In all fairness, I want to point out a very important difference between the training of Counselor Maggog and Doctor Grubnyak. Maggog got his training in law in the law office of an older Maggog. Consequently his law clerkship was an apprenticeship in the very vilest cunning of the race.

For *his* apprenticeship, Grubnyak had to go to a hospital. And, luckily, almost all of the hospitals in America, even those supported specifically by Jewish donations, are under the direction of gentiles.

By getting his internship in a goyish hospital (not because he preferred it but because there was no other alternative) Grubnyak got a fairly clean start.

Like any other physician, therefore, our Grubnyak had to devote at least a year of his time to the practice of medicine in a hospital, almost as if he were doing it, to increase his skill, or, much more remote for Grubnyak, for the love of the profession.

For that long year he observed about him the best traditions of his profession. But it was not long before he was, in the language of the street, wised up.

It was not long, you may be sure, before he was handing out his private cards to the patients in the hospital and fleecing them outside the hospital hours.

Once in my teens I suffered a mild rupture and was advised to go to a public hospital in our neighborhood for treatment.

When I had been coming there patiently for two successive weeks, I approached the attending physician and asked him how long he thought it would be before I was completely cured.

"Do you understand Yiddish?" he asked me. I nodded.

"Well, if you keep on coming here," he said to me in Yiddish, "you may never be cured."

I was frightened. "But why?"

"Because" he replied, "I am not permitted here to give you the particular attention your case needs. This is a free hospital, and, as you can see for yourself, we have more patients than we can afford to take care of properly. Better take my card."

A few days later, in the privacy of his own office, I found him in the possession of the English language again.

But he seemed not to be interested as much in my state of health as in my finances and the finances of my family.

When I had communicated to him the information that I earned only four dollars a week and was estranged from my immediate family, his zeal for treating me privately vanished miraculously.

He even discouraged my coming to the hospital again. After devoting a rather hurried examination of the part of my anatomy affected, he gave me his opinion that I was really well enough to forget about the rupture altogether. I followed his advice and "forgot" about my rupture. Unfortunately the rupture has never altogether forgotten me.

In European countries, in England particularly, the honor of the medical profession is guarded so jealously that you are not supposed, in practice, to even hand your physician money when he has finished treating you.

You do, of course, make arrangements for payment with his secretary or his nurse, but theoretically the English physician is above such consideration.

The noble intention is apparent. It cannot be expected of a physician to be a business man and healer at the same time.

The American physician has wandered far from his European ideal. Only in his hospitals has he managed to preserve some of the dignity and sanctity that used to attach to the profession of healing. But the average Jewish doctor, our own Dr. Grubnyak, has left the ideal so far behind him, he is practically pursuing his calling in a different country.

To Grubnyak, being a physician is merely running a business with many complex ramifications. He appraises the sick who come to his office not for the use he can be in healing them of their ailments but for the source of income for himself he can make of them over a long stretch of time.

Let us look him over more closely, this little man with the solemn looking black bag who is called upon to perform the miracles of science no matter what may be the nature of the illness in one of the families who have become accustomed to calling him in in case of trouble.

He has office hours from ten to twelve in the morning, and from five to seven in the evening. But his telephone jangles pretty nearly all day—and all night.

Dr. Grubnyak has just returned from several calls which dissipated his afternoon. Visits one makes to patients who call a doctor on the telephone are almost always unsatisfactory.

The people are either old patients with whom he has already established a price, or they have been recommended to him, which amounts to the same thing. Old patients pay him three dollars for a call, as they did when his office was in a cheaper neighborhood. It is difficult to explain to them that the upkeep of his new office is so much greater than the upkeep of the old one.

Old patients are sometimes even ungrateful enough not to heed the suggestion that the prescription be filled at a certain drug store—the drug store which gives him a solid rip-off.

So he gets back from his daily wandering to his office, with a sense of relief. For the office is always the source of possible adventure. A stranger may walk into office who will make him rich. Dr. Grubnyak is always looking forward to the appearance of such a stranger who will enrich him, as he opens the door leading from his operating room to the waiting room to see what patients are waiting for him. Only rarely is this hope rewarded.

Usually he sees only the faces of old patients, old faces torn by the same ills. But this is one of those golden days.

There are only two people waiting for him this afternoon. Old Mrs. Skulnick who has come back to him with her ancient lumbago, and a man he has never seen before.

The man is middle-aged, well-dressed, and has all the appearance of a solid citizen. Dr. Grubnyak pretends not to even notice him.

"Come in, Mrs. Skulnick."

"Again you are eating too much, Mrs. Skulnick," he says tapping her playfully between her shoulder blades. He helps her with the most tremendous delicacy to bare her back for him; that is a consideration Dr. Grubnyak crafty knows she gets only from him, and is almost worth to her the price of the occasional visit.

"Just as I thought," he murmurs. "How long is it since you've taken the medication I prescribed for you?"

"Only a month. Shall I get the same stuff again?"

"No. There's a change now. I'll have to prescribe something else for you. But you must make a promise, Mrs. Skulnick. You've got to stop eating so much fats."

He gives her the very same prescription, only instead of writing it in three lines he does so in five. "Don't forget where to go with it," are his last words to her, as he pockets the two dollars for the visit.

Once more he opens the magic door. "It's now your turn, sir."

He notes gratefully that there are no other patients waiting impatiently for him.

This stranger really looks like a good prospect. He would like to give him a solid sales-talk.

The stranger comes forward and introduces himself. "We'd better get acquainted immediately, Dr. Grubnyak," he says.

"I'm Gay Meltzor. Took the Penthouse around the corner last week. Someone told me you're a wonder with lumbago."

"This seems to be lumbago night," muses Dr. Grubnyak. Aloud he says: "People will exaggerate Mr. Meltzor. I can treat lumbago up to a certain point.

"Beyond that I can only give you the co-operation of the very best specialists, under my constant care. Let me see what's the matter with you."

(You may not know it, but that was a pretty slick speech. Grubnyak cannot charge more than two dollars a visit. But there is no limit to how much money he may divy with a so-called lumbago specialist.)

Curiously enough Meltzor's case is very much like that of Mrs. Skulnick. But there is this difference. It was useless to expect more than an occasional two dollar out of Mrs. Skulnick who is still taking in borders in order to make ends meet.

But this new patient can be told of the new treatment for his species of lumbago, invented by Dr. Krochmal. Dr. Krochmal is a rather expensive specialist, Dr. Grubnyak explains. But the fact is that he achieves the most marvelous results.

What Mr. Meltzor is not told is that Dr. Krochmal has agreed to turn over to Dr. Grubnyak at least twenty five percent of the moneys he will receive for treatments from the accommodating patients recommended by Dr. Grubnyak.

Dr. Grubnyak has five interesting ways of extending his income as a physician beyond the unsatisfactory two dollars he receives at the office and the three dollars he collects on his visits to the homes of patients:

1. If he suspects his patient of having money, or of being able to raise money, no matter how, Dr, Grubnyak insists on calling in a specialist, another Jew who has agreed to share with him whatever they can both wheedle out of the patient.

2. He has either a drug-store of his own, or he has an interest in one. To this drug store he recommends his patient to go with their prescriptions.

At the very worst, he has an arrangement with some neighborhood druggist who returns to him an interest on the money he gathers from his prescriptions.

3. No matter what ails his patient, Dr. Grubnyak recommends an X-ray examination, the photograph to be taken either by himself or by another Jewish doctor in the neighborhood who has agreed to return to him a generous percentage of the income from such recommendations.

It costs approximately seven cents to develop an X-ray picture. The average charge for it is five dollars.

4. When the patient has been X-rayed hollow, Dr. Grubnyak, undaunted, has an absolutely new set of treatments for him. "Something to revitalize you, fill you with new life," he says, and reveals his Alpine lamp to him.

This Alpine lamp in the hands of Dr. Grubnyak is like that older more famous lamp in the hands of the boy Aladdin. He only rubs it and presto—there is wealth.

An average Alpine lamp treatment costs Dr. Grubnyak a fraction of a cent. The average charge he makes for a treatment is three dollars.

5. The young girl of unsteady morals is Dr. Grubnyak's legitimate prey. Poor thing, she never knows whether she's coming or going, so shifting and uncertain are her lunar derangements.

If she is really *enceinte,* Dr. Grubnyak sends her to his favorite abortionist who returns to him almost half of the charge for the operation. If she is not, he sends her to the abortionist anyway. A Jewish abortionist I know, confided in me that a good percentage of the girls the Dr. Grubnyak of the neighborhood sends to him are not in need of an operation.

But he pretends to perform the operation, the unfortunate creature pays dearly for it, and no one but he and Dr. Grubnyak are the richer for it!

The rapaciousness of Dr Grubnyak is not due to the fact that he is merely a family practitioner. The specialist and the surgeon of his sort are no better. For they are at all times moved by only one passion: greed for money.

A famous Chicago surgeon, a Jew, was about to perform a very serious operation on a young married woman whose husband had deserted her.

Because of her obvious poverty, he had consented to take two hundred dollars, although, he explained to all parties concerned, for such work he was accustomed to getting at least five hundred dollars.

The young woman was already on the operating table, and the ether had been administered to her, when the surgeon turned right about face, stormed into the waiting room where the young woman's mother was agonizing, and announced vehemently that the operation was off.

The mother looked up with alarm. "Why?"

"Your daughter lied to me," the doctor rasped. "She said that she was without means and I have just learned differently."

"But my daughter is penniless. The two hundred dollars she gave you I lent her."

"That's just it. And you have more than three thousand dollars in the bank."

That moment the mother caught sight of her daughter, still under ether, being wheeled out of the operating room.

"But you don't understand," she cried despairingly. "I'm a widow. It's all the money I have left in the world. I may never again be able to earn another dollar. The, if I give this money away, what shall I do in my old age?"

"I don't care. She's your daughter, not mine. I get three hundred dollars more or I don't operate."

The mother looked up sternly. "You will risk my daughter's life that way, doctor?"

"Why not?" coolly.

"But suppose something happens to her, and I tell the medical association how it came about?"

The doctor's face changed instantly, all his coolness vanished. He hadn't thought of the possible harm to himself. Without another word to the mother, he had the young woman wheeled back into the operating room, and proceeded to perform one of his most marvelous operations. He had to!

I was recent in the home of a local Jewish physician who does not mind discussing his business with a layman. He had just come in from his office, and he was extremely disturbed. "I've just made a very serious blunder," he explained.

'I recommended a patient six salvasans for fifty dollars. But I guess it just hit him too high. If I had said thirty-five dollars it would have been a sure sale."

Salvasans (popularly known as 606 treatments) are essential to the cure of syphilis. "But didn't you tell him that it is the only reasonable sure cure?" I asked in wonder.

"Well," came the astonishing reply, "We're not yet sure that he has syphilis."

"Then why did you recommend the salvasans?"

"Why not? They couldn't do him any harm."

"Whatsoever house I enter," says the Hippocratic oath, *"there will I go for the benefit of the sick, refraining from all wrong-doing and corruption, and especially from any act of seduction, of male or female, of bond or free."* But the education of Dr. Grubnyak goes back farther than Hippocrates.

It goes back to the ancient rabbis who knew enough about medicine to keep it out of the hands of the priests, and insisted that the most important phase of the practice of medicine was the profit to be derived there from. It is from the rabbis that Dr. Grubnyak learned that "a physician who charges nothing is worth nothing."

The history of medicine is full of ever renewing restrictions against the practice of medicine by Jews. Mohammedans forbid them as early as 853. In 1335 the Synod of Salamanca declared that the Jewish physicians offered their services only to kill the Christians.

It is only natural that Jews should complain of such accusations. But the truth is that they owe much to the glaring untruthfulness of their Christian critics.

If Christians did not bother to rake up against the Turkish people charges without foundation in Jewish nature and practice, it might occur to them to hit on the real evils the Jews practice on them. Then it might be much more difficult for Jews to accomplish the miracle of survival.

No. Dr. Grubnyak's business is not exterminating Christians. It is much more terrible than that. His business is really to capitalize the ills of all people who come within their reach, be they Christians, Mohammedans or even Jews. You cannot buy honest advice from Dr. Grubnyak any more than you can purchase honest advice from Counselor Maggog.

John William Draper, whose work *The Intellectual Development of Europe* is excessively friendly to the Jews, is authority for the statement that French animosity against Jewish physicians led directly to the banishment of all the Jews from France in 1306.

If the Jews are ever expelled from America it will be on account of the evil practice of Jewish doctors and Jewish lawyers.

The Jew and the Land

XII THE JEW AND THE LAND

The Jew is a gypsy with a weakness for real estate.

The very first promise the Lord made to Abraham was a promise of land: land already occupied and the lawful property of the peoples who had fertilized it. *Genesis* and *Exodus* are crowded with specific references to the many peoples who lived in the land of promise before the birth of Abraham, and before its fierce invasion by the seed of Abraham under Joshua.

At no time in the narrative is the matter of the titles of these ancient proprietors of Canaan brought into question. But the most microscopic study of the texts reveals not even the hint of a plan by which, when the Jews were to possess the land, the title to it was to pass legitimately to them. There was no offer made for outright purchase, such as Abraham himself had made for the burial ground of Machpelah.

No offer of a periodic lease either. It was deemed sufficient to repeat the oral legend that the Lord had promised the land to Abraham, Isaac, Jacob and their posterity, forever. On this slender pretense (which reminds one of the extraordinary reason given by Norman William to his home-legislators for invading England) the Jews marched into Palestine, slaughtered most of its inhabitants, and proceeded to make a pig-stye of the whole country.

Suppose the records of this first great conquest of Israel were not as detailed and as indisputable as they are? Would there not be an inclination on the part of the more civilized Jews of our day to dispute that it really happened? Instead of adopting the story as sacred scripture, I conceive that Jews might even have advanced the theory that it was nothing but a false series of accusations, the ancient world's peculiar contribution in advance to anti-Semitism. But the Jewish history, that to throw doubt on the Jewish Conquest of Palestine would shake the world's belief in our very identity as a race and as a nation.

That's why, instead of trying to deny the shameless story, the Jews are trying to re-enact it—in a more modern and more moderate setting.

I began by saying that we Jews have a weakness for real estate. I mean real estate as distinguished from land. People with a love of land are anxious to work it. They have a passion not only to live on the soil but pierce it and fructify it. But, as I have already shown, the Old Testament is a solemn testimony of the Jewish People's hatred of work—particularly agricultural.

In the wilderness, on their march to conquest, God had to practically rain food down on the Jews in order to keep them going. A hundred times, under the reluctant leadership of Moses who must have hated them bitterly, they refused to take another step forward. And the Lord, in order to get them to go on, to save the sweet breath of the desert, was compelled to promise them that their labors would be at an end on reaching the Promised Land, where the cities were already built for them, the vineyards planted and ready to nourish them.

Jewish historians and apologists make a hue and cry about the Jews having been barred everywhere from the ownership of land, during the Middle Ages, and even in some countries in the modern world. They would have you believe that the Jew's extraordinarily repugnant ghetto character is not the result of an inner evolution from a bad kernel but the result of hostile, frustrating outside forces that have molded him into the terrible anomaly he presents before the world today so that he is the blighted flowering of a fine sowing.

This is not true. The Jews did not seize the opportunity offered them by Edward I, to rent English land and till it. Nor have they seized opportunities in England and in America in our own time.[29] The reason why? Jews know only one use for the ownership of land—or of anything. Speculation. And there you have the real reason why the Christian world is so reluctant to permit the Jews to buy land;

---

[29] *It will be objected, that there is quite a population of Jewish farmers in the United States. Most of them were taken from Russia by Israel Zangwill's ITO and placed on farms which they promptly turned into summer boarding houses. Tilling the soil and living by its labor is still strange to the habits of life of the modern Jew.*

and why, as I write these words, Arabians are marching through the streets of Jerusalem protesting against the English government's threat to allow Jews even more freedom of movement than they already enjoy in Palestine.

In the things in which the gentile world does not mind speculation it has allowed the Jew every liberty of enterprise. In those few things, however, in which the prejudices are against speculation, it has restricted the Jew decisively and sometimes violently. Now I have no set opinion on whether speculation is good or not for the welfare of society. But I do recognize that there is an indefensible evil in the speculation of land. Let me illustrate.

I am the owner of a precious robe. One day, finding myself in need of money, I sell this robe. I care not who buys it from me or to whom the purchaser will eventually resell it, precious as may be the memories the robe holds for me. Suppose, as in its multiple career of sale and re-sale, it should came about that it falls into the possession of a Satzkin?

I might even be so unfortunate as to see it beloused over his cankerous shoulders, yet I wouldn't care. I have sold the robe, and therefore I am through with it. On the other hand, I own a piece of land next to the land on which I have built my own house. Suppose under the same need of money, I sold this piece of land to a fellow Jew? Might I not awake some morning, and, looking out of my window for a glimpse of the bright sky, find by the agency of a hateful face seen through glass, that the new house built on the land next to mine, belonged to such a Satzkin? Do you now see my point? Is it not apparent to you that my whole life might thereby be made quite unbearable for me?

That is only one of the reasons why the world is reluctant to permit Jews to own property. Civilized people attach a certain mild sanctity to the ownership of land—a sanctity the Jew can be depended upon to violate every time.

So that when the Jewish apologist whines:

"If we had not been forbidden the ownership of land during the Middle Ages we would not today be a nation of idlers," he lies in his throat. We were a nation of idlers to begin with. Our sole interest in land has always been in its speculative value as a turnover.

But about fifty years ago a miracle took place in Israel. Almost a generation before the birth of political Zionism, a group of Russian-Jewish students left their homes, families and prospects of a future, to wander on foot to Palestine, to till the soil there, and so spend out the juices of their natural lives.

Two powerful forces moved these marvelous young men on this momentous march of despair: the persecution of the Czar's government from without, and the sight of the awful depravity of their own people from within. It was given to them to realize, in a flash of unhappy inspiration, that no matter what happened to the world or to themselves, they were lost.

It was futile for them to hope to reconcile themselves with the insane whims of the Imperial Russian government as with the slovenly and degrading conduct of the real Jewish world into which they had been born. Traditionally, Palestine was the only Jewish home they knew of. So, without consulting national or personal wisdom, they set out on their unprecedented journey. There was not even a glimmering of personal ambition in what they did, or of a political vision. They were going to Palestine to work with their hands and die. They were the *Halutzim*.

I have before me a Hebrew book entitled *Yizkor* which is a simple memorial to the poor *Halutzim* whom I hesitate to call Jews. Were they really Jews? I hardly know. But I will stake the immortality of my soul that they were amongst the most beautiful people on the face of the earth.

I see them starting out of their humble homes with just enough money to purchase them water and crusts of bread on the unfriendly highways. Certainly they do not take along with them money with which to buy favors. When they reach Palestine they approach the land as did Jehudah Halevy, four centuries before them, on their hands and knees. All they ask of the Turkish masters of the land is the freedom to till the wretched centuries-neglected soil alongside of the poor Arabs. The Turks offered them little real opposition. Even the Arabs, distrustful of everything else in an apparently treacherous world, learned to like them.

Poor *Halutzim* and their vain vision of life of peace! They thought that by escaping from the Ghetto into Palestine they had got away from the meanness of the Ghetto, and there it was in full bloom before them in the Jewish Quarter of the city of David.

Before the coming of the *Halutzim* the only Jews in Jerusalem were the charity (*Halukah*) Jews, who lived by a special fund collected from the boxes posted on the doors of the Jews in Russia and in Poland. The intention of this charity was, while the law made it possible, to preserve a Jewish population in Palestine—as a reminder to the world whom the land really belonged to. Much money was brought into Palestine yearly from these tin boxes, but the charity Jews added to this source of income by soliciting alms at the Wailing Wall.

So ugly was the sight that Sir Moses Montefiore, on his visit to Jerusalem, was moved to protest. They seemed to him, he said quite plainly, no more than a degraded set of paupers. He was instrumental in building for them schools and houses and a mill outside of the city near Birkel-El-Sulta, or Lower Pool of Sihon, but the poor wretches were too lazy to take advantage of the opportunity and it all went to ruin. The *Halutzim* knew when they started out that there were Jews in Jerusalem. But it had never occurred to them that they would be even lower in the scale of civilization than the Jews they had run away from.

Those old Jerusalem parasites hated the *Halutzim*, and they had two very substantial reasons for hating them. In the first place, the *Halutzim* refused point-blank to subscribe to the synagogue and its rigid procedure. And in the second place, those outrageously independent young fellows actually worked, and with their bare hands. Such a thing had never been heard of among Jews. It would certainly never do to let the goyim see.

What evil might not fall on themselves if the Turks and Arabs, by observing the *Halutzim*, got the grotesque idea that Jews might be expected to work like other people. As a consequence the charity Jews conspired against the poor unsuspecting *Halutzim*. They told the Turks that the poverty of the *Halutzim* was only a cleaver disguise. The *Halutzim* were the agents of European Jewish bankers who had their eyes on the ownership of Palestine. The first step in their program was to organize the Arabs against their ruler. The Arabs, on the other hand, were led to believe that the *Halutzim* were really spies in the pay of the Turks, so that every movement of theirs might be noted and suppressed. Otherwise, how was it that the Turks treated them with so much more consideration than they had ever before extended to foreigners? The result of this bit of Jewish scheming was that the bones of many poor *Halutz* prematurely whitened the Arabian desert because of death by sudden violence.

The movement of the *Halutzim* grew. Once they had settled themselves on the legendary Jewish soil, they wrote back to their friends and relatives in Russia: *The soil here is hard and bitter. The Jews one sees in Jerusalem are even shabbier than those to be found in the kremlach of Minsk and Lemberg. But it's a lovely thing to have land that you can till even if three quarters of the land is desert. What a relief, after centuries of Goluty, not to have to barter and hawk. . . . For whether it is in the market place or in the court room the business of a Jew is to barter and to hawk. . . . It is beautiful here by comparison. . . .*

And so more and more young Jews wandered out of Russia and Poland on this extraordinary pilgrimage of labor.

Meanwhile Jews all over the world, but particularly in Eastern Europe, began to organize societies called *Chovevi Zion* meaning Lover of Zion. The Lovers of Zion were a direct offshoot of the passion of the*Halutzim*, but it was not the passion of a pure heart, it was the old lustful bestiality with which Joshua had laid waste Canaan. The Jewish passion for real estate was reasserting itself in the modern world.

The Lovers of Zion had no economic or political program: they were actuated by an undirected lusting after land. It was not through these mean little people that political Zionism came into being. Theodore Herzl, whose pamphlet *Der Judenstaat* created the Zionist movement, was in body and in heart like one of these *Halutzim* of whose very existence he did not become aware until he found himself, overnight, the new leader of the Jews.

History will always speak of Theodore Herzl with love and respect. He was a Jew whose life mingled easily with the life of the gay sophisticated people of Vienna, the city of his birth. He was a handsome man, a witty conversationalist, and the most brilliant journalist in Central Europe. The Dreyfus affair recalled him to the fact that he was a Jew. In Paris, whither the *Neue Freue Presse* had sent him to report the Affair, he saw the most humiliating posters ridiculing Jews, displayed in shop windows. He heard Parisians marching through the streets crying *Death to the Jews*. He came to a very simple conclusion. If we are so hopelessly offensive to the world, he pleaded, why should we continue to impose ourselves on it? Let us go somewhere (he did not, in the beginning specify Palestine) where we may build up a world of our own.

The First Zionist Congress, of which he was the natural leader, settled on Palestine as the land. But Herzl was studying his Jewish history, and he was learning very quickly about the Jewish People and Jewish methods from direct observation. This was not going to be another blind, violent grab as Joshua had engineered before him, he determined.

He set down before the Jewish People two unalterable conditions under which he would lead them: 1. The Jewish homeland must be legally secured and legally assured. 2. No individual Jew must be allowed to own land, so as to be able to sell it. All land in Palestine was to be purchased from the Arabs from a common national fund and remain the property of the whole people for all time.

Herzl was probably the first honest Jew in the public life of the world in two thousand years. From the moment he became known to the general Jewish masses Herzl was transformed into a living Jewish legend beloved by the extensive communities of his people all over the world but secretly hated by every individual leader of Jews—except, of course, Zangwill, *the good Zangwill* as Herzl always referred to him.

Here was the rarest of all terrestrial things, a Jew without the itch for money or real estate. A Jew who worked all day for Zion and spent his nights writing for the Viennese press, as a means of making his livelihood, for he not only refused to accept money for his work as a Jewish leader, he insisted on being the first contributor to every fund that was created for Jews. A Jew who, offered by Colonel Pond fifty thousand dollars for a ten weeks tour of America, replied that he could not sell the ideas of the Jewish People.

An irresistible leader was Herzl. There was nothing for Jews to do but follow where he led. The Rothschilds yielded to his every whim. The Baron of Hirsch, that obdurate old man, listened to Herzl wonderingly and affectionately. Even the goyim yielded to his spell: the memoirs of Kaiser, Sultan, King and Pope praise the sweet honesty of the man. Yes, even the yellow little Satzkin followed him. (Does it make much difference whether you pronounce the name Satzkin or Ussischkin?)

They followed him, but true to their deeper natures they kept up a dismal yelping at his heels. Their evil faces, by showing themselves before him from morning till night, constantly reminded him of the meanness of his burden. I know what it is to look at the face of one Satzkin.

Herzl had to look at hundreds, thousands of them. Herzl was not physically delicate. As the leader of any other people he would have lived to be a hundred. At the head of a nation of Satzkin he was doomed. After seven Jewish Congresses, they broke his heart. In 1904, when he died, there was practically nothing left of Herzl to bury in the cemetery of his beloved Vienna. The Satzkins had eaten him alive. The death of Herzl doomed the Palestine of the *Halutzim*. Under the guise of honoring their dead leader's memory, at first they began purchasing land individually and in groups. After a while they even abandoned creating pretexts for their purchases.

And buying land in Palestine became a race between Jewish investors and the Jewish National Fund which was practically paralyzed into inactivity. Until today Palestine is not the land conceived in the heart of Herzl but another evil concoction of the Ghetto.

William Zuckerman, a correspondent for the *Jewish Morgen Journal*, creates in a recent issue of *Harper's Magazine* a devastating picture of what is happening today in Palestine. It has become a center of speculation such as the Jews have never created anywhere else in the world before. Every day new businesses are being opened and machinery is being installed.

It would seem that every Jewish businessman in Poland is planning to move his business from Poland to Palestine.

That they are practically uprooting themselves in one land without the certainty of being ever able to take root again in the other, doesn't seem to bother them at all. It is the old gypsy with a weakness for real estate on the move again. Several kinds of booms are taking place at the same time. There is, for instance, a building boom. Wherever there is an empty lot an empty house springs up overnight. Not that there are people waiting to occupy these houses. It is just that Jews who were accustomed to speculating in Warsaw, in Vienna and in London are trying their luck with speculating in Jerusalem. Another speculation is in orange-groves, not restricted to Palestine.

All over Europe and even in America, where we have become a trifle suspicious of manufactured booms, Jews float orange-grove companies in which stocks and shares are sold.

It was bad enough when the old charity Jews confounded the Palestinian landscape. But there was one comfort, with the charity Jews. A charity Jew could only live a certain length of time, when he died there was nothing left of him, he left no heir.

The new Jews who have come to exploit Palestine are just as mean as the charity Jews, probably meaner. But they bring their wives with them, and, what is terrible, reproduce their kind.

"Already on arriving in Tel-Aviv," writes Mr. Zuckerman, who apparently was an eye witness, "one is surrounded by a swarm of brokers, real estate sharks, business entrepreneurs, high pressure salesmen, money lenders, usurers, and speculators of every kind, each offering a new business venture, each outbidding and denouncing his competitor, each greedily seeking to grab a commission and to snatch a share of the wealth which he did nothing to produce."

"Was it not," inquires Mr. Zuckerman, "in order to escape from the futility and the contempt which go with the non-productive ghetto occupations that Zionism was devised? Of what use would it be to the people even to gain its livelihood—assuming that such a fantastic event were possible—if it loses by it the soul which it has begun to regain?"

If this is the bitterness of a New York Jew, picture to yourself the feeling of the poor *Halutzim* who journeyed to Palestine with their bare feet, as they witness the rape of the holy land by the old Ghetto.

The Ghetto has placed everything in Palestine for sale—even the memories of the *Halutzim* who died for it. So often have they sold the weary lots of Jerusalem that you have to pay, in the business section of this town, with a population of less than fifty thousand, twice as much per lot as you would have to pay in the heart of New York City which has a population of more than six millions and enjoys a steady water supply. Houses are built every day. But where are the people to live in them? Factories of all kinds are opened, but for whom are its products to be manufactured? More orange-groves are being organized than could be planted in Palestine with Sahara Desert appended to it as a province.

At first the *Halutzim* protested. But they realized quick enough the stubborn temper of the people they tried to interfere with. Now they stand aside to watch with narrowing eyes the approach of catastrophe. They know what usually follows any inflation of industry, as a result of pure speculation. But this will not be the usual sore of economic crash. The deceit practiced in Palestine was not of a people on itself, but of a people on another people, of the Jews on the Arabs. What will happen when the Arabs discover that land which they have been told is worth fifteen hundred dollars a lot isn't worth that much an acre? Do you think they will merely smile good-naturedly and mildly discuss ways and means out of the confusion into which their lives have been thrown?

Of one thing the *Halutzim* are quite certain. The Satzkins and all their speculation will, in the fury of a disillusioned people, be broken up and crushed to the earth. Those who escape slaughter will be banished like so many diseased cattle. With them will go the terrible industrial stench with which the shores of the Jordan are today troubled. What, then? Will everything go? Will the loving toil of the *Halutzim* have been entirely in vain? Will the destroying fury stop nowhere?

I believe that a stopping-place has been created for the fury of the Arabs. It is the University of Jerusalem. Already the Arabs regard it with a certain amount of pride and affection. The Arabs are no fools. They will not wantonly destroy the instrument of their own salvation.

The Arabs, I predict, will allow to remain untouched the simple buildings of the University of Jerusalem. Around them a new civilization will arise. But it will not be a Jewish civilization. Nor will it be an Arab civilization. It will be something new created of the mingling of Jews and Arabs.

The dim signs of hope in Palestine are these:

1. The *Halutzim*, a few honest Jews who are still trying to stand off,

in the midst of the horrible commerce of the transplanted Ghetto, the oceans of filth which are pouring into the streets of Jerusalem through the medium of the Zionist Organization;

2. The University of Jerusalem which, with its slender means, is opening the doors of universal knowledge to Jews and Arabs alike;

3. The presence, as the virtual head of the University of Jerusalem, of Judah L. Magnes.

Repeat that name for yourself. Judah L. Magnes. It is a name which will grow more and more glamorous every day. It is a name which links itself with all that remains left of beauty in the Jewish world today. Do you remember when Judah L. Magnes was the spiritual head of the richest Jewish congregation in America, and the furor caused by his resignation in which he quietly intimated that it was impossible to be a rabbi and remain an honest man?

In *Now and Forever* which I dedicated to Magnes in 1925, before he took up his duties at the University, I ventured the opinion that if there was to be a Jewish national future in Palestine it would probably not be a purely Jewish future but the result of a mingling of Jews and Arabs.

In a recent dispute between Jews and Arabs I was thrilled to read that Magnes took the same stand. The Jews, he announced to the utter confusion of the Zionist, must share Palestine with the Arabs. Apostate! cried the Satzkins. But they have not dared to move him from his high place. For it is pretty generally realized by this time that the headship of the University of Jerusalem is high only because Judah L. Magnes occupies it.

Magnes will see the flood of blood turn from the marketplace in Jerusalem on the Mount of Olives. It will flow upwards till it almost touches his feet. But he is seated too highly to be touched. I hope he will have the stomach to see the last of the Satzkins drown without the turning away of an eye.

* * *

As I correct these proofs the situation in Palestine grows daily in intensity. Jews who went to Palestine from America are coming back. Is it because Palestine is becoming unsafe? Or is President Roosevelt's New Deal—offering thinner, but a greater number of dollars—doing the trick?

The Vision

XIII THE LIFE AND DEATH OF WILLIAM FARO

The iron door closed heavily behind me. The sound of a huge key rasped in the lock. I looked straight ahead of me, and about me. I was in a vast steel cage about twenty-five feet square. The bars, set six or eight inches apart, and making the web of walls and ceiling, must have been a half an inch in diameter.

There were about thirty narrow, iron beds, covered with a brown army blanket, in three rows; approximately a foot of space between every two beds. The long steel platform in front, must be, I conjectured, the common dining table.

Behind the guard and myself followed another prisoner with a mattress and two blankets. "We're a little crowded right now," explained the guard. "But some of these mugs will be leaving soon. Until there's a bed vacant, you'll have to get along on the floor. Don't worry. You'll like it."

"Four months of this," ran through my mind. There were prisoners ranged in odd groups about several of the beds. Card and checker games were in progress at the sides and ends of the long steel dining table.

I might wander into one of these groups and, providentially, lose myself. But no, I was too tired. I turned to inquire of the guard if it was against the rules to lie down in the daytime, but he was already gone.

I arranged the blankets over my mattress, where the prisoner had dropped them, and lay down.

But sleep I could not. I lay, instead, for I don't know how long, maybe an hour, maybe two, in that terrible borderland between sleep and waking in which the tortured mind places itself on trial before and dumb and paralyzed court of shadows. It must have been the agony of my body that forced the opening of my eyes; I sat up.

The afternoon had darkened considerably, but it was still daylight by which the world was apparent. On the bed next to which my mattress had been placed sat a grave middle-aged man reading the latest issue of *The Nation*.

How shall I explain to you the nature of the relief which suddenly swept through me at this sight? Even if you disagree with the editorial opinions of *The Nation* (as I do so often, especially when they relate to me or my business) you should understand what it meant to me to see someone reading it. There is only this to say: it gave me courage to know that someone who occupied that beastly cage with me wanted to read such a paper, and that the authorities in charge had no objection to it. The man had evidently been observing me, too, for his eyes met mine as I looked up, and he greeted me in a mellow, matter-of-fact voice.

"How're you feeling, Roth?" Another miracle. Someone knew me.

"A lot better than I did a moment ago, I can tell you. You weren't here when I came in, were you?"

"No, I work in the kitchen downstairs. I've just got back. My name's Bill Paro."

"Glad to know you, Bill. So you're in the kitchen. What sort of grub do they dish out here to the guests of the government?"

"Pretty terrible stuff, unless you happen to be lucky enough to have a job downstairs in the kitchen, the laundry, or the commissary. Then you can eat what they cook for the warden and the guards. If you think you'd like it, I'll try to get you one of those jobs."

"No, thanks. There's a book I've been wanting to write all my life. I think I'll take advantage of this enforced vacation to at least get into it. Who knows, I might, here in prison, be able to accomplish what I have not been able to even approach with all the freedom of the outside world. It will have been worth while eating the rubbish they'll serve me up here if I can turn my prison sentence into a fine book."

"Alright," he said. "You go ahead with your writing. Maybe I can arrange to smuggle some good food to you. It's been known to be done here."

Bill was not an idle promiser. Before his release several weeks later, he had not only managed to get some fairly decent food delivered to me, but he had done many more things to befriend me, and to make my stay at U. S. Detention Headquarters more bearable. About himself, I had learned from him that, as the result of a series of misunderstandings, he had become estranged from his wife and four children.

The loss of his position in the U. S. Post Office, held for nearly thirty years, was to him a catastrophe trivial by comparison with this bitterer loss. The only thing he really wanted to accomplish in life was to regain the respect and affection of his wife and children.

I wanted to do something for Bill Paro in return for his considerations to me. On the morning of his release I called him over and talked over his prospects with him.

"I don't know," he said dubiously. "It seems to be pretty hard for everybody out there if you judged by the newspapers. I wonder what there can be for an ex-convict past fifty to look forward to?"

"Tell you what, Bill," I said. "I like you, and it would please me very much if I could help you. I think I can. When you get out of here, do your best to find work. If you're still jobless when I am released, come to see me."

You cannot have completely forgotten what things were like in 1930, after the three celebrated Wall Street crashes. Bill Paro was among the first people to greet me when I finally reached home after an additional eight weeks in Philadelphia. He was not only out of work but in a pitiable state of destitution.

"I'm going to give you a job, Bill," I told him. "And it's going to be more than a mere job. I'm abandoning the publishing of special and limited editions, to go into general publishing. To do that, I'll have to organize a new corporation. I'm going to organize the new corporation in your name, with you as president. The company will be known as *William Paro, Inc.* Your salary will be exactly what you'll be worth—you'll start at twenty dollars a week. But I'm going to do my best to teach you the publishing business, and your salary will go up as your usefulness increases. We'll make *William Paro, Inc.* among the most successful businesses of its kind in America. And then I dare your family to keep up its aloofness to you. What do you say?"

It was fully a minute before Bill could find the words with which to thank me.

I had my attorneys file papers of incorporation. Bill was to join me and my wife several days later in signing them in the offices of my attorney. On the morning set for the signing, he met me in the lobby of the office-building. He was obviously agitated. "I'm afraid I can't sign, Sam," he said dolefully.

I was surprised.

Paro proceeded to explain. "I'd really like to, Sam. But I had a talk with a friend of mine about it. He's a lawyer. He pointed out to me that you have many enemies and that you've already lost several decisions on books. If I went in with you, I'd be liable to prosecution whenever anyone thought a book of yours was objectionable. And if you lost a case I'd get a long stretch as a second offender."

I could not quarrel with Bill. What he said appeared to me entirely reasonable. But I wanted no further delays, especially in the matter of the incorporation of my new business. My first book for the trade was already being set up. I had to put an imprint on it. I had to make plans for its sale. To save the need of filing new papers for incorporation that might be necessitated by the change of names, I suggested to my attorney that he simply wire Albany to change the P into an F, and that I would undertake to answer to the name of William Faro.

In view of the amount of scurrilous lying that has been done on the subject, especially in a book entitled *The Truth About Hoover,* I offer the above as a true account of the genesis of *William Faro, Inc.*

The first publication of the new company was my revised version of D. H. Lawrence's *Lady Chatterley's Lover.*

This novel had become, without being made accessible to the general reader, one of the most famous books in the world. Because of the attitude of our laws, the objectionable words in the story made it anybody's property. It was apparent to me as well as to several other publishers, that there was a vast market for a cleverly revised edition. If *Lady Chatterley's Lover* were revised so as not to impair either the narrative or its vitality, it might even become one of the sensations of a publishing season. The biggest of the publishers, however, had decided against the enterprise, on the theory that only Lawrence, now dead, could have accomplished such a change in the book. So I set myself the task of doing it.

The usual procedure in such a matter is to ask for permission from the author, or, the author being dead, his estate. But to do so, I decided, would be to recharge outside interest in the project and lead, possibly, to its issuance by one of the bigger publishers capable of making a heavy advance of royalty.

I remembered how it was with the publishing of *The Well of Loneliness* in America. Alfred A. Knopf had set the book up; but, upon the solicitations of the vice crusader, had abandoned publication. For a time it looked as if the book would be completely abandoned. Then I put in a bid for it. Instantly other bids began coming in, and I lost out to CoviciFriede.

I therefore proceeded with my work of revision and publishing, without proper authorization; and, without as much as a newspaper announcement of my intention, threw the book on the market where it became a favorite overnight. My best hopes for it were realized. For not only did the book sell rapidly; it was granted on all sides that I had accomplished my revision without real injury to the book either as a sustained story or as a work of art. One of my first acts in opening the books of *William Faro, Inc.* was to create a royalty account payable to the D. H. Lawrence estate.

The instant success of my very first trade book was gall and wormwood to both my seniors in the publishing business, and the conductors of literary reviews who had sworn enmity to me and mine on other, older scores long before. They raised a hue and cry about my having tampered with a work of art without having consulted the corpse of its author, and in other ways made a bloody nuisance of themselves. Well, they couldn't threaten me into being respectful towards them. Nor could they stay me from continuing to make money. But one thing they could do, and did: they could blackball my future publications. And when my next two publications, *Celestine, a Chambermaid's Diary* by Octave Mirbeau, and *Body* by Daniel Quilter, appeared, they were reviewed in a manner that can only be described as vicious vilification.

Encouraged by the hostility of the press towards me, my old friend the vice crusader grew bold, and, in the May of 1931, swooped down on my offices at 96 Fifth Avenue, arrested me and a member of my staff, and accused us of publishing, in *Lady Chatterley's Lover,*

Celestine and *Body* books of a lascivious and filthy nature. The book came, luckily, before Magistrate William Dodge, an intelligent man and a fearless judge who dismissed the case as unwarranted by the books themselves, which had been placed before him for examination.

Defending myself and the books cost me over two thousand dollars. But I felt that it was fully worth it. Once and for all time it had to be proven to the vice crusader that the courts would not sustain him as a censor of literature. I was advised on all sides to sue him for false arrest, but I did not feel that I wanted that. I had beaten him beautifully and decisively. That was enough for me.

I celebrated my triumph over organized virtue by publishing, next, a collection of the short stories of the columnist Mark Hellinger. I had been an interested observer of Hellinger's career from his genesis in *The Daily News* to his settling down to the more mature and more deeply humorous incidents in his columns in *The Daily Mirror*. I had not succumbed to the easy temptation to underrate his particular kind of charm because he had happened to use a tabloid as his medium.

I was afraid only, when the enterprise first occurred to me, that Hellinger might be too prejudiced against me by what he had read in the literary columns to let me publish a book of his. I could not, as a matter of simple pride, undertake to argue .him out of whatever notion of me might have been preconceived for him by his friends. But nothing could stop me from telling him why I liked his sketches and why I thought they'd make an excellent book.

I did. And though he had heard of my reputation as the *enfant terrible* in publishing, and had offers from some of the bigger publishers, he was sportsmanlike enough to see me in my own light as a creative publisher, and let me have his book. The only other author whose work I have enjoyed publishing as much as Hellinger's is Voltaire who has been dead several centuries. At this writing, Hellinger is only sporting a crutch.

The success of *Moon Over Broadway* (the title of the Hellinger book), which I saw through four editions, encouraged me to produce a dollar reprint of *Venus In Furs* by Sachor-Massoch, a translation of Lila and Colette by Catulle Mendes and a prose poem by Anthony

Gudaitis entitled *A Young Man About to Commit Suicide*. These books were certainly not produced with only a hope of profits in view. They were not the sort of books one can hope to make much money on, in the first place. But when a publisher has made money on one book he is tempted to get out a few purely good books as a sort of altar-offering to the angry gods of the publishing business, or by the way of showing that he is not insensible to the more delicate aspects of his business.

* * *

The next big phase of the life of *William Faro, Inc.* was the publication of *The Strange Career of Mr. Hoover: Under Two Flags* by John Hamill. There has been as much lying about this as there has been about every other part of my business; so I shall tell you how it came about.

There was during the winter of 1930, in the Mayfair Theatre building, a book shop conducted by a young man who had frequented my wife's ill-fated Book Auction at 28 East 12th Street. I liked talking to him about books, and whenever I saw a movie in the vicinity of Broadway I made it my business to drop into the Mayfair book shop for a chat.

One night this young man told me of a strange man who had walked that day into his shop, with a manuscript. "A strange-looking Irishman, Sam. And what do you think the manuscript is about?" I could not guess.

"President Hoover."

"Indeed. What's the matter with little Herbie?"

"I can't say exactly. Coherence is not one of this man's solid virtues. But he seems to have some sort of case against him. If half of what he says that I understand is true his book should be of excited interest to any publisher. I told him about you, of course, and he's anxious to get together with you. Would you care to meet him?"

I met Hamill (for he it was) at this book store one afternoon several days later, and took him to drink beer with me at Steuben's around the corner. He told me that the President, long before the inception of his political career in America, had been associated with numerous questionable business enterprises that would seem to make him unfit for another four years of the high office he was holding in Washington. "The country will be interested," he said. "The question is, have you the guts to publish the facts?"

"If the facts are facts," I said, "I will publish them. You will have to first of all convince me of their genuineness. Then I will have to see a good reason for bringing out such a book in the midst of an economic crisis."

"I can only undertake to give you the facts," he said gruffly, and went away.

A few days later, according to promise, he appeared at my office in 96 Fifth Avenue. He had with him the facsimiles of court documents that fairly opened my eyes. There was no doubting the truth of Hamill's assertions. As for good cause to publish the book, a local wag was singing "Four years more of Hoover and Gandhi will be a well-dressed man," and that seemed good enough cause for the while. I could visualize a book that would open the eyes not only of America but of the whole civilized world.

When I announced my intention to publish this book, nearly everyone was horrified. Of all my undertakings, it was declared, this was certainly the maddest. Mr. Hoover, it was painstakingly pointed out to me, was one of the richest men in the world, and his position certainly made him the most powerful.

Even if everything in my book were true, it could have no chance of success. The newspapers would certainly refuse to advertise it. The book reviewing columns would give it scant encouragement. I would be lucky to be able to get even a few obscure book stores to handle it. On the other hand, as punishment to me for daring to bring the book out, there was no means of calculating in advance what ills might not befall me.

My reply to all this was to make a contract with John Hamill. Besides the usual royalty arrangement (and, because he knew nothing about that end of it, I gave him a better contract than I had ever given an author) I paid him fifty dollars a week for the ten weeks in which he was to write the book. There must, under the circumstances, be someone courageous enough to publish such things. If not I, who?

A few days before the actual appearance of the book, an attorney who was at that time advising me, proposed that, since nothing would keep me from doing this rash thing, it would be safer and wiser for me to withdraw from the company. "I have looked through your book," he said, "and I have no reason to doubt its truthfulness or your sincerity. But I must warn you at the very start that you are leaving one very wide loophole through which the enemy may be able to get you and even destroy you. Yourself. Suppose your facts are unassailable, as I believe they are? Then your fight is won—unless they can divert interest to a phase of the book which is not invulnerable—the character of its publisher. They'll just have to pretend, in order to defeat you, that the arguments are unworthy of notice because they are advanced by a man who has served three prison sentences. No one will ask why you served the sentences; if you try to explain no one will listen to you. Prison sentences are forgiven only in the heroic dead."

"What would you have me do?" I asked.

"Resign from *William Faro, Inc.* Then let them dare drag you into the issue."

I considered the matter. "I can see your point," I said. "But it doesn't seem to me good sportsmanship to attack a man and keep one's self entirely safe from attack. Don't you see," I added, "that if I were not already an officer of the corporation publishing this book, it would be morally necessary for me to become one?"

My lawyer could not see anything other than that I was laying myself open to an attack that would once more give my enemies an unfair advantage over me. All I could see on my side, however, was that if there were any evil consequences to be suffered as a result of the publication of the book, I should be there to take them. I wish now I had not been filled with so much airy bravado.

For weeks after the appearance of *The Strange Career* I could not take a step outside of my office and home without being followed by a member of the Department of Justice. Even on the sidewalks of the city I was jostled, harangued and threatened. My private and office telephone were tapped and listened in on. The Post Office sent its inspectors to search through my books for guilty stains of obscenity, and my mailings were so hampered that for a while I had to give them up altogether. The climax came when one morning, on entering my office in the penthouse of 1140 Broadway, five men who had evidently been waiting, rose to greet me.

"I'm from the income-tax department," said one of them showing a Federal badge.

"What is it now?" I asked.

"We have a complaint," he replied, "that you have not filed income tax returns."

I smiled. "Don't you know?" I asked.

"We're here to find out," he announced breezily. "Let's see your books."

I tried to block his way to the inner office. "It seems to me that you should have definite information before you come on such an errand. Either I did file income tax reports in which case they are on file at the Custom House, or I did not. Now as a matter of fact, income tax returns have been filed my myself, my wife, and my business. I can't understand your wanting to look through my books."

The spokesman then took out a paper which he said was a search warrant and proceeded with his followers into my more private office where they began rummaging quickly through all the books they could lay their hands on. To this day I do not know the object of their search. After a while one of them made a pretense of calling up the custom house where, he told me, they had just found the mislaid income tax reports. When I showed the warrant to my attorney the following day he pointed out to me that it was fraudulent, for it had not been made out as of a definite date.

But all my troubles did not come from the subject of the book. Its author was the source of some real embarrassment to me. It appears now that before he came to me, John Hamill had approached a certain ex-policeman, with Democratic connections in Brooklyn, and had interested him, as he was later to interest me. They had come to an agreement whereby the ex-policeman was to write a book from Hamill's facts, publish it and give Hamill a substantial share of the profits. In compliance with his part of the contract, the ex-policeman had financed for Hamill a trip to England, advancing him more than two thousand dollars.

You will therefore have no difficulty understanding this ex-policeman's indignation when he learned that Hamill himself had written a book and that someone else was due to make the major publisher's profits there from. I had, of course, never heard of him or of his arrangement with Hamill whose contract with me assured me that no one else had any claim whatever on his manuscript. When the ex-policeman wrote me about it and demanded that I immediately abandon the project I could only sympathize with his loss, for I had already invested even more than he had, in advances to the author, in setting the book up in type, in printing, paper and binding. I could not see that it was my moral obligation to throw away all this because Mr. Hamill, playing no favorites, had lied both to the ex-policeman and myself.

I discussed with my attorney at great length a plan whereby we might compel Mr. Hamill to repay the ex-policeman out of the royalties earned by the book. But my attorney had no sooner introduced himself to the ex-policeman in court than the latter assumed such an unruly and violent attitude that it became clear that it would be impossible to deal with him on that basis.

Our defense against the ex-policeman's attempt to enjoin the sale of the book cost me thousands of dollars in attorney's fees. But that was not the worst of it. It gave the friends of the President, who were otherwise at a loss as how to defend him against the accusations in the book, an easy way to belittle.

It was only necessary to point out to a gaping country that the author of the book was an obvious liar and cheat: almost a whole issue of *Colliers* and several serious books were devoted to this sort of thing, which had its effect by retarding the sale of the book.

But Mr. Hamill had not yet reached the highest development of his peculiar character. He had sold out the ex-policeman's interest to me. He was yet to sell out my interests bodily to the friends of the President.

One morning I received a telephone call from a New York Republican ward leader, whom I knew slightly. If I would have lunch with him, he said, there was something of great interest to be revealed to me. As we were eating he asked me if I had given thought to what would happen to me if the President failed to be re-elected.

"Why should that worry me?" I asked.

"It is pretty well known that the President feels that your book has done more to prejudice the country against him than anything else. If he's defeated, he'll blame it on you and prosecute you."

"Prosecute me for what?" I asked with astonishment.

"Libel."

"But there is no libel," I cried, "and every one of you damn well know it."

My friend across the table looked shrewdly at me. "Did you know," he inquired blandly, "that John Hamill has confessed that the whole of his book is a fabrication of his own, intended to harm the President?"

"I don't know, and I don't care," I declared. "I didn't believe Hamill to begin with. I might have libeled Hoover if I had published everything Hamill wanted me to publish. But I only published what appeared to me true from indisputable documents and company reports. What difference does it make to me how many confessions Hamill signs?"

I called up Hamill that same day. He denied the allegation vehemently, but there was something suspicious about his very vehemence. A few days later Mr. Hoover delivered his famous Cleveland speech in which he referred to the Confession. Then there was no doubt in my mind that Hamill had once more given rein to his peculiar imagination.[30]

---

[30] *I have in my possession a copy of this alleged "confession." It is 187 pages of pompous bluster in which I could not find that as much as a single fact in* The Strange Career *is controverted or even called into serious question. That would explain the reason why, for all the noise they made about procuring it from Hamill, Mr. Hoover's friends have never dared to publish it. During the trial of the ex-policeman's suit against William Faro, Inc., a futile attempt was made to make America conscious of the existence of this "confession." Mr. Hamill was placed on the witness stand by the little Jew attorney who, for reasons best known to himself, had maneuvered the all-too-willing Hamill into that curious 187 page tract. He began asking him a series of questions whose answers were meant to make exciting reading for Mr. Hoover's friends. But Hamill had a stroke either of conscience or perverseness, for he refused to make the scheduled answers, and the press went home without a story. All but the good old* New York Times *which prints only "news fit to print." This great newspaper had Hamill answering the questions as he was supposed to, and certainly not as he actually did. To one who was actually at the trial and saw what happened, the full column which* The New York Times *devoted to it the following morning, read like a fine work of the imagination. Evidently those week-ends in which Mr. Hoover entertained Mr. Ochs at the White House*

But even that speech did not save Mr. Hoover who suffered that year the deadliest defeat ever meted out to an American President who made himself a candidate for a second term. I had braved so much in publishing the book; it had given me so much trouble, that 1 looked on the outcome of the election of 1932 as a sort of personal triumph. I had favored Mr. Smith against Hoover in 1928, when my imprisonment made it impossible for me even to vote. And I had not only survived that unjust imprisonment. I had materially helped to defeat Hoover far more seriously than he had defeated Smith.

* * *

The financial success of *The Strange Career* made it possible for me to realize one of the earliest ambitions of my life, to publish in a smaller and more beautiful format, the ten volumes of Voltaire's *Philosophical Dictionary* which had been the chief literary and ethical guide of my boyhood. I realized that thus far my success had always been due to the intrinsic sensationalism of my publications: whatever sales I achieved came in spite of the discouragement of the reviewers. Voltaire's work required a greater investment than I had ever made in one enterprise, and it was in no way sensational. Had I the right to risk it?

The truth is that I thought I had a pretty good knowledge of how far the literary press would go to hurt my business. They might, I said to myself, justify themselves in snubbing my ventures into sensationalism, dip though they are in the gold of glamour and adventure. But how could they disregard an enterprise of such a purely literary and philosophical nature?

I had the *Dictionary* set in two magnificent volumes. The setting cost nearly two thousand dollars. By the time the edition had gone through the bindery it had cost me over four thousand dollars, almost half of my cash savings.

Then I launched it, to learn that I had underestimated, in my enemies, either their hatred of me or the extent of their indifference to literary values. *The Philosophical Dictionary* evoked no comment at all in the press. Because I was its publisher, *The New York Times* did not even mention the book. Voltaire's great work got less reviewing

---

were not for nothing. Why should gentiles fear the Jewish power of the press when the latter can be procured so easily?

from the press of the Hansens, the Gannetts and the Soskins that I would have got if I had reprinted a cheap thriller from one of the pulp magazines. The whole edition fell dead at my feet the very first week I issued it.

With my funds getting thinner and thinner, I continued to issue books in the hope of hitting one that would make up for the loss sustained by me in the publishing of the *Philosophical Dictionary*. I published two magnificent biographies: the *Life of Pope Joan,* and *The Adventure of Fritz Duquesne,* both by Clement Wood. The shifting about of the chronicles of the Church of Rome so as to make it appear that Joan never really lived had always seemed to me like murder. In Clement Wood I found for the loveliest of the world's fair scholars a champion to my heart's content. *The Woman Who Was Pope* must eventually take its place with the very finest biographies ever written. It was Wood himself who mentioned to me Duquesne's name for the first time. I was instantly fascinated by the story of the man who, to punish it for the rape of his family and fortune during the Boer War by a Kitchener regiment, had sworn vengeance against the British Empire and fought it single-handed for over thirty years, and I asked Wood to write the story for me, which he did in *The Man Who Killed Kitchener,* with such grace and vigor.

I also published the autobiography of Lord Alfred Douglas and the memoirs of my friend Dr. Ralcy Husted Bell. But business was getting worse and worse. And, due to the silence of the press concerning my publications, they were not catching on. Then a manuscript come to me through the mails which promised to get me out of my financial difficulties. It was an ugly scandal which involved one of the three great motor magnates of America; and moreover, a story of a grave injustice, a bigamous marriage and false imprisonment which the motor magnate had spent a fortune to keep from the public. And there it was in my hands, written by a close relation of the motor magnate.

I hesitated to publish the book for only one reason: the injustice did not seem to me important enough to warrant a whole book being devoted to it. With a book I had just helped to save my country from the strangling hold of a man who had all his life been a menace to the finest things in our civilization. Was I now to expend the same amount of energy in order to iron out a petty quarrel? But undoubtedly there would be tremendous national interest in the story, and I had almost decided to publish it when something happened to stop me.

I was in Cafe Royal one night when a young Jewish publisher whom I knew but did not particularly like, walked in. Nevertheless, when he asked me what was troubling me, I told him about it.

"Going to use real names?" he asked.

"Of course."

"Well, you'll make money alright," he said drily.

"You think people will really be interested?"

"What do you care whether people will be interested? That's not why you're publishing it, is it?"

"I can't see any other reason."

"Stop trying to kid me, Roth. You know that motor magnate will give you at least a hundred thousand to withdraw the book from sale."

I discussed the matter no further with him. But my mind was made up. My business might if it liked, go to the devil. But I was never going to publish that book.

Well, my business did go—to the Jews.

* * *

Towards the end of the year 1932, I realized that the business of *William Faro, Inc.* was sliding into real trouble. It had outstanding, and payable over a period of three months, notes aggregating some seventeen thousand dollars. My estimated income during three months, as business was at that time, would be sufficient to meet only about a third of that amount. Our chief creditors were: a printer, a binder, a linotyper who set most of the type of our books and a paper house, which had supplied us with all the paper for our books. We owed various small sums to other concerns, too, but the records of them would be of no consequence to this story.

There seemed to me no cause for alarm, either to me or my creditors. Our stock of books, under any kind of liquidation, was worth at least forty thousand dollars. Besides that, there were tons of linotypemetal, and valuable copyrights.

The solution to this difficulty seemed to me very simple. The production of new books must come to an end. I must begin to liquidate the stock we had on hand, and arrange extensions of time on the notes held by our creditors. At the rate money was coming, it might take nine months for us to meet all of our obligations. But since nearly every other business in town was in pretty much the same position, I did not doubt that the creditors of *William Faro, Inc.* would cooperate with us.

I had done, I could tell them in all sincerity, what under the circumstances was pretty nearly heroic. I had withdrawn all of my family savings from the bank and thrown them into the business. No one could go further than that—just for a business.

When I came to my creditors I encountered, apparently, difficulties only inherent in the financial situation. The printers and binders, having been hard hit themselves, had disposed of all of my notes to third parties.

The linotyper made arrangements with me to collect the balance of the moneys due him at the rate of fifty dollars a week for ten weeks, and a hundred dollars a week thereafter, until some seventeen hundred dollars was paid up. The paper house owned by a German-Jew, made a similar arrangement with me, by which it was to get a hundred dollars a week. Since the amount owed the latter was in excess of four thousand dollars, I mortgaged to it the standing type of eight of my best books.

According to what I had learned in *Perok* (in the Wisdom of the Fathers) when I was a boy, my association with these people was in itself proof of my guilt, and my worthiness to keep my business. *Perok* says: *If a man is brought before you in a court of law, accused by one or more of his fellows of irregularity of conduct, regard him as guilty until he has managed to prove his innocence.*

The sense of this stern admonition is this. A man who is brought to court by associates in business is at least guilty of associating with the sort of people he cannot arrange things with amicably outside of court. But let me not make the mistake of characterizing these people. Let their actions do that for them.

During the first years of my business association with the binder whom we will call Parrach, he did business as The Art Bindery. Later, merging his business with that of two other binders, he began billing me as Union Binderies. This was followed soon by the Parrach

Bindery, which in a few months gave way to still a fourth name. It is about a half a year since I have seen a billhead of his, so there is no telling how many other names Parrach has worked under since. It was during the Union Binderies period that something sinister occurred which would have warned any sensible publisher of danger. Robert Sherwood, a wholesaler of books at 24 Beekman Street, called me on the telephone and informed me that a young man had just offered to sell him fifty copies of a $3.75 book of mine for seventy five dollars.

"What did you say to him?" I asked.

"I told him to bring me the books at four o'clock and I'd buy them from him. You can then do anything you like with him."

At four o'clock two men from police headquarters saw a dark young man tow in a package containing fifty copies of my book. When he had taken the seventy-five dollars in cash from Mr. Sherwood, they nabbed him, marched him to the nearest station house and called for me.

When they pointed him out to me I did not recognize him. But he had no hesitation in recalling himself to me. "You don't recognize me," he said, "because I am usually in work clothes when you come into the shop. I work in the shop. I'm -------'s son."

He named one of Parrach's partners.

"And how long," I asked him, "have you been a partner in my business?"

He swore that this was his maiden effort. He had only done it because business was so bad that neither he nor his father had been able to draw pay for four weeks. His mother was dangerously ill. He had just taken his bar exams. If, because of this charge being pressed against him, he would not be admitted to the practice of law, it would literally kill his mother.[31]

---

[31] *The next time you read about a particularly bloody pogrom and pause to wonder how Christians, dedicated to a religion of mercy, can exercise so much brutality against the Jews, remember that the Jew wheedles all the mercy out of his neighbors in the ordinary course of business. He lies and cheats until he is caught. When caught, instead of accepting punishment, he moans and tears his hair, invokes the sores of ancestors in their graves and living relations at the point of death in hospitals, until the wronged gentile, nauseated, lets him go. Then, thumbing his nose at the gentile behind his back, the Jew goes about his business the same way, lying and cheating now doubly to make up for*

Instinctively I knew that the Jew was lying. There was a huge discrepancy between the number of books we had printed and the number which had been delivered to us by Parrach. It ran into thousands of books.

Still, even though there was only the faintest chance that he was telling the truth I would not press the charge. I could not risk being the author of such awful consequences, even to regain so much money. And so I did not press the charge, and the police freed him.

I was a fool, of course, to let him go. It was my only chance to get an honest reckoning from Parrach and get rid of him altogether. Furthermore, by nipping this young Jew's career in the bud, I would have prevented another Jew vulture from infesting the courts of the State of New York.

I repent this more than anything else. If the New York Bar Association has any interest in this matter, I am prepared to turn the facts over to it, in full.

* * *

One by one I met the people who had taken over the notes we had given the printer and the binder. In almost every case, when I had explained the situation and offered a scheme of payment, there was no difficulty coming to an arrangement. But occasionally I would run into trouble. Usually it was some lawyer—a Jew shyster.

A typical instance concerns a note for a hundred and fifty dollars I had given the printer, who had in turn paid it over to his attorney, a crafty old Jew with an office on lower Fifth Avenue. This printer still assures me that he gets along marvelously with him, but my experience with this lawyer was singularly depressing.

We will call him Counsellor Pinsky. I tried to explain to Counsellor Pinsky over the telephone just how things stood, but he would not listen to me.

"I don't care how bad business is," said Counsellor Pinsky. "I want cash for my note and I want cash immediately."

"But why don't you let me come to see you," I pleaded. "I'm sure we can arrange things amicably."

---

lost time. A pogrom is usually the climax of years of such relentless goading. Do you wonder that when the final reckoning comes the gentile is absolutely merciless?

He seemed to consider my suggestion. "Alright, then. How long will you remain at your office?"

"I'll wait for you till you come," I said.

"I'll be over in twenty minutes," he assured me.

In less than twenty minutes a young woman walked into my office and announced that she was from the office of Counsellor Pinsky. Having been introduced to me by my secretary, she handed me—a summons.

In the midst of this difficulty, Parrach, the binder, came to me with a summons from his attorney, whom we will call Mr. Black. It was a matter of the utmost importance that I see him and talk things over with him.

The first thing you notice when you come into Counsellor Black's office is a picture of his wife on his desk: a matronly Jewish woman who you feel could allow herself to be the wife only of a man of the utmost austerity. The office of a Jewish lawyer is usually devised with great cunning. In addition to the stock portraits of George Washington and John Marshall, there is usually a picture of a child or, if possible children. If the lawyer is unmarried he displays a picture of his mother. This is calculated to give you confidence in him. It is by way of saying: You see in me a man of family, true to all my pledges; you may speak your mind to me with the utmost confidence.

Mr. Black opened our conversation with the remark that he had been given to understand that I was having considerable difficulty with creditors.

I told him that I seemed to have been very careless in my choice of creditors. I had given several of them series of checks with the understanding that the checks were not to be deposited without my office being consulted, to ascertain that funds were available at the bank to clear them. One or two of them complied with this arrangement.

The rest, pleading that necessity had compelled them to turn checks over to others, didn't. The truth was that it was difficult to persuade these Jews that when I said there was no money in the bank there really was no money. One of the minor results was that the bank had tactfully but firmly asked me to withdraw my account.

Mr. Black appeared to listen to me thoughtfully, but when he spoke suddenly I realized that his listening had been only an attitude. He had a definite plan in his mind. He had not been considering what I was saying to him.

"There is only one way out for you," said Counsellor Black with the dramatics that shyster lawyers flatter themselves with in the privacy of their offices. "As long as you continue doing things as you are doing them now, you will be in hot water. Here is a solid idea and a sure way out for you. Form a new corporation. Turn over to this new corporation all of the stock of *William Faro, Inc.* Then let the new firm dictate terms to your old creditors."

"I don't see," I remarked, "what difference it will make to my creditors under what name I trade, since it will still be the same business."

"That's just it," said Mr. Black. "It will be the same business, but your creditors will have to accept new terms because you will not be running the business under the new name."

"And who, may I ask, will be running the new business?"

"Oh, we'll find someone to run it. We'll hold the stock of the new corporation in escrow for you in the interest of my clients till the old debts are paid off, that is to say your debts to my clients."

"And who," I asked him, "are our clients?"

He named the binder and the paper house.

"And what about my other creditors?"

"They would have to wait till my clients are paid and the business is restored to you."

"But suppose you never fully clear the debts of your clients? Then you need never restore my business to me. Isn't that so?"

Counsellor Black looked hurt. "Don't you trust us?" he asked softly.

I rose to go. "I don't like your plan," I said. "It does not seem to me to be either rational or necessary. My business is worth a hundred thousand dollars. I owe your clients about five thousand dollars, which is fully secured to them. Is it reasonable that I should be asked to turn over to you a business worth a hundred thousand dollars so that they may collect a twentieth of it and ruin it utterly?"

"But the fact is that you are not meeting your obligations," he argued.

"I am meeting my obligations," I replied. "But like everybody else nowadays, I am taking a little more time doing so. Forgive me if I can't stay any longer. I don't think following your advice will get me out of my present difficulties. On the contrary, I can see worse difficulties I might get into."

Back at the office, when I returned, I found the agent for the paper house, an ugly little socialist-Jew with burlesque Jewish accent and manners. "Well how did you make out with Black?" he asked.

I told him what had happened.

He seemed chagrined. "It's a good idea," he muttered. "You should have taken it."

I told him it would be quite useless to argue the point with me. "I don't like the whole business. I don't see how I happen to have got mixed up with a lot of plug-uglies like you and your friend Parrach to begin with. I shall sacrifice a lot of my stock at lower prices and see if I can't get rid of both of you."

I said this in the manner of jest, but there was real feeling behind my words. The ugly little socialist-Jew whom I shall refer to as Isaac Ratte pretended not to notice my rancor. "If you're going to liquidate," he said, "I've got another proposition for you. Why don't you get someone to help you?"

"Anyone who could help me," I said, "would cost too much."

The socialist-Jew seemed to brighten. "Well, there's Lousse. He worked for you before, and understands your business. I met him a few days ago and he and his wife are literally starving. He told me he'd work for you now for twenty dollars a week."

It was certainly true that I had taken a great deal more work on myself than I could possibly do well. I was helping my wife run four branch outlet stores along Broadway in addition to all my other duties as a publisher. But I was not so pleased with the suggestion about Lousse who had left my employ at about the time I issued the book on Hoover. It was just such a plea (that he and his wife were starving) made to me by a loose-thighed Jewess I met in Cafe Royal, that had procured his first job with me. His work had been satisfactory to a point; but he had always given me the impression that he was planning how to steal my business away from me, so that when he announced that he wanted to go into business for himself I was inwardly happy to get rid of him. The prospect of re-employing him was not a bright one. But the truth was that he did know my business pretty thoroughly, and twenty dollars a week would not be too great a tax on my business. At least I would not have to teach Lousse the rudiments of my business.

I paid out nearly five thousand dollars of the obligations of *William Faro, Inc.* in the next three months. Then because of an irregularity it is not necessary to discuss here, I discharged Lousse.

* * *

Two or three weeks later I was awakened at eight o'clock one morning by the ringing of the doorbell of my apartment. I opened the door only slightly and asked who it was. A young woman came within full view of me and asked if I was Mr. Roth. I said I was but that she would have to wait a few minutes if she wanted to see me. "I don't have to see you," she said, and stuck a summons through the opening I had made in the doorway.

The summons was a complaint based on two notes, for two hundred dollars each which I had given to Parrach the binder. The complainant was a Yiddish bookseller on East Broadway, a Mr. Jankewitz about whom I had heard many things. I indignantly called Parrach on the telephone and asked him how he happened to have turned over those notes to this man. Parrach replied that he did not know Jankewitz. He had given the notes to Ratte who in turn had given them to Jankewitz.

In answer to my call, Ratte came in to see me. He had already discussed the matter with Mr. Jankewitz. It had been agreed between himself, Ratte, and Mr. Jankewitz that if I paid sixty-eight dollars in two checks of thirty four dollars each, and gave a new ninety days note for the balance, judgment would not be taken and everything would return to *status quo*. I saw no other way out because I could not spare the cash with which to get those notes out of the hands of Mr. Jankewitz. And so, trusting Ratte to carry out the agreement, I gave him the checks and the note and dismissed the whole unpleasant affair from my mind as something too unwholesome to entertain in a short lifetime.

But a new difficulty had arisen. Parrach, after another one of his prodigal failures, had turned his plant over to another bindery. In this bindery he was not really owner. He just collected an agent's commission for work done. The new binder had delivered to me a thousand dollars worth of work against fifteen hundred dollars in notes, the extra five hundred being advanced by me to help Parrach out of one of his usual difficulties. And just as things seemed to be going smoothly again I found it impossible to get books from the bindery. I went to see the new binder. The trouble he said was with Parrach. Parrach was not attending to his business. When I saw Parrach he said the trouble was with the real boss of the works. He had heard that I was having difficulty in meeting my notes, and so was reluctant to let more books go out till I showed myself capable of paying some of the notes which would soon come due.

"But if I cannot get books my business will come to a standstill," I argued.

"I'm not boss here, you know that," was all I could get out of Parrach.

It became obvious that I would accomplish nothing till I got these two Jews and their stories together in the same room. I found myself spending days and weeks trying to accomplish this. Now and then I would catch one of the office force snickering behind my back. They certainly knew what was going on. On Thursday, April 20th, Ratte, the Jew paper agent who had mysteriously disappeared after getting the check and the notes came to me with a proposition. "I understand that you can't get books from the bindery, "he began innocently.

"True."

"You know why, don't you?"

"I've been told a few reasons."

"Well the truth is that the new binder is afraid of you. But there's one way you can prove to him that you don't intend to default. He knows that you have no money. But he knows that your wife has a claim for more than nine hundred dollars against the bankrupt estate of Louis K. Liggett. If you'll get Mrs. Roth to turn over this claim to us, we'll see to it that you get instant delivery of books."

"I wouldn't like to do that," I said. "My wife and I have already deprived ourselves of all the benefits of cash. This is a poor time to leave oneself penniless. And the money from Liggett's seems to be the only cash left for us to look forward to."

I realized by this time that there was something foul in the wind. But I had put everything I had into the pot; it would be a mistake to let the fire go out too soon. Let me not hesitate, I said to myself, over my final bit of money. If I am to get into trouble, let it not be because I hesitated to throw in everything I have. I therefore, finally, and most reluctantly, consented to let my wife turn over to the paper house, which was already fully secured, the assignment of her claim against the Liggett Estate. This assignment, we had agreed, was to be held in escrow by someone we trusted mutually until the first shipment of books came to me from the Bindery.

"No escrow arrangement will be necessary," Ratte suddenly interposed. "You'll get your first shipment tomorrow."

The following day, Friday, Ratte came to the office of *William Faro, Inc.* in the company of Parrach. Ratte had with him the assignment for my wife to sign, pretended to be in a hurry, and Parrach assured me that he had seen a truckload of books leave the Bindery, for my warehouse. But I told them bluntly that no assignment would be signed till the books arrived. Hours passed in waiting. About once an hour someone in my office would telephone the Bindery to ask what had happened to the shipment. And someone on the other wire would always answer that it was on its way.

Then it became quite plain that all this knavish nonsense had been prearranged, I suggested that I was still ready to leave the assignment in escrow till shipment at a later date. The escrowee was settled on, a Jew who paid me twenty five dollars a month for space in my office. The agreement was drawn up by an attorney who happened accidentally on the scene. But because additional papers, showing how this money was to be accounted for by the paper house had to be drawn, the agreement could not be consummated till the following morning, Saturday, April 22nd. Ratte took the assignment from me Saturday morning. Saturday afternoon I was served by his attorney with papers asking for a receivership of the business of *William Faro, Inc.* The demand was based on an affidavit by the discharged Lousse that I was misappropriating the funds of the corporation with the intention of cheating my creditors.

That was not all. I was to learn several days later that on Thursday of April 20th, the day before we sat around waiting all afternoon in my office for a delivery of books, all of the stock of *William Faro, Inc.* had been sold out on a marshall's levy to the binder for three hundred and eighteen dollars.

The marshal's levy was based on a judgment obtained against me by Jankewitz on the original summons with which I had been served. Ratte had taken my sixty eight dollars and the new note. But, without notification to me, Jankewitz had proceeded to take judgment on the note, the one for which I had already settled, and was to be returned to me. When asked by an attorney of mine why he had not given *William Faro, Inc.* notice of his levy and sale, the marshall replied that he did not know our address, and that it was not possible to communicate with *William Faro, Inc.* In spite of the fact that I had fairly lived at the binder during the past two weeks, and that I had been there at the very time the alleged sale was supposed to have taken place. Furthermore: *William Faro, Inc.* was listed in at least two of New York's telephone directories.

Evidence enough here, you will say, to hang any set of conspirators. Apparently not enough, though, in the Jew-run courts of New York.
* * *

This is how the papers asking for a receivership of *William Faro, Inc.* were served on me.

Having delivered in escrow for the paper-house the assignment of my wife's claim to the Louis K. Liggett Estate, I got a call from the bindery. If I wanted an immediate shipment of books it would be necessary for me to meet Parrach the binder at the office of the paper house. I accompanied Ratte to his employer's headquarters where Parrach and the owner of the paper house were waiting for me. The latter, a German Jew, looked elated. I fancy that in Germany today many a Jew like him is paying heavily for just such experiments in the administration of the human spirits.

The telephone rang even as I sat down. It was a message for Parrach. Mr. Black his attorney wanted us over at his office. In view of what I had already seen of Counselor Black, the prospect of getting together with him again was not enticing. But business had become very ugly and seeing this legal sycophant seemed to have become an essential part of it. Only Parrach accompanied me on this trip. Ratte had accomplished, to his complete satisfaction, his part of the business for the day. No sooner was I seated before Counsellor Black's desk than, to my utter amazement, he resumed discussing the plan he had outlined to me the first time I called on him. He talked lengthily, apparently to make time. I observed him with growing perplexity. Obviously he was not really interested in his own words. I was aware of a sinister movement the very nature of which I could not guess at. Firmly he paused and looked at me.

"What's the use of going over all that?" I asked. "I now owe my creditors five thousand dollars less than I owed them when you first broached this matter to me. Surely you don't think I can be more inclined, under the circumstances, to entertain your plan?"

"But the situation has changed on our side, too," he said mysteriously.

"How?" I asked.

"I can't tell you," he said. "I can only hint to you that I am acting for a majority of your creditors. Very important things have happened, and are happening."

"That sounds like a threat," I replied. "As for your representing a majority of my creditors permit me to express a doubt."

"Then the only thing there is left for me to do is to warn you to accept my proposition."

I became angry. "If you want me to accept a proposition of yours, why not try to make an honest one? It seems to me to be very poor legal ethics for you to sit there and try to threaten me out of my business. You're not practicing law."

He looked up dramatically. "What do you think I'm practising?"

"It looks to me a little more like blackmail."

He rose. "I don't care what you think of my practise. I represent your creditors, and they do not think you are competent to run your business well enough to pay them what is due them."

"Which of you," I asked, "thinks he can run my business better?"

"We have a man," said Black looking down on his carpet.

I grew suspicious. "Who?"

Counsellor Black paused a moment before answering. Then he uttered the ugly word: "Lousse."

"Do you happen to know," I asked him, "why I discharged Lousse?"

"Yes."

"And yet you want me to turn my business over to him?"

"We're not asking you to turn the business over to him. But to us. We want you to have confidence in us."

"I see," I said. By this time I realized that something really vicious was afoot. I decided to fight for time, myself. I turned to Black. "Let me think about it. I want to consult my attorney."

"I'm an attorney," said Councellor Black.

"Yes, but not my attorney. You understand that I'm entitled to an attorney who will consider my interests in this matter?"

"Yes. But why can't you trust me?"

"I only want to take the ordinary precaution of having someone representing my interests, Mr. Black. Here is the name and telephone number of my attorney. Please call him Monday morning. Whatever he is willing to arrange with you, will be alright with me."

Counselor Black pretended to see my side of it. We shook hands and I left his office. I had no sooner reached the street than I realized that I was being followed. I stopped; a young man came up to me and asked me whether I was Samuel Roth. I replied in the affirmative and he served me with the receivership papers, returnable the following Wednesday morning. The whole thing had been arranged so as to make it possible for me to be served that afternoon.

* * *

It was now almost six o'clock. Lower Broadway, together with the rest of the world, was darkening before my eyes. Across the street was a United Cigars store. I went towards it to communicate with my attorney. It was too late to get him at his office, so I telephoned his home. A maid answered that Mr. Lavine had left with his wife the day before for Washington, D.C., and would not be back till Tuesday morning.

I thought that it might be too late to get together a reply if I waited till Tuesday, and remembered Mr. Hyman Burtel. I knew that Mr. Burtel, who had been for thirty days a magistrate under Tammany Hall, would want a big fee, for I had retained him once before. But since I had only recently helped Mr. Burtel earn a five hundred dollar fee from another publisher, I thought that he might consider my impaired finances and help me in this matter.

I called Mr. Burtel and he consented to see me at his home in Essex

House the next morning, Sunday. I introduced the matter by telling him that it was a matter of life and death for me to win this action, and I wanted him to undertake it only in that spirit. He studied the papers for about fifteen minutes, then threw them on the table. If what I told him was true, he said, it would be a simple matter for me to resist this move. He would take the case, but I must give him a retainer of five hundred dollars. "Cash," he added. "I wouldn't take a case like this from anyone else for less than a thousand dollars."

The only concession I could get from him was time till Tuesday afternoon to have the full amount in his office.

The following day I paid Mr. Burtel half of his retainer. The day after that we learned about the sale of all my assets. Mr. Burtel immediately prepared motion papers returnable in Municipal Court the following Monday, asking why this sale should not be set aside as fraudulent, and why the "purchaser" of the property of *William Faro, Inc.* should not be restrained from disposing of it.

The presiding magistrate, a negro, granted the second motion, but wanted time to consider the first. Naturally the "purchaser" of my property was represented by Counselor Black. After the memorable court meeting between Mr. Burtel and Mr. Black in court that morning it became practically impossible for me to see Mr. Burtel again.

In spite of the fact that copies of the court-order forbidding any disposition of the property were served (at my suggestion, not Mr. Burtel's) on Parrach, Lousse, Ratte and all other parties concerned, I was approached by booksellers all over town who told me that my property was being sold on all sides.

It was now in order to bring Parrach, Lousse and Ratte into court for contempt for disobeying a court order. I also urged upon Mr. Burtel's office that proceedings should be taken against Lousse for violating the criminal statute forbidding an employee from using, as Lousse did, information obtained while in the hire of an employer.

But, as I have already mentioned, I could not get to see Mr. Burtel who behaved as though, as far as he was concerned, the matter was closed. Mr. Gottlieb, a clerk in the office, who received me for Mr. Burtel, told me that it was inadvisable to take any such action at the time. When the proper time came they would let me know.

At my instance, all of my creditors (whom Counsellor Black had pretended to represent) got up a petition to be presented before Judge Valente when the motion for receivership came up. This petition asked that I be permitted to continue running the business of *William Faro, Inc.* and was granted. The request for a receivership was denied.

The negro magistrate was daily putting off the decision on the question of the validity of the "sale" of my property. One morning Mr. Gottlieb called me on the telephone. The magistrate, he informed me, had finally decided to put the question up to a referee.

"Has a date been set?" I asked.

"No," was the reply. "When a date is set we'll let you know."

One of my creditors was, in the meantime, persuaded by his attorney that at the rate I was managing things, Black and his crowd would have sold out all of the assets of the corporation before I could get to them, and advised bankruptcy as the safest means of rescuing what was left of the property of *William Faro, Inc.* At the request of this creditor and two others, the Federal Court appointed the Irving Trust Company as the receiver, and the latter designated Mr. George Mintzer as its acting attorney.

I turned over all of the papers in the case to the attorney for the Irving Trust Company, trustee. Office of Mr. George Mintzer. After several days, he informed me that he saw no grounds on which to proceed against the people who had defrauded me because on the surface everything seemed legal. To dig into the matter meant an investigation and an expenditure of moneys which were not in the estate.

"But you don't need an investigation," I cried. "They have been selling my property all the time in violation of a court order."

He promised to look into this immediately.

Several days later this attorney recalled me. The books were being sold, he informed me, but it was perfectly legal. The motion as to the validity of the sale had come up before a referee in the Court of the State of New York, and it had been decided against me by default. Neither Mr. Burtel nor anyone representing his office had appeared before the referee to argue the motion when it was called.

The Jew is Amused

XIV THE JEWS, THE THEATRE, AND THE WOMAN-MARKET

On Shaftsbury Avenue, London, within a strong man's stone's throw of Piccadilly Circus, there stood, in 1920, a very elegant house which conducted its peculiar business in a manner picturesquely unusual.

The young dandy (or the old baldhead) patron turned over an admission fee of a crown to a man on guard before the entrance, and in return for it got back a little yellow slip which gained him admission to the office in the first floor. One's first entrance to this office was inevitably sensational.

There was absolutely no furniture in sight. Nor was it attended by any living human being. Just before one entered, the yellow slip was taken away from one by another attendant at the door whom one did not see when one approached and could not find, if one wanted to, a moment after this transaction with him was over.

Once inside the patron found himself in a sort of picture gallery. There were thirty seven photographs in all, each of a young girl in a more or less nude and lewd state of undress.

To every one of the pictures was attached a white electric button with a black number on it. If the number was alight when you approached it, it was understood that the lady was disengaged. The patron pressed it, and the light instantly went out. He then had only to seek out the room of the same number as the one on the button, and he would find the lady of his fancy waiting for him there, stretched out on her dark red velvet cot in precisely the state and position assumed in the photograph.

The owner of this unique and highly successful enterprise was a continental Jew who, I was told, conducted similar establishments in Paris, Berlin and Vienna. The most ravishing English girls were at his command. He had only two rules by which he chose them, one a

191

positive, the other a negative. To get into the establishment the girl had to be very beautiful, and she must not be a Jewess.

In 1923, upon my return to New York City, I went to an opening of the Ziegfeld Follies in the New Amsterdam Theatre. The Follies were always the most sought for review in town, and it had, not without justice, got the reputation of also being the most decent. So fancy my surprise, when the late Mr. Ziegfeld's delighted chorines streamed out into the limelight of that vast stage, to see a large readable numeral engraved in silk on every pretty costume. The program that was handed to me did its part, too.

It listed every girl's number next to her name to enable a man to identify, for whatever evil purpose he might have in mind, the girl who happened to catch his eye.

The next morning I bought the newspapers to see how the critics took it. I was not mistaken.

The critics, too, understood perfectly. They railed, jeered and bantered the producer about it. What led the producer to the abandonment of the practice I do not really know.

The girls might have objected. It might have been the irony of the critics. And it might have been the iron arm of the law.

Of all the Jewish producers on Broadway, the late Florenz Ziegfeld probably came closest to exhibiting a real streak of genius of showmanship.

His chief asset, as it seemed to me was an unfailing feeling for delicacy in human *ensemble*, especially feminine. He selected his peculiar miniature style of beauty in women so unerringly that he might almost be said to have created it.

I think it was Sir Francis Bacon who, in his *Novum Ogganum*, pointed out that, in the very last analysis, man does not ever really add anything to the world.

What we call a creator is, according to Bacon, a man with a genius for rearranging the things in the world which please him. Looking at the matter in this light, Ziegfeld was, as an artist, infinitely superior to Sargeant. In his review, which he alone of all the showmen in the musical comedy field gave any semblance of character, he made not only the least vulgar of all theatrical displays: he actually touched what we call the aesthetic sense.

If he did not possess positive good taste (and that's really too much to ask of even the best of Jews, which Ziegfeld was not) he was at least shrewd enough to realize that one might please America with woman-stuff without staggering its sense of appreciation with droll demonstrations of anatomy.

But the Jew in him had to come out, as it did in that single and singular performances of the Follies which I witnessed in 1923.

However humble may be Isaac's position in Wall Street, on Broadway his position is unquestionably that of an uncrowned sultan. If you buttonhole Isaac and ask him what he is doing on Broadway he will reply that he is staging the entertainment of a continent.

"But you are apparently such a sad fellow, Isaac," you say to him. "How have you suddenly become so merry?"

"I am not merry," he replies majestically. "In my heart, every day, it is as sad as on the ninth of Ab, the anniversary of the destruction of Solomon's Temple."

"But I am holding down this job because I alone have the secret. I know what the public wants."

"Yes," Isaac continues mournfully. "I am the only one because I am the only one who knows how to do it."

"Indeed," you say.

Make no mistake about it either. He knows what the public wants, and he supplies it at a very reasonable rate.

It's a very valuable secret, I assure you, and he is even generous enough to share it with that continental Jew who runs those interesting houses in London, Paris, Berlin and Vienna.

Every great race and nation has made some significant contribution to the development of the drama. for the theatre is the only church to which all the nations and races come independently, with the understanding that they remain on equal terms.

What is goodness in the theatre in Portugal is also goodness in the theater in Rome. What men applaud in a theatre in Brussels is also applauded in a theater in New York.

The variance in the prices of admission make no difference in the standing of the sites: the silk hats, if I remember correctly usually occupy the orchestra seats front, yet the ambitious mimes usually play the gallery.

All the absolute human values are recognized in this international church, the only one in which no sides are taken, wherein no embarrassing questions are asked.

The very first plays we know of, those of the Asiatic Indians, attained an enviable literary excellence. Centered about the fantastic working of a dominant and domineering fate, they resemble in effect the sea stories of the late Joseph Conrad: they lack only the element of personal charm. They aspire to a very lofty ethical life, and but for their lack of humor one might almost call them modern.

The Chinese, on the other hand, conceived of their stage pieces as festivals and made a performance by combining songs and dances and stringing them together on a very flimsy story.

But for their quaint habit of taking it for granted that the characters in the plays speak not only for themselves but for their authors, too, the Chinese might have made more of the business of the drama for the drama and for themselves.

As is their worst in other delicate matters, the Japanese, in the theatre, did exactly like the Chinese only that they employed a coarser language and made infinitely more noise.

The Japs lack sensitiveness in their moral attitude towards individuals and nations, and yet, by reason of their European contacts, the need for it makes itself felt in their very use of words. The violence and noisiness of their stage life is their subconscious effort to drown out the insistence of this "still small voice!"

The Greeks, of course, gave us the very best we know of in tragedy, comedy, and satire. How the Jews, living as near as they did to the Greeks, failed to be infected by the fever of this yielding to form and rhythm—unless they were by nature incapable of being touched aesthetically—I cannot understand.

But it is significant in this respect to remember that the Greeks created their theatre long before the drama was conceived of as a means of making money, and the Jews have never devoted themselves to anything which did not offer an immediate prospect of profits.

In Rome—in spite of the efforts of Terrence, Plautus and a score of other minor dramatists—the drama begins the decline which became so absolute in the Middle Ages. Like Europe later on, it weltered in a series of miracle plays that were almost obscene in their stupidity.

But the spirit of renaissance in the drama sprouted early in Europe: for Corneille and Racine raised gay banners in France, Ariosto in Italy, Lope de Vega in Spain, and Shakespeare and his vital mob in England.

All this time, what were the Jews doing? They had failed to learn anything from the Greeks.[32] And now, while a Frenchman was putting the story of Queen Esther into immortal verse, they were writing and enacting Purim plays[33] as a form of refined beggary, and inventing droll stories of what happens when a Jew met an Italian, an Irishman or a Frenchman, or all the three at once.

It was not till the drama ceased being a form of religious observance and began to become a part of the business of professional entertainment that the Jew began to conceive a real interest in it. No one was required to pay for attending a religious festival.

But when it came to partaking in a night's entertainment, money could be asked. That made quite a difference—for the Jews.

The Jew makes his appearance in the theatre of the world as the Hebrew comedian of the old Irish Joke Books.

If he may be said to have created a theatre of his own, it is that which is known as Burlesque. Only it does not seem proper to say that such a thing has been created. Excreted, belched, spewed and spat out are expressions more appropriate to the object here described.

Equipment for entering the theatre the Jew had very little of. No sense of form or even the capacity to enjoy its expressions in others. Ditto traditions.

No spiritual experiences to explore and set into a fine mold. No reverence for dramatic performances of the past or even hope of the future. The Jew had only one thing—a secret. He knew what the people would pay to see.

[32] The Book of Job *is occasionally set forth as an example of Hebrew contribution to the drama. But Horace Meyer Kallen, a Jew and Zionist leader, has proven amply that* Job *is really an obscure Greek play that was adapted by a Hebrew writer.*

[33] *Purim is the Jewish holiday which celebrates the victory of the Jews over their enemy Haman—the Hitler of his day in the court of the great Persian monarch Ahasueres. The Purim play, of which there are literally thousands, simply reiterates drearily and unimaginatively, the incidents leading to Haman's humiliation—*ad nauseum.

Had he not been running brothels for Europe ever since anyone could remember?

The Jews succeeded in the business of the theatre in no small measure. Three quarters of the millions of dollars made every year in the entertainment world goes into the pockets of Jews.

This money is made in night-clubs, in vaudeville, in burlesque, in private entertainments run for the blasé rich, and in stag affairs run for the vulgar poor; in reviews such as Ziegfeld's *Follies* and George White's *Scandals*, all glorifications of the spirit of burlesque.

Now and then something very fine blunders its way into one of these reviews: the dancing of a Harriet Hoctor, the lariat-philosophizing of a Will Rogers.

But in the main the Jew has only one contribution to make to the theatre. By making it, he links up the theatre with the rest of his charnel houses in America and on the continent.[34]

I have no doubt that the presence of a Jew in the theatre is the one great impediment to the development of the drama on its more spiritual side. You have only to glance at the history of the theatre to realize that the art of playwriting and the arts allied with it flourished only where the Jews were not in a position to interfere with them. Because it was a sort of state church the Greek theatre was absolutely Jewless.

Whatever Jews lived in England and in France during the sixteenth and seventeenth centuries kept themselves well under cover. They certainly would not risk outraging Christians with appearances as public as attending the theatre.

The moment the Jew enters the theatre a sort of impotence falls over the scene. Witness contemporary England where the stage is

---

[34] *I do not want to appear to minimize the importance of dramatic creations such as mark the productions of* Habima, The Wilna Troup *in Europe, and Maurice Schwartz's* Yiddish Art Theatre, *in America. But what do these theatres offer the world in general? The scope of* The Dybbuk, *for instance, is as wide and deep as anything in Greek or in English. But presented in any but a Jewish language, it yields nothing but gossip for the curious. When* Yoshe Kalb, *the delight of the present-day Jewish world, is produced in English (as Mr. Schwartz himself must if he is ever to lose all the money he has made out of its presentation in Yiddish) no one will benefit unless you count the scene shifters, ushers and ticket-choppers.*

held by trite luminaries such as Shaw, Galsworthy and St John Ervine with the Jew Pinero as a sort of mock crown over all; then compare with the dramatic achievements of the Scandinavian countries where Jews are comparatively few, and almost entirely out of the theatre.

In America, the Jew is in the theatre and on top of it. Occasionally beauty comes to Broadway, of course.

But when it does, it is in spite of the obstacles placed in its way by the Jews who run the street. The Jew has not the simple divination with which to recognize, before actually seeing it produced by someone else, the merits of a fine play.

If he did recognize a really vital drama he would not have the gallantry to promote it properly. For the Jew, the theatre means only two things: an easy way to make money, and a woman-market.[35]

Broadway is the richest woman-market in the world. It supplies, first of all, the wants of the thousands of rich manufacturers and brokers in the domestic market.

And it is quite a market, my boy. This is, as you probably know, a monogamist country. As if that were not bad enough, we are also in principle opposed to a red-light district in which illicit love might be conducted in an orderly and hygienic fashion. Unfortunately, morality does not change human nature.

So our gentlemen of means and leisure, unable and unwilling to maintain harems, and forbidden the luxury of the licensed brothel, take as a substitute the next best thing, the house-of-call. The house-of-call gets its recruits from the theatrical agent who, nineteen out of twenty instances, is a Jew.

The surplus of these poor delightful things is shipped out, with our over production of cotton, potatoes and copper, to China, Japan, Panama, South America and every port-of-call in the obscure regions of the Pacific Ocean where woman-hungry men willingly pay dearly for the dainty white meat of Broadway.

What I am telling you here is known to every good newspaperman in New York, Chicago, and the coast. Occasionally, after slobbering

---

[35] *At this point I can almost hear some rabbi begin to lecture me on the Jews' conception of the sanctity of womanhood and the home. Yes, I know. But the Jew, alas, believes only in the sanctity of Jewish women, and in the sanctity of the Jewish home. This aggravates, rather than lightens, the case against him.*

around some night-dive into the early hours of the next day, the boys get drunk enough to write the story up. But to date no editor of a newspaper has been drunk enough to publish such a story.

The printing of one such story the editor knows, would be quite enough to ruin his newspaper and lose him not only his present job but the hope of ever again finding another one.

In America, the Jews do not any longer have to pay agents for getting them recruits to the numerous brothels with which they dot the planet. Shanghai-ing, expert pimping or even coaxing are no longer necessary.

The victims come of their own accord. They come to Broadway to become an actress. The come to Hollywood to become movie stars. They are the sweetest and most beautiful women in the world. Mainly Christians, too.

Jewish parents are very strict in forbidding their daughters to leave home. Besides, remember our continental Jew's prejudice against admitting Jewesses to his fine establishments?

Actors and actresses, for stage and cinema, are rarely hired directly by producing companies. Usually they come to work, on the lot, or in the theatre, through special agencies.

To these agencies, with offices on Broadway and in Hollywood, streams the feminine beauty of America.

A few, indeed, are picked for legitimate roles. The rest? It would be the human thing, of course, to tell them to go home, and try their luck in domestic pursuits.

The agents might do that—if they did not have a further, more profitable use for them.

But how, you may ask, is this evil accomplished? These girls come to Broadway and to Hollywood to act, not to whore. They think of glory; how can they possibly let themselves sink into such ignominy? That's just it. The poor girls are thinking of glory. And the agents sell them glory—in somewhat the following fashion:

Agent: Hello, girlie. Here again, bright and fresh as usual. Don't get me wrong girlie. You know what I mean by fresh.

Girl: Of course. Is there any opening today?

Agent: No, not today.

Girl: But you've been saying that for six weeks.

Agent: I gotta, girlie. Why? Because you got no stage experience. There's plenty of calls for girls with stage experience. But I can't say you've got acting experience when you haven't, can I? I'd be getting in wrong before I knew it. See?

Girl: But a girl's gotta get a job somewhere some time if she's ever to make a beginning.

Agent: Say, girlie. I don't think I ever noticed it before. But you've got spunk, guts. You're alright. I guess I've simply been overlookin' you. I always thought you was a swell looker, good figure and all that sort of thing.

But you've got lots more than that, I can see. You've got real guts. You're really out to make a career, aren't you?

Girl: I told you that at the very beginning.

Agent: Sure you did. But that don't mean a thing. Just because a girl wants a career don't mean she's willing to go through with experience in order to get somewhere.

Believe me, we can't take stock in every girl who comes in here. But you look to me like the real thing. So I'm going to let you in on something real, something good.

Girl: Wonderful!

Agent: How would you like to appear in a music hall review?

Girl: Would I? Just try me.

Agent: Thirty dollars a week to start with.

Girl: I'd work for half of that to get the experience.

Agent: But you don't have to. I treat my girls right. It's thirty dollars a week.

Girl: When do I start?

Agent: In about two weeks. That's how long it'll take you to get there. But you'll be paid for your time and the traveling expenses.

Girl: Two weeks? Where can it be?

Agent: Panama.

Girl: Panama!

Agent: Why, what's wrong with Panama?

Girl: I don't know. But it sounds so strange. . . .

Agent: What's so strange about Panama? It's America, isn't it? Or don't you know that Panama is American? Sure. It's as good as being in the United States.

When you come back from there you'll be prepared to do almost anything. (This is literally true. And if her sense of decency is too sharp, she'll probably never have the face to come back at all.)

Girl: I don't really know.

Agent: There you are. It's just a question whether you got the guts or not. You want stage experience. I'm offerin' it to you. Take it or leave it. If you take it, it'll mean the beginning of a career.

The girl can resist almost everything but this. She might put aside scornfully offers of jewels, automobiles and penthouse apartments. But almost never does she put aside the offer of a career. And what is the career the agent offers her?

Not much more than the dull, pitiable routine of a south sea brothel where every vestige of decency and moral cleanliness is sure to be blotted out in her.

By far the greatest number of these innocent seekers after lighted careers on Broadway and in Hollywood are distributed either among the local call houses and night-clubs, or shipped out to foreign ports.

Their spirits broken by their experiences abroad, these girls eventually return to the United States to join one of the hundreds of traveling companies of girls who play one-week stands at the thousands of little traveling brothels throughout the country. These places guarantee their patrons a change of girls once a week.

If we have produced in the American theatre nothing beyond the rough, arrogant, unauthentic moods of Eugene O'Neill and the thin (though occasionally gratifying) whimsies of Phillip Barry, it is the fault of the Jew who, because of the instinctive timidity of good taste, is permitted to set the standard of entertainment in America.

The average American play-writer and producer, who feels deep in his heart the need of recreating in artistic miniature the life forces which move him, has to face this very grave problem: how far may he dare to stray from the obvious titillating of the Jew, and still hope to be able to survive competition with him?

It is not such an easy matter for the honest play-writer or the honest producer. For the Jew has entrenched himself on Broadway not merely with the elementary vagaries of the Minsky family.

If all that the Jewish showmen had to display was high chests and bare behinds, the indignation of the good sense of the mass

XIV Theatre and the Woman-Market

of theatre-goers would have wiped them out long ago, so that the problem would have solved itself.

But for every whirl of a hip in the Eltinge Burlesque there is a Ben Hecht swashbuckling violent Chicago nuances into hilarious comedy, drama and melodrama.

For every lifted skirtlet in the Republic Theatre there is a Morrie Ryskind inventing political conundrums with familiar questions that are easier to answer in a theatre lobby than in a voting booth.

For every off-color song screeched out in the blistering darkness of the Central Theatre, Samuel Hoffenstein devises a quip which brings him closer to the heart of Minsky and still farther away from the spirit of Heine to whom, when he started out on his Broadway rounds, he bore such startling resemblance.

I have just thought of a really sound and happy example of how the working of the Jew on Broadway interferes with the development of an American national dramatic literature.

It is the case of George S. Kaufman, the most cunning contriver in the theatre of our generation, and, let us hope, for a long time to come.

It was reckoned up last year in one of the more reliable Broadway columns that Mr. Kaufman's average earnings from the play and screen royalties of such favorites as *Dinner at Eight, The Royal Family, Beggar on Horseback* and *Once in a Lifetime* come to approximately eight thousand dollars a week. I believe I have seen every play Mr. Kaufman ever produced on Broadway, which is an admission that he has entertained me, for I do not go to the theatre out of habit or on principle.

I will go even farther and say that Mr. Kaufman's plays have entertained me hugely. No one can go to see a play of his without being caught in the web of his rambling good humor; but neither can you help feeling, on leaving the theatre, after a performance of one of his plays, that you have only witnessed some very remarkable pranks, that the whole business was meaningless, and as pointless for you as it must have been for Mr. Kaufman unless he happened to be thinking of his eight thousand dollars a week.

Don't misunderstand me. No damage is done by giving Mr. Kaufman eight thousand dollars a week, for he probably provides his family well by it and invests the balance wisely and well. I suggest, however, that it would be better policy for the American people to pay Mr. Kaufman eight thousand dollars a week on the promise that he will not write plays as long as he gets paid.

For as long as Mr. Kaufman continues to collect a revenue of eight thousand dollars a week from his plays, he sets a very dangerous standard for those American play-writers who might really enrich our theatre. Eight thousand dollars a week is a lot of money with which to attack the imagination of the hungry play-writer.

The Barrys, Howards and O'Neills know that it is useless for them to hope of ever achieving such a figure. But they cannot help asking themselves occasionally, during their dramatic ruminations, how far they can stray into the temple of art and yet not get too far away from this precious figure.

That is probably the real reason why the work of Sidney Howard still mantles chaos, why Phillip Barry threatens to remain whimsical into his gray beard, and why Eugene O'Neill, like an evil chemist, continues to brew Ibsen and Freud in the same pot.

In Hollywood as in Broadway the Jew is the dominant figure.

Is it anything less than a misfortune that the motion pictures should have developed into an industry out of the penny arcades of the Jews?

How much more precious a development might we not have witnessed had the first pictures been planned, at least, in the studio of photographers curious about the artistic possibilities of their medium?

As it was, the penny-arcade owners, sensing that there were fortunes to be made in the extraordinary phenomenon of pictures moving about like living people, sought financial stimulus in the clothing industry.

The net result for the United States is that whereas there is a creditable cinematic art to be found flourishing in Germany, Russia and France (and an occasional fine picture comes from time to time, even out of England and Italy) America, which practically dominates the industry, has produced maybe two or three good pictures—and these only under the direction of European actors and directors imported for short spells into Hollywood.

But nature has her own way of taking her little revenges for these things. Recently one of these Russo-Jewish pants pressers, who rolled up a fortune in the manufacture of stamped celluloid, decided to erect an office building to serve as a monument to his triumph.

This office building was also to house a huge theatre for the showing of the productions of his own company.

The erection of this monument and its furnishings cost well above five million dollars. The very best architects in the world were called in to devise it.

But man, like God, can create only his own image. In spite of the talents of artists and advisers, this gigantic monument to a stupid and obscene industry, reared on one of the busiest corners of the world, resembles, seen from afar, the figure of a humped Jew.

Maybe the image is also that of the Jew who runs those interesting houses in London, Paris and Berlin.

The Allrightnik.

XV THE RAPE OF LAKEWOOD, LONG BRANCH AND ATLANTIC CITY

If I were asked to name the chief social characteristic of my people, I would say that it is the habit to want to be where we have no business to be, and most particularly where we are not wanted. Westchester golf-clubs, exclusive summer and winter resorts, Christian college fraternities, even the most orthodox of the churches, are all beleaguered by Jews straining nerve and sinew to break through. But for our ancient prejudices, Jews would be even more numerous and more frequent churchgoers than their gentile neighbors. Indeed, the most fashionable of America's churches are so solidly frequented by Jews, that to the more conservative elements in Christendom is has become a matter of querulous concern.

I met recently, by pure accident, the spiritual head of one of the more important Fifth Avenue churches, and asked him if it were really true, as I had heard bruited about, that he was favored by a steady patronage of Jews.

"Yes, indeed," he answered. "It is most gratifying."

I realized that he was merely trying to be polite to a Jew, so I did my best to appear skeptical. "I could understand your gratification," I said, "if they came to you as converts. But you do not really look upon them as converts, do you?"

He looked startled. "Certainly not. But I assure you they contribute color and charm to our services. They do even a little more than that. They can really be relied upon to come regularly every Sunday, as if they were charted pew holders.

"That is much to be grateful for. Have you any idea how it must feel to mount the platform on a Sunday morning, your sermon all prepared and studied, and find yourself looking out upon rows of empty benches? Thanks to the Jews many of us are saved this embarrassment."

Let it not be told in Gath, however. The Jews have only to learn that the churches welcome them, and it will be the last you have seen of them in church. Jews do not go to church out of a religious feeling. If Jews had any need of religion they would pay some attention to their own synagogue which, in America, has become an obsolete institution.

The whole point in Jews going to church is that they are really not supposed to be there. Their getting in without being thrown out is one of their most precious social triumphs.

In the colleges, especially the oldest and most traditional, a certain number of Jews, usually the sons of the newly rich, try, once a year, to crash the exclusive fraternities. Invariably they are turned down. Without fail, they cry "Anti-Semites!" and raise a terrific hullabaloo calculated to impeach the democracy of the particular institution they are attending. To all appearances they are very indignant and proudly wrathful. But the following year, having forgotten the snub of the previous year, they go through the same horrible motions all over again.

I remember the time when a rich Jew (and, what is rare among Jews, a sportsman) donated a new building to one of the greatest eastern universities. It was, and it still is, the most glamorous building in that campus. Its library in particular is both rich and commodious. This building had no sooner been dedicated to the best interests of the university, than the Jew students seized upon it as though it had been erected especially for their use, and made it their natural *habitat*. They streamed through its broad halls and into its reading room at all hours, brought their lunches and dinners with them, and so infested the gracious spaces with newspaper wrappings, banana peels and other forms of picnic garbage that an extra force of attendants had to be hired to keep it clean.

As a result of the increasing protests of the gentile students, the university authorities (who only too bitterly know in advance the consequences of any interference with Jews) finally had to intercede. They announced that the university expected in the new hall the same standards of conduct and cleanliness observed throughout the rest of the buildings on the campus. As was to be expected, the Jews on the campus rose on their hind legs and howled. The rabbis denounced the college to the empty benches of their synagogues. But the university authorities had their way.

Five years never elapses when American Jewry does not make some national protest against the limitations set to the number of Jews who are permitted to attend Harvard, Princeton, and Yale in any one year. Harvard, which, as the most exclusive of the eastern American colleges, has borne the brunt of the attack of the Jews, has defended her position with the most unswerving rigidity. Unlike her sister colleges, Harvard has not yielded one inch of sacred ground. And so Harvard is today the only American institution of learning which may be regarded as a unit of culture.

The rest of the colleges of the country rank in importance according to how successfully they have been able to resist this influence of the Jewish student element in their midst. The very lowest degree of culture is, therefore, achieved by the College of the City of New York, ninety percent of whose attendance is Jewish. One never hears of poetry, painting or music having its origins on the campus of this institution. The philosophy of its average student is to get as many facts as possible crammed into him and acquire as quickly as the mechanical passing of the requirements of the curriculum will allow, the precious coveted degree that will entitle him to begin the momentous struggle to get back to Israel from the laps of the goyim the wealth that the Lord Jehovah really intended for Israel.

But eager as may be the Jewish merchant's effort to get his son into an exclusive college his zeal is as nothing compared with his own itch to get into the swanky summer and winter resorts in which he is most definitely not wanted.

There are many reasons why the gentile does not want the Jew in his pet playgrounds. I will enumerate four:

1. The Jew temperamentally knows no dividing line between business and pleasure. Let a Jew edge into a drinking party and he will unfailingly turn it into a business conference.

2. The Jew's general appearance, like that of the negro, the mongolian and the gypsy, is hostile to the peaceful state of mind of the gentile trying to relax and play. The state of the Jew may not be as lowly as that of the negro, and it is probably not as splendid as that

of the moneyless but hilariously happy gypsy. Nevertheless, it breeds ill-at-easedness.

3. However good a Jew's intentions are, however soft his heart, his manners are those of a barbarian. I am not unmindful of the fact that there are Jews whose conduct is in consonance with all the laws of good breeding and behavior. Sir Phillip Sassoon, an English Jew, is England's official host to visiting royalty from the continent. I have met Jews like Sir Phillip Sassoon, too, and I wish to report that I find the manners of my own Galician schnorrers infinitely more bearable.

4. The Jew in unclean and he makes unclean any place which he learns to call home—even temporarily.

The latter embodies a very serious charge. I know that I am not the first one to make it. But I am not repeating it in a spirit of malice. It is a conclusion that comes to me out of the limited experience of my own life among Jews.

I happened to be in Parksville, a Jewish[36] village in the Catskill Mountains, during the fall of 1912. One morning, early in November, I was wandering aimlessly down the yellow road when a neighborhood farmer greeted me from the eminence of the driver's seat of a one-horse runabout, and asked me if I would not exchange the pleasure of my society at his side for a privileged view of the countryside in its change-of-leaf season.

His business for the next few hours, he said, would take him as far as Livingston Manor on the crest of the hill opposite us. The Manor, if it run more to stone than to sap, could match the exuberance of the general landscape with a passionate flaring up of the spirit of its mankind in the form of a local, bitterly contested election.

"Of what use is any kind of an election in a foreign country?" I asked, climbing up beside him.

The farmer smiled significantly. "You say that who do not know that elections in Livingston Manor cannot be considered in the category of ordinary elections."

"I say that," I replied, "who find no interest in elections of any kind."

---

[36] *The majority of the farmers in Parksville are really gentile. But Jews have to constitute no more than twenty percent of any community to thoroughly Judaise it. I have shown how it was in (N)utscha. And what is true on the influence of Jews in Russia and Poland is also true in the United States.*

"Have you ever been in Livingston Manor?"

"No."

"Well, you're going there now."

I had been trudging the dirt road since the early hours of the morning, without discovering tiredness. But once I sank back in the comparative comfort of the driver's seat, the feeling of relief mingled with the weariness of the morning's pleasantry threw me into a lethargic state of autointoxication. I had barely managed to get into the leisureliness necessary for one to enjoy the bright darkening of the dry shining wings of the earth when I noticed that we were passing through a low white gate, and I knew that we were in Livingston Manor. In a few moments we drew up before a broad expansive white building which I judged to be a hotel. The farmer dropped the reins and leaped down.

"I'll be back in a minute," he cried and disappeared through a doorway.

I looked about me, to discover the secret of so much quiet charm in the noisy Catskills, and I was about to remark to myself the extraordinary neatness of the road and the houses within my view when my eyes encountered a surprising oil-cloth sign, in large heavy lettering, strung across the facade of the hotel:

IF LIVINGSTON MANOR VOTES AGAINST LIQUOR WE'LL TURN OUR HOTELS OVER TO THE JEWS.

"What a remarkable threat!" I thought. I stared and stared at the sign, as though I hoped that the letters would somehow explain themselves, and I was still staring stupidly when the farmer, having finished his business inside, rejoined me.

The farmer grinned broadly at my perplexity. "I thought that would interest you," he chuckled.

We resumed our journey.

"What I can't understand," I said, "is why it should be such a terrible thing to turn a hotel over to the Jews."

He looked at me and stopped laughing. "I must take you through this place," he said drily. And we drove about the several streets which wound themselves about and through the Manor.

Of beauty the village had none whatsoever. But it had a sensitive neatness which is so close to beauty in a town, that it is to be seriously considered as a substitute, especially on a continent which is still without a positive architectural heritage, where care today may become the mother of beauty tomorrow.

As we were emerging through the little gate into the wider road the farmer looked up.

"Well, what do you think of it?"

I shrugged. "What is there to think of it? It's neat, almost a pretty village. But nothing to get excited about."

"How would you say it compares with Parksville?"

"Oh, well. Parksville wouldn't be so bad if it weren't so damn dirty."

The farmer laughed. "That's all the hotel keepers in Livingston Manor imply in their sign. If the voters outlaw liquor and force them to give up their business they will sell out their holdings to the Jews who may be trusted to pile up in Livingston Manor a state of dirtiness very much like what you can behold, anytime you wish to, in our own dear village."

"You're cynical," I protested. Parksville is dirty, of course. But that is because it is Parksville. If the Jews ever take over Livingston Manor they will keep it clean if not cleaner, because it happens to be Livingston Manor."

The farmer chuckled deeply. "The Zionist in you was bound to come out. Not content with keeping us Jews, you would also have us become clean. Let me tell you this. You will have to be contented with our being Jews. As for cleanliness it will remain perforce the goyim's nextling to godliness. But we don't have to really be clean. And, as a matter of fact, if we had to be clean, we would not know how. Unfortunately there is no way to prove such an argument. But some day the Jews will take over Livingston Manor and you will be able to see with your own eyes what they will make of it."

I happened to be passing through Livingston Manor twelve years later, and the substance of this gay conversation was forcibly brought back to the surface of my consciousness by what I saw, by the decadence into which the houses, the streets and even the sky of this peaceful village had fallen. The whole landscape seemed to have been chocked up by some indefinable anarchic re-arrangement of the fibers of the universe about it. But I understood, without asking, what had brought this change about.

I am told, as I write this, that the last bank in Lakewood, New Jersey, has been closed down. If you have never lived east of the Alleghenies this will mean nothing to you. To those who know what Lakewood was once, the news spell tragedy. Don't misunderstand me. Lakewood was never one of the really great pleasure resorts of the world. No one would think of comparing it with Nice in Europe or even with Atlantic City in the United States. But that is half of what constituted the charm of Lakewood.

A place of amusement to which you took your family for the winter holidays, it was as quiet and as unostentatious as if it were your own winter cottage somewhere in the trackless wilderness. Lakewood offered the choicest of amusements with a promise of rest not to be dreamed of elsewhere.

Up to about twenty years ago Lakewood was closed to Jews. Now and then, by giving a Christian name and registering as a Protestant, a Jew would manage to "crash" the hotels. But usually he was quickly discovered, quietly snubbed, and life was made so uncomfortable for him that he might continue to boast of the conquest for many years, but for no consideration would he be tempted to repeat it. One day a Jewish king of finance—and otherwise a man of the most unusual human qualities—appeared at the desk of a prominent Lakewood hotel. He had wired for reservations. He knew of the existing prejudice. But he was certain that his great name would pull him through.

The clerk was polite. "Sorry, sir, but we're all filled."

"But I wired for reservations."

"And we wired you our regrets. It's a pity you did not receive our wire. We're sorry you have been put to so much needless trouble."

"Sorry hell. You know damn well you're being rude to me because I'm a Jew. You have more rooms vacant in this hotel now than is comfortable for you."

The clerk maintained a respectful silence.

"Alright then," said the great Jew. "Keep your rooms. I'll go on to Atlantic city. But I'll show you that you can't keep me or any Jew who can afford to pay for good service out of Lakewood."

The Jew kept both threats. He went to Atlantic City. And he built a hotel for Jews in Lakewood.

To get the land for his project in Lakewood, the Jew had to pay for it practically three times what it was worth. When work on the new house had been begun, one of the leading Lakewood realtors sought him out in his office on lower Broadway.

For the ease of this narrative we will call the rich Jew Brown and the Lakewood realtor Chandler.

Something like the following conversation took place between these two:

Chandler: I have come to offer to buy back from you the land you are building on in Lakewood.

Brown: Sell it after all the trouble I had getting hold of it? Besides, I have signed building contracts.

Chandler: I have seen your building contracts. They are good. I am prepared to take those over, too. You'll find that I'm a thoroughly responsible person.

Brown: I remember you very well. I tried to buy your hotel from you—the one that refused me reservations.

Chandler: Please believe me, but I am really sorry about that. Clerks, as you probably have found for yourself, know only one way of obeying orders. If I had been there when you came, I assure you I would have extended to you every courtesy at my command. I really have no objection to a Jew of your caliber being a guest in my hotel.

Brown: It's very kind of you to say that. But suppose you had let me in? Your guest would have been crueler than your clerk.

Chandler: But that, you see, would be quite beyond my control.

Brown: That's why I'm glad I'm building the new hotel. Lakewood is America's most beautiful winter resort. Why should a half witted prejudice keep my people from enjoying it?

Chandler: I know very little about the nature of the prejudice, Mr. Brown. Sometimes I suspect that we live by it. I sincerely wish it were possible for you and your people to share Lakewood with us. But surely you wouldn't want to destroy Lakewood just for the pleasure of seeing Jews living in it?

Brown: No. But who talks about destroying Lakewood? We Jews do not destroy. Wherever we come we build. The coming of the Jews to Lakewood will probably mean a new prosperity to you—a prosperity you don't deserve.

Chandler: I know you well enough, Mr. Brown, to realize that you really mean what you say. I have no doubt that if you did not think your hotel would benefit Lakewood you would not build it. That is why I must convince you of the very contrary. Have a little patience with me. Do you happen to know where Lakewood derives its patronage from?

Brown: The surrounding states, I presume.

Chandler: Yes, from New Jersey, New York, Pennsylvania, Delaware, Maryland and Washington D.C. States with a combined population of about twenty million people. How many Jews would you say there are in these states?

Brown: Probably two million.

Chandler: I need not tell you that everybody cannot come to holiday in Lakewood. One must have the money and the leisure. Also an inclination for the sort of quiet which Lakewood offers in a garish world. At present twenty million people produce just enough patronage for Lakewood, to keep us going. Do you think your two million Jews are so superior to the other eighteen millions that they will be able to replace this power of patronage?

Brown: Is it your opinion that non-Jews will stop coming to Lakewood as soon as the Jews get in?

Chandler: I don't think it's fair to put it that way. But there are so many other resorts, exclusive ones, to which they can turn to.

Brown: From the way you talk one would imagine that Jews are a plague. On the exchange I find more non-Jews about me than Jews.

Chandler: Forgive me Mr. Brown. That's on the Exchange.

Brown: Plenty of them invite me to their homes, too. I cannot accept half the invitations extended to me.

Chandler: Why shouldn't people invite you to their homes, Mr. Brown? You're a very interesting and charming man. But a home is not a public place.

Brown: I see. You gentiles are more sensitive about what you do in public than what you do at home.

Chandler: Put it that way, if you like.

Brown: And the moment I get into Lakewood, non-Jews will run out. Is that your point?

Chandler: Unfortunately it is so.

Brown: Suppose what you say is true. Did it ever occurred to you that Jews alone might be able to do more for Lakewood that is now being done for it by the rest of the neighboring states?

Chandler: They might—if they all came to Lakewood. In that respect I appear to know your people better than you do. Jews now clamor to come to Lakewood because it is forbidden them. Just show them that it is only like any other resort to which they are admitted, and it will have no further attraction for them.

Brown: Sorry, Mr. Chandler. I don't believe that. Nor do I believe that the gentiles will get out of Lakewood as soon as I get in.

Chandler: Don't you? Well, I'll prove it to you. How much did your broker offer me for my hotel?

Brown: Two hundred and forty thousand dollars.

Chandler: I refused to accept, didn't I?

Brown: Yes.

Chandler: Well, when you have opened your new hotel, you can have mine for fifty thousand dollars in cold cash. Think it over Mr. Brown.

The Jew thought it over and decided that he was in the right. He saw his new enterprise rise out of the frozen ground and rear the Jewish star of David over its imposing front gate.

And as Chandler had predicted the rest of the hotels in Lakewood, with the exception of two or three, were immediately announced for sale—at rates that made people rub their eyes with surprise. But there were no bargains consummated.

For the gentiles left Lakewood, and all the joy of the resort went along with them.

I mean here, by joy, Lakewood's desirability as a winter resort. Mr. Chandler seemed to have been right in everything. The Jews had been attracted to Lakewood not by prettiness of its winter landscape but because of its exclusiveness.

It lost all of its magic for Jews the moment it lost its power to keep them out. The value of Lakewood property deteriorated more and more. The conduct of the community became shabbier and shabbier. Its business thoroughfares began to look like Grand Street and ended up by looking like Rivington Street. For almost every maple tree in Lakewood a garbage can sprung up as if by magic.

Lakewood having been conquered, the Jews moved on to Long Branch where even greater havoc was wrought. Lakewood has, to this day, some old and exclusive hotels—reminders of her pristine glory. But Long Branch has been so completely Judaised that an old resident would find great difficulty recognizing it.

Lakewood attracted the rich powerful Jew like the Mr. Brown we described. These Jews are a fairly civilized people. Having attained a certain standard of wealth and power they begin to disgorge and soften. Having become conquerors, they begin to imitate the ways of the conquered. The tragedy of Long Branch was that she attracted the middle class Jew, the Jew with a going business and several savings accounts aggregating ten or fifteen thousand dollars.

There is still banking being done in Long Branch. But the heart of Long Branch has been stone a long time.

Let us not, in the meantime, lose track of Mr. Brown. He moved on, in accordance with his threat, from Lakewood to Atlantic City. He went to Atlantic City to holiday, and remained to proselytize.

Now Atlantic City never really excluded Jews—or any other nationality or race. It was never Atlantic City's ambition to be exclusive. The ambition of Atlantic City was a much greater one. Atlantic City has always advertised herself as the playground of America. America meant everybody, blacks as well as whites, Jews as well as gentiles.

To that end the Jews had been allowed to settle a part of the Boardwalk, the lower part, with the Breakers Hotel as a sort of local capitol. Jews had been quite satisfied with this arrangement. At any rate there had never been any symptoms of dissatisfaction. The hotels might have prejudices. But the Boardwalk belonged to the whole nation. There was no doubt about that, and the Jews were kept pleased.

As usual, Mr. Brown had his mail forwarded to him to the hotel, that winter. One morning he noticed an application for the renewal of the mortgage of one of biggest Atlantic City's hotels on the other end of the Boardwalk. Mr. Brown, I should had, was the president of one of the most powerful banks in America. The finances of this particular hotel, as Mr. Brown knew, were in very good shape. Ordinarily, he would have approved the application without a second thought. But, as I have already mentioned, Mr. Brown was in a proselytizing mood. He pressed a button at his side. To the clerk who appeared he said: "Get Mr. Martin on the telephone. Tell him I want to see him here at once."

"If he asks me what it's about, what shall I say?"

"Sound anxious. Say nothing."

One o'clock that afternoon Mr. Martin, his hat in his perspiring hands, was facing the genial Mr. Brown. "There is something wrong, Mr. Brown?" he asks genially.

"Of course not," smiling.

"And the mortgage?"

"I have already approved a renewal. Here it is."

"But you wanted to see me about something?"

"Didn't my secretary tell you? How stupid of him! My wanting to see you was purely personal. Your predecessor at the hotel set a precedent which makes it practically impossible for me to be a guest of yours."

"But I assure you, you would be most welcome, Mr. Brown."

"I know, Mr. Martin, and I appreciate it. But I cannot afford to go to a hotel in which Jews are not admitted. Why don't you forget that stupid prejudice? I'm pretty sure it keeps some very profitable patronage from your hotel."

"I may loose some good patronage, too, Mr. Brown."

"Why?"

"I am not responsible for it, Mr. Brown, but you must know that the prejudice against your people in resorts is a pretty powerful one."

"I know, Mr. Martin. But I am sure you will do much better to disregard it. I want to be friendly with you. And oh, yes. I meant to point out to you before. I am renewing your mortgage for only one year. Don't it let it alarm you. When it falls due next year I may be able to work out a plan for another ten years."

"I understand, Mr. Brown."

There were many things Mr. Martin could have done about it. But Mr. Martin was a very amiable man, and he did the easiest thing under the circumstances. He acquiesced. Once they realized that the Jews had been let loose in the hotel, his best gentile clients deserted him. The Jews, finding this hotel patronized only by Jews, decided that since it was now practically a Jewish hotel they might as well give their patronage to a Jew, and moved back to the Breakers.

In this fashion the hotels were one by one taken over by the Jews—and broken. Until, as I write this, practically the whole of Atlantic City is bankrupt. The difference between being the playground of America and being the playground of American Jewry is the difference between being patronized by a hundred and thirty million people and being patronized by four million Jews.

Before the Jews seized it, Atlantic City was one of the world's most envied communities. Today, under a Jewish mayor, it is broke and criminally involved in an issue of "scripp" which has neither moral nor metallic foundation. Real American money is practically never handled by its thousands of merchants.

What is there to say to all this except that a Jew may be a king of men in a manger but, when he forces himself into a society which does not want him, he unfailingly makes a damn pig of himself?

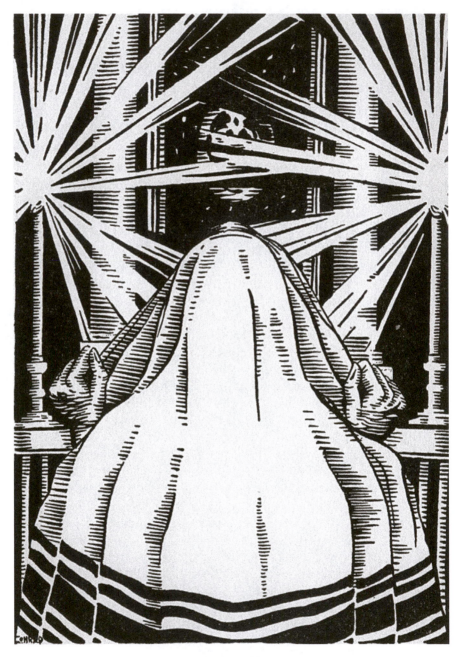

Farewell!

XVI FAREWELL TO JUDAS

For you everything has finished itself out, I said to myself. Everything that has had a beginning has ended. Curiosity itself has had for you a beginning and an end. All the shapes within your vision, pleasing and unsightly alike, are pitchers you have seen filled up with rain-water, then emptied out by the pitiless sun. If you had a stouter heart, and a hammer, you might do a good job of breaking them. But are you going to spend the rest of a restless day watching the heat lick them fawningly into a mass of colored fragments?

If you had, yourself, at least, a cunning for withstanding the shattering light! But there you go, running off headlong into a shade of doorway. . . . Could you but make one last tumultuous effort, lift up that two hundred pound corpse of yours, place it on a comfortable ship, and see what a power of wind and water would do for you. Why, man! you needn't ever be yourself again! The ocean is a mighty and savage cleaver. There might be nothing left of you when you reach the other shore but what is needed to identify you with the photograph on your passport!

1

On the deck, a few steps away from me, a corpulent elaborately dressed young man, with a good natured east-side face, was photographing a group of giggling friends. They waved white handkerchiefs, laughed, jostled one another, and tried to maintain a homogenous group on the shore. The ship was absolutely motionless.

The gray moldy woodwork of the pier rose devastatingly over everything. I was still in New York. By unchangeable schedule I would continue being there another three quarters of an hour.

The prospect was intolerable, and suddenly a way out of it shone on me. I wheeled about, tripped down to my cabin, and turned in. When I reopened my eyes I was in the embrace of a huge somnolent rhythm that pleased me. The light was streaming in through a triumphantly free porthole. I dressed hurriedly, fairly ran up the deck, and looked about me. Neither before nor behind us was there a glimpse of shore. But behind me, I knew, lay America. Before me was Europe, Europe that I had not seen for a quarter of a century.

People, all strange to me, were scattered in groups everywhere. I looked them over casually, quizzically, consciously trying not to see any one of them.

Well enough did I realize their importance. For at least a week, I knew, they would be my mental and social horizon, all the world to me. I would be a little slow discovering them, and they would be a little quicker finding out my usefulness for them. Eventually, it would be the world and me all over again, as it has always been. The story of creation was beginning anew.

The ordered magnetic chaos of the Atlantic, gray, vast and darkening, was before me. Looking far out, I saw deep into my own soul. I had left America and was heading for England, a country in which I knew instinctively they liked neither Americans nor Jews, and I was both.

But that did not really matter. I was going back to Europe which my people had cradled from infancy, and which, as a return favor, had cradled me. That was the arrangement, I decided. Nothing must alter it. As a mark of my resolution I sought the bar.

2

A pock-faced mottle-headed steward they called Jim brought me a double scotch with some ice in it. I observed the ice melt as I finished a cigarette. Two passengers, one large, grisly-faced and morose, the other slim and dark-eyed, both engineers returning from the Far East, sat down at my table.

They drank quickly, as people do after a fan tine, and when my glass was emptied, ordered Jim to fill it up for me. They had spent about a month in dry America, and were glad to be getting back to England.

Jim brought many more drinks, and my newly acquired companions began to talk freely. Nothing in America had pleased them, not even

XVI Farewell to Judas

the women. They deliberately drew me into the conversation, for I seemed to them American, and good game.

"Why, what have you got in America, anyway?" the older of the two demanded. His mouth had acquired an ugly twist.

"For one thing," I replied, "some one hundred million rather nice people!"

They stared at me with open mouthed wonder. They had expected me to boast of the Woolworth Building and of winning the great war. Undoubtedly they had, at their fingers' tips, fondly cherished arguments itching to reply. "You don't sound at all American," the younger one drawled.

I made a risky experiment. "Well, to be absolutely correct, I am not entirely American, being also somewhat of a Jew."

The effect of this speech was electric. My two easily acquired companions exchanged significant glances, gulped down the rest of their liquor, and without another word staggered away from the table. The taintless instinctiveness of their procedure amazed me. My stupefaction was interrupted by the impersonal appearance of Jim, on whose plate I flung a two shilling piece.

"Any change?"

I looked up into his face and shook my head. The realization that I was on an English ship settled fully in me. I went below.

3

In the long elegant saloon people were getting their assignments to tables, asking questions with reluctant timidity, ordering children about, and slowly, inevitably drifting into one another.

I noted with satisfaction that there was not a pretty woman in sight. A pretty woman usually spoils everything by attracting to herself more attention than legitimately belongs to her. Like a tree standing out in a finely etched landscape. It may be a good tree. But it ruins the landscape.

I do not mix easily. Besides, I should see whether my baggage had been sorted out and brought to my cabin, in good order. My trunk was being dragged in by a pleasant-faced, pleasant-mannered steward, as I arrived. There was already a trunk, under the bed I had napped in. A strange trunk. Here was something I had not counted on at all. "Is there someone else in this cabin with me?" I asked.

The steward paused to look up at me. "Yes, sir. And you're lucky, in having only one."

"Well. Have you seen him? What's he like?"

"Oh, you'll like him, sir. He's a young gentleman, a Scotch engineer. Got two gold medals in Japan."

"Two gold medals, eh? That's going it some, I'll say."

"Oh, he's a fine lad, sir. . . . He's with the rest of the engineers now, sir."

Just then the gong sounded for dinner. I turned to the dining room feeling skeptical about the possibility of this Scotch engineer being "a fine lad" for all of his gold medals.

4

Opposite me at the table sat two familiar strangers. One said he was German. The other pleaded cosmopolitanism. The German was fair and fleshy, and spoke English with a substantially German accent. The cosmopolitan, at least ten years older, dressed with neat and scrupulous tightness, and displayed a shining baldness rimmed by *paye*-like hair. He appeared to be a super tailor, that is to say a tailor turned real estate agent.

I rather liked him. At my right sat a hard boiled, past middle age Canadian with whom I enjoyed altogether one brief conversation. He asked me had I ever been to Montreal, and I asked him where was Montreal. At my left sat two mulatto girls who dressed like Spanish grandees and apparently got away with it. Very appropriately, it seemed to me, they coquetted with the German and the cosmopolitan.

At the head of the table, a vivacious little woman, all black hair and black eyes, explained that she was English and didn't like Jews. On both sides of her, as if she were chaperoning them, sat a fair slender English girl and her tall grave fiancé whom I always think of as the Churchman; he was forever describing "our cathedrals." But in a corner, out of the vision of everybody, it seemed to me, was one whom I had almost escaped seeing such is the modesty of real beauty. To begin with, she was the only woman at table not in evening

XVI Farewell to Judas

clothes. She presented a Queen Anne bust, a white collar rising from her white waist towards her high neck. Her hair, almost a metallic silver, parted in a straight line in the middle of her head, and fell back in two long twisted braids. She ate as if she were preoccupied entirely with herself. She sat too far away for me to judge of the smoothness of her skin. It was absolutely impossible to meet her eyes, for she did not once raise them during the hour at the table, as though she were guarding them from some imminent danger.

Table talk was dominated by the churchman who, among other things, had a goodly knowledge of Jewish affairs, and was cordial to the point of insisting that General Allenby's conquest of Palestine was the most glorious chapter of Jewish history.

But I quickly tired of his spurious courtesy, and, in order not to hear him, set myself the task of making out definitely the mysterious beauty of the girl with the silver hair. But beyond the placid loveliness of her face I could make out nothing, and she had left the table in one motion of flight before I could pierce the image of her.

"What cool, impersonal beauty," ran through my mind. It was the sort that I had never had in my life, and perhaps never would live to attain.

5

A heavy mist had settled over the sea. Our ship seemed to move through it with round-shouldered timidity. Only a few people were on deck, those who had not yielded to the fascination of unpacking their belongings for the journey.

They paced to and fro in short semi-circles, and puffed away in silence at brief cigarettes. Here and there, on a deck chair, a man could be seen sprawled out, his hands folded over his stomach, eyes half-dosed. Now and then the ship-whistle sounded shrilly over the soft lapping of the sea about the ship. The air seemed dying out.

Upon this trivial monotone of sound and movement I imposed myself for a few minutes. I could not make up my mind whether I wanted to rest or find something to do. The bar, as I passed it, had been absolutely deserted. The deck afforded not much more encouragement.

The manner of the few who promenaded about was almost mystical in its seclusiveness. They talked in the hushed voices of people who are tired, rather than of those who are afraid of being overheard.

Back in the cabin I ran into the young engineer who was to share it with me for the rest of the voyage. A tall blond broad-shouldered fellow who narrowed down towards his feet. He had a big head, a square fleshy face pointed with a slight blonde moustache, blue eyes and a full sensual-lipped mouth. From a pair of broad shoulders he narrowed down alarmingly to a slender waist, thin legs and ridiculously small feet. "So you're Roth," he said abruptly, as I walked in.

"Yes," I replied.

"Well, you slept in my bed."

"I'm sorry. I didn't know it was your bed."

"My luggage was under it when you came in."

"I must have failed to see your luggage. Why don't you take the bed that hasn't been slept in, then?"

"I don't have to. I've changed the bedding around."

"Nice boy," I thought, and began pulling off my things. "I should warn you," I began jocosly, "that my feet, under the burden of two hundred pounds -"

"I won't bother about your feet," he interrupted, "if you keep your Jew head out of my affairs."

I looked up at him, and with great effort resisted a reply. Here's fate's little messenger, I vowed to myself. All ready to drag you into the Jew business again on the slightest provocation. Well, let's see how much fate can accomplish without your cooperation. I'll let this damn little squirt wilt before I take up this quarrel again.

6

A knock on the door of my cabin awoke me the next morning. It was the steward. "You've overslept, sir. I thought I'd call you before it was too late to get you something nice from the kitchen, sir."

"Good. Get me some ham and eggs and the exact time."

He returned, within ten minutes, bearing a tray laden with ham and eggs, toast, marmalade and coffee. "You'll find the coffee real good sir. We've a good chef this trip." He paused in the doorway. "One more thing, sir. Shall I reserve you a deck chair? It's a crown for the trip and that includes cushion and blanket."

"Alright," I said. "And there's an extra five shillings in it for you if you get it next to a really pretty woman."

"Very well, sir. Blonde or brunette?"

"I have no petty prejudices in the matter of women."

I ate, shaved, and sauntered out. At the end of the saloon, I found my steward waiting for me, a broad contented grin on his face. "I see that you've earned that five shillings," I said, pressing it into his hands. The number of my reservation was 76. "What's she, 75 or 77," I asked.

"I didn't notice, sir. But she's a beauty."

My heart rose in me with a strange hopefulness. Might it not be the girl with the silver hair?

"Good. How's the sea this morning?"

"In fine fettle, sir. Only that she looks a bit too coy."

"What does that mean?"

"Usually it means rough seas ahead, sir."

"Well, we'll take care of that in time." I ran eagerly up the easy circular stairway leading to the upper deck.

Morning on the deck was dazzling. The sun absolutely prodigal. The waters seemed to be on promenade. The atmosphere, crowded with the flow of flesh, steel, silk and water, was like a flawless mirror. I walked about for a few minutes in a daze of happiness, for it is happiness when you lose yourself in mingling with the world to the point of complete forgetfulness.

I stopped to watch a ping-pong game and noticed the number on the deck-chair nearby, 121. That reminded me. I had a quest ahead of me. I walked on slowly, watching the numbers dwindle. My mind was on the silver image of the night before. If only it turned out that it was she who occupied the chair next to mine.

A young woman in brown, her face half hidden by an old brown tamashanter sat in the deckchair to the right of 76. To the left the chair was not occupied. The glimpse I first caught of the face was pleasing. But she turned to look at me, as I sat down, and I saw that she was very lovely. "Beautiful morning," I said.

She smiled brightly, and I got a glimpse of small white teeth and copper-colored hair. "Yes," she replied. "English ships invariably play to good first mornings. But as omens of the weather to come they are not to be trusted."

"You're English, I presume. You see I'm hopelessly American."

"No. There's something about you which is super-American. I can't say just what it is."

I could have told her just what it was. But I realized that fate was handing me my cue again, and I was more than ever determined not to take it. I had only to say: *Oh, yes I'm also a Jew,* and the old battle would be on. But no, this time I wouldn't say it. "Probably the result of my first shave on board an ocean-liner," I said. "But to get back to the weather on English ships. Why don't you do something about it?"

"Oh, but we have. We've thought out a perfectly grand solution to the problem. We've simply sold out the stocks in our companies to the Jews."

"Delightful arrangement," I murmured. "And I suppose the Jews lose whatever money is lost on these ships."

"Oh, no. You see, losing is not their business."

"Traveling alone?"

"Oh, no. I have a sister with me. We missed you at breakfast."

"Missed me?"

"Yes. She saw you at the table last night. I was too ill to eat, myself. You can imagine what an impression you made on her because I recognized you from the minute description of you she gave me."

Hope burned bright within me. "Where is she now?"

"Walking the deck with her fiance. He's been in the Far East for more than a year. We traveled all the way over to New York in order to meet him half way back. They're to be married as soon as we reach London. There they are now."

I looked up. It was she, and yet the impression was now an entirely different one. The night before she had seemed to me so slight, almost a wisp of beauty. And now. . . . But of course I had only seen her face; and the perfection of her features framed by her silver hair gave her an elfin littleness.

But really, she had such majestic feminine form and bearing, and as she approached us, on the arm of her escort, her walk suggested the movement of deep waters. "This is Alma," said the girl next to me. I'm Ada. And permit me to introduce Mr. Stewart."

I proceeded to introduce myself, and Stewart, my cabin-mate, was obviously not particularly pleased to meet me formally. I made no effort to appear enthusiastic myself, but happily Alma appeared entirely oblivious to this difference between us, and sank happily into the vacant chair next to mine.

Stewart grudgingly sat down at the right of Ada. "Ada paints, you know," began Alma. "She'll tell you that she paints badly. But every year she gets one or two pictures into the Royal Academy exhibition. I told her last night that she simply would have to have you sit for her."

"And you?" I asked.

"Oh, I divide my time between doting on Ada and preparing myself to be a good wife to some good man. And you?"

"I write."

"Do you write the sort of books that keep children frozen stiff in their beds?"

"Good heavens, no. What gave you that impression?"

She hesitated. "I guess it must have been the way you stared at me last night."

"I'm sorry."

"Please don't. I wouldn't have missed it for worlds. I assure you I had never been so thrilled before. Promise me you'll never stop staring at me that way."

"I don't see how I can very well stop," I said.

"Alma's much too easily scared," said Ada dryly, turning from a whispered conversation she had had with Stewart. "But if your stare is anything like Alma describes it to be, I shall most certainly insist on your letting me pin it on canvass. Before you know it you'll find yourself hanging in the Royal Academy."

I bowed. "If I must hang, dear ladies, let it be in the Royal Academy."

7

The rest of the morning was given over to talk of pictures. Ada spoke slowly, hesitantly, almost as though she were not sure of herself.

But the eyes of Alma were on me, and I knew that I had to find some way of saying things which it would be difficult to find a regular way of saying. I knew that Stewart was observing me microscopically. But you know how it is when you try to get away from doing the inevitable. You only succeed in drawing the cords of fate more tightly about you.

So it was that, without any prewarning in my own mind, I suddenly settled on Rossetti and made him my favorite English painter, to the consternation of Ada and Alma, and the secret delight of Stewart. After all if I was going to show such abominable taste in pictures. . . .

I might have let the matter rest there. What difference would it make to me now, I ask you, what these people thought of my taste in art? But there was that damn bitch fate working away at my side, like the ghost of Abraham's wife impeaching me for slander. . . .

I went on to explain: "My choice must depend, of course, on what I can get out of English painting. I certainly would not go to English art in order to increase my enjoyment of the spectacle of nature. Even if one had to learn French in order to enjoy a French picture, it would still be easier to gather delight from the meanest of the French naturalists than from the illustrious but tiresome Turner.

As for the new dimensions which the moderns have been digging out of paint and marble, I would not try to learn new tricks from people who have not yet fully mastered the old ones.

"Isn't Augustus John learning to do today what Theodore Rousseau had learnt to do perfectly a half century ago? But what Rossetti gives me I cannot find anywhere else in the world."

"And what does Rossetti give you?" There was just a tinge of contempt in Ada's voice.

"English women," I said. "The most beautiful women in the world."

"Hurrah!" cried Ada. "Britannia rules the waves."

"Please explain yourself," urged Alma.

"Don't you dare," warned Ada's eyes severely. "You know damn well you're only going to make love to the poor child."

"I must," my eyes answered her. "I simply can't help it." I spoke without looking at Alma, but that only made the application of my words more obvious. "I think Alma is right. This is too lovely a morning to burden with anachronisms. Why shouldn't the things we utter have some of the properties of the sunlight which is falling so abundantly about us?

"Rossetti's English women have come to mean so much to me not because they are more English than the women of many another English painter. It is just that the things which I find most delightful about English women are in Rossetti's pictures most singularly emphasized.

"You will notice, for instance, when I name you Rossetti's five most English women, that no one of them is really English in origin: Lilith, who came before Eve, and wouldn't be acknowledged by the rabbis because, they claimed, she had no soul, was originally a Jewess. Pandora whose curiosity, Juvenal claimed, had no spiritual side to it at all, was Italian; as were also, Boccaccio's Fiammetta, and Pluto's bride Proserpine. Venus, the Goddess of Love, was, of course, Greek. Yet every one of these five women, whose origin in the mind of mankind is associated with sensual objects, Rossetti reproduces in the fresh and rich purity of a kew orchard in first bloom.

"What, for instance, does Rossetti let us see of Lilith? A lovely placid woman in a white nightgown, combing out her long brown hair before a hand-mirror held almost vertically in her left hand. The eyes, perfectly elliptic and brown, are wide open; out of them seems to flow the light by which you see her. The lips, curved and full, suggest no passion; they are lips with which to modulate the voice, not to kiss. Of his Pandora you see eyes, lips, neck and one hand, the most exquisite hand but one in the whole world. Her bosom is covered, and I swear to you that the curiosity in her eyes is purely intellectual. Nor would you know, from looking at her, that this Fiammetta of his had ever known a man with as sensual a memory as that of Boccaccio. In the midst of a shower of spring flowers, she stands tall and erect as if she had grown there in that garden. The arms, long, cold, and naked, are not such as you would wish to enfold you. Her limpid eyes are two small pools of moonlight in her delightful little head. In Proserpina, Rossetti gives us the head and shoulders of a frightened girl who is too dignified to show it. Two half closed eyes, a soft cheek, a long strong neck and a partly peeled pomegranate in a hand that might as well have been coolly gloved. Finally he gives us Venus, the naked bust of a woman whose breasts are as fresh and cool and unlicentious as apples. The lips are not parted, but no one in the world would want to part those lips to kiss them. All the attributes of love are here, all the things a man dreams of in his wildest of solitudes, the things he learns soonest he will never attain. Now this silver-haired Venus of his, Rossetti, who was as swarthy as I am, seems to have endowed with all the attributes most precious to himself. He endowed her features with a perfection made up of the miniatures of mighty things: a nose, like a white crystal; a brow like a pearl; cheeks like pale rose leaves, and a neck like a delightful white pendant. Can you tell me why, since I find so much to gild my passions in Rossetti, I should struggle for art with labors that appear to me to be only a half-hearted pageant of pomp?"

"I never saw those picture in that light before," said Alma breathlessly.

"If you ask me," said Stewart, "I think it's downright obscene."

"You mean Rossetti or myself?" I asked.

"Both of you," he stormed.

"But you notice he didn't ask you," put in Alma severely. "I think I want to take another turn about the ship before we go down to luncheon. Will you take me?" she asked, turning to me.

I saw the scowl darken on Stewart's brow, but there was nothing to do but take Alma's arm.

"Have you known many English women?" she asked.

"Besides the five I have already described," I replied, "there are a few I have read about."

"Then you have never known an English woman in the flesh and blood?" she cried.

The gallantry of the words *flesh and blood* thrilled me. The warmth of her arm against mine became sweet and personal. I didn't dare look at her. "I hope to—in England," I said.

No other words passed between us, till we returned to Ada and Stewart who said that it was time to go down to the dining room.

8

Luncheon, lightened for me by the discovery that Stewart would not be at our table, for sharing one set aside exclusively for the engineers, was full of the zest of trivial talk and venture. From where I sat I could see Alma clearly. She had changed places with her sister, and smiled continually at me. The churchman, whom we had not missed, came late, and he was full of story.

There had been quite a bit of excitement in first class which, this trip, was particularly well spotted with society, dramatic and film celebrities, among them a certain famous and temperamental Polish Pianist. There were also, returning as guests of the line, the four amateur pugilistic champions of England who had come over to America and had wiped the floors of the Commodore with America's four amateur fighting champions. The Pianist and the ship's captain, who was making this his last voyage, were old friends, the Pianist had always graciously consented to play for the Seaman's Fund, which was quite a prize for any voyage. They had been standing on deck that morning in the midst of a breezy conversation when the English amateur heavyweight champion hove into view. "There's a lad I'd like you to meet," cried the captain who was a great boxing enthusiast, and called the fighter by name.

The fighter came up and shook hands with the captain. "Mr. Przenski," he said proudly, "I want you to meet the amateur heavyweight champion of England, Mr. Isaac Cohen."

The Pianist stood stiffly and made no move to touch the young hand that was outstretched for his. "You will excuse me," he said, "but I think I will go back to my cabin. I see that you will have no difficulty whatever filling your Seaman's Fund quota this trip."

"Does that mean that he won't play this trip?" asked the black-eyed, black-haired little woman.

"Certainly not," said the churchman. "The captain followed him immediately and apologized. He might really have known better because Przenski's attitude towards Jews is very well known."

"Well, thank God it won't keep him from playing," sighed the little Englishwoman.

"What about the Jew?" asked Ada.

"Oh, he's going about with a chip on his shoulder. He had his things transferred immediately to second class, and he threatens that he'll ruin Przenski's concert by fighting someone here that night. He's got a good prospect too in Battling O'Brien—see him at that table to your left—who was once light heavyweight champion of America. And if you ask me, a good fight will outsell a good concert anytime."

"That would be a dirty Jewish trick!" exclaimed Ada.

I looked at the German and the cosmopolitan but they were staring deep into their plates. "Why?" I asked.

"Do you think it was very nice of Przenski to snub Cohen so cavalierly?" I demanded.

Ada's eyes seemed to narrow into a hard glint. "You're a Jew, aren't you?" she said.

"I don't see what difference that makes."

"Only this. You wouldn't ask such a question if you were not a Jew. And if your Cohen fights O'Brien I hope O'Brien knocks his damn head off."

I looked at Alma, but I couldn't find her eyes any more. A whole world of loveliness seemed to have passed out of my life. "Alright," I said, turning back to Ada. "I'll give odds on Cohen."

"I'll take you," she snapped. "It'll be a pleasure even to lose against you."

There was nothing to say to this. As soon as I could I got away from the table. I avoided the cabin, because I wanted to see as little as possible of Stewart, and I felt unable to face the sunlight of the deck. So I spent the rest of the day at an open window of the ship's library. Fate and I had had our first open clash, and, as usual, I had come out second best.

As if to utterly confound me, everyone came to dinner that night in evening clothes. The negresses looked more than ever like Spanish grandees. The dark little Englishwoman showed surprising lines of voluptuousness. Even Ada looked soft in her aloofness. But Alma— Alma succeeded herself for the third time in my fancy. The first time I had fallen in love with a dainty silver bust. The second time it was Rossetti's *Proserpine* which drew my eyes. This time it was Whistler's *Girl in White*.

She greeted me as she approached the table with Ada, but it seemed to me a formal greeting, so I returned it in the same spirit, and did not venture to speak to her. Only a casual word now and then passed between her and Ada. In fact no general conversation developed at the table, so before we could realize it, dinner was over. I had no fancy for pacing the deck alone, so I got myself a magazine at the news stand and went into the bar.

Several small drinking parties were already in progress. I could recognize no one I knew, so I sat down at a little table occupied by a tall swarthy looking fellow about whom there was such an air of dejection that I thought I guessed who he was. "You're Mr. Cohen, aren't you?" I said.

He turned to look at me. I could tell by the wetness of his mouth that he was hostile to any intrusion, and that he had already drunk considerable for that day. "Well, what's it to you?" he growled.

"Nothing. But as one Jew to another, I don't think you've been very tactful. In fact I'm afraid you're going to find it rather rough sailing."

He made an ugly grimace. "Me find it a tough trip? You're crazy. You think they've counted me out because I happen to be a Jew. I can count myself out if I want to. But *they* can't count me out, see? I've got something on them, but they've got nothing on me. I'm not just a bloody Jew, see? I'm a fighter. I don't care what they think of Jews.

"When they see me fight they'll go crazy over me. Why? I got something to give them no other Jew can. There's that guy Einstein people talk about. What can he give them? Ideas. Or Lord Melchett; he can only give them money. But me, I got something to give them that they want more than ideas, yeh, even more than money. You know what?" He paused dramatically as if to wait for an answer.

"I'm sure I haven't a notion."

"And yet I heard them say that you're not only a Jew but a writer," he said contemptuously. "This is a Christian ship, isn't it? And these are bloody Christians, mostly, traveling on it, aren't they? Well, what do Christians like even more than love and money? You don't know. Well, I'll tell you.

"It's blood. And when I fight I give them blood, plenty of it. You wait and see if they don't go nuts over me."

"I hope so," I said. His vehemence had astonished me and taken me completely off my guard.

"Have a drink?" he asked me. Jim had come up alongside us.

"If you let me set them up," I conditioned. "And I should warn you," I added when Jim was gone, "that if you pass out on me I'm not sure whether I'm strong enough to carry you back to your cabin."

"Don't you worry about having to carry me," he growled, and drank down the new glass of brandy at a gulp. "If you're not careful you're gonna be in a hell of a lot more trouble yourself."

"That's very interesting."

"A few of those English engineers were in drinking this afternoon. That's how I heard about you. One of them sounded particularly sore. Talk about my not being tactful. How about your going off with that engineer's dame the first day of the voyage?"

"That's ridiculous. I've barely exchanged greetings with her."

"I don't doubt you. But you know how touchy those fellows are about their women."

"That boy seems an utter idiot to me," I said, "and I'm not taking any further notice of him."

"Well, he's taking plenty of notice of you, I can tell you. If you really don't want to get into trouble with him I'd advise you to keep away from that dame of his."

My indignation was rising. "You mean to tell me," I cried, "that he sat here discussing me and his fiancée so that you could overhear him?"

"Overhear him. I'd have to be deaf not to hear him. But he was a bit drunk, I can tell you. And so were his friends. It looks as if they're going to make one grand souse out of the whole trip."

"I see where I'm going to have a grand time," I murmured.

"Afraid of him?"

"Not exactly. But you see, he shares my cabin with me."

"That is sure tough," he said sympathetically, and suddenly leaned forward with a bright suggestion. "They gave me a cabin all to myself down here. Why don't you ask your steward to move your things in with me?"

"I'd like to," I said. "But I'm afraid I can't."

"Why not? It'll be alright with the steward. You haven't any idea what an English steward will do for five shillings."

"I'm not worrying about the steward, Cohen. But about myself. I've never run away from anything in my life, before. Do you think I can afford to start with this fool of a young Scotchman?"

He scowled. "A question of courage again. How is it that when cowards meet it is always courage that is most talked about. Here we are talking courage, a couple of prize cowards. Yes, and in the very stuff we count ourselves heroes—this Jewish-ness of ours. I go about the world calling myself Cohen, and you let on to innocent bystanders that you're a Jew—like a leper who tells you that he's a leper not to warn you but to extract sympathetic alms. You know what a Cohen is? When I was a kid I learned that to be a Cohen was to be like a priest, a Jewish priest, a sort of holy man, a holiness one is born with. Well, if I was born with holiness, it's been shot so full of holes the best Cohens in the world couldn't recognize it. And you call yourself a Jew. You make me laugh.

"Let me tell you something about this hero, drunk in my chair on his fifth glass of gin. As a kid, would you believe it, I was a particularly good Jew. And holy? Holy smoke! I believed practically everything I was told on the business of holiness. I used to spend Saturday afternoons with my nose against the windowpane waiting for the sun to go down before beginning the new week's devilry. You see I'd been told what it meant to be a Cohen, and I tried to live up to the bloody thing. All the hell in me was frozen to a sort of white holiness.

"Both of my parents are dead now. So if you must make copy of some of the things I'm going to tell you, go right ahead and be damned. Tell the world that One-Punch Cohen was a religious kid, and a yellow little Jew at heart. Dead afraid. And of what? You'll laugh when I tell you. You wouldn't guess in a million years. I wouldn't tell you in a million years if I wasn't stinking drunk. I was afraid that I wasn't really a Jew. Did you ever hear the likes of it? It's true, though.

"It started the day my father first caught me whistling behind the barn on a Sabbath afternoon. We had a particularly good dinner, and mother had made me happy by pinching my neck in a way she had when she was really pleased with me. I had wandered out of the house in a daze of ecstasy, with the day drifting over the meadows before me like a ship. I felt so pleased with myself there was only one way to express it, with no other children about to play it out with. I whistled.

"I whistled a holy tune, the Friday night *Lechu Dodi*. When my father, who I thought was dozing in his bed, appeared, I stopped whistling even before I realized that I was doing something wrong. But there he stood glaring at me, his face purple. *"Shaigetz! Goy!"* he cried, and slapped me twice, once on each cheek, a slap with each epithet. I think the words hurt more than the blows.

"The next time he hurled those words at me was when he caught me swinging my legs under the table at meal time. What does a boy think of when he swings his feet under the table that it can merit punishment? It seemed as if I could do nothing to please myself without arousing the anger of my father. There were always blows. And with the blows always came those terrible words: *"Shaigetz! Goy!"*

"It grew worse as I grew older. If I went out into the windy sunlight without a hat, which was always a glorious thing to do; when, while begging my mother's pardon for some accidental rudeness, I sank down on my knees before her; everything that was beautiful to me seemed goyish to my father. And I began to be afraid that there must be something wrong with me. I seemed instinctively to do the things which were un-Jewish.

"One night mother told us the story of the *Ger Tzadick*, a gentile who fell in love with Jewish ways and sacrificed the rest of his life in service of Jews. Not a poor gentile, a man of title, a man who by becoming a Jew lowered himself in the esteem of the world. It's dangerous enough to practice being a Jew when you're born into it. But to try to be a Jew when you're actually born Christian. That's why the Jews love him so much, my mother explained to us.

"'But do you think he was a good Jew?' I asked her.

"'Why not?' she replied. 'He was more than just good. He was beautiful. Beautiful, I tell you.'

"To me the story was a great relief. I no longer had to be afraid of whether I was a Jew or not. Because, if a goy could be a Jew and a saint . . . At worst, if I lived honestly and sincerely, I would be a *Ger Tzadick*, and entitled to a certain amount of love . . .

"There is a legend, I think, in every man's childhood up which the rest of his life crawls like a vine. If you look back into your own origins you'll find some such tale which began by striking your fancy, made itself at home in your mind, and became the unconscious guide to every growing action of yours ever afterwards. My mother's version of the *Ger Tzadick* was mine. It grew up with me and I grew up with it.

"Without having any inkling of the matter myself, I became a *Ger Tzadick* in my own sub-consciousness. I began to divide the world into Jews I didn't like and those who were *Ger Tzadickim*, like myself. All the Jews around me were just Jews. But when a Jew I met said a fine thing or gave expression to a beautiful gesture I thought immediately he was a *Ger Tzadick*.

"It is a strange sort of fantasy to discover roaming about in one's blood. But we must live by what we have, for we can live by nothing else. Day by day I found myself consciously growing away from the ordinary type of Jew. When my mother died I left my father's house altogether and went to live by myself. It was because I couldn't bear the old associations, I told the people. And it was true. I couldn't stand the horrible Jewish faces about me.

"It tormented me, of course, this repulsion of mine for my own people. I remember that there was a man in Cambridge, a Jew whom I confided in, and he tried to talk me out of it. "The feeling is unworthy of you and contemptible he said. "As a Jew you have every reason to be proud of yourself. Think: you are racially one with Rambam, Spinoza, Heine, Karl Marx and Einstein.

"'I would be,' I replied, 'If I were certain they were really Jews.'

"He looked amused. 'Even Houston Chamberlain does not deny us Spinoza.'

"I tried to explain myself: 'I grew up among Jews like you,' I said to him. 'The Jews I saw and listened to every day were shrewd, ambitious and law-abiding at home, but perfect anarchists abroad, outside their own homes. When I met a Jew who was sober, orderly and scrupulously honest he never looked to me like a Jew, or even sounded like one.

"When I began reading the Old Testament I found myself thinking the same way. Abraham, Isaac and Jacob were Jews alright. They were hardy, domineering, profoundly calculating, and instinctively thieving. But Moses did not seem to me, at all like a Jew. Neither did Isaiah nor Jesus.

"'When I was fifteen I was struck in Genesis by the peculiar wording of the description of Rebekah's pregnancy: *"And the Lord said unto her: Two nations are in thy womb, and two peoples shall be separated from thy bowels."* How, I asked myself, could two nations be in a woman's womb unless two nations had placed them there? Was that possible?

"'I might have gone to the rabbis with my perplexity. Luckily I didn't like them. So I went to the teacher of biology in my school, and he explained the matter to me, to my complete satisfaction. A woman, a promiscuous woman, could have twins of two different fathers. The author of *Genesis* could have had nothing else in mind, for he goes to such pains to show that, both by his heritage and because of his glorious personal qualities, Esau was certainly not a Jew.

"'I do not imply that all Jewish women are lusty promiscuous bitches like Rebekah. Towards the production of a whole stream of Esaus in Jewish life, this is not an essential condition. Every generation of Jews is plentifully pogrommed, raided and raped, so that the seed of Esau is constantly sown in the womb of Rebekah. It is my sincere conviction that it is of this sowing that Jewish mothers give birth to Montaignes, Spinozas, and Heines who bear no resemblance whatever to the unbearable merchants and swindlers who spring everlastingly from the seed of Jacob.'

"I did not convert this Cambridge friend of mine, any more than I am trying to convert you. But I have always believed it myself. So you see how my carrying on under the name Cohen is the sheerest and emptiest bravado."

I told him that I had really had no intention of posing as a hero. That nasty little Scotchman might, for all I cared, get as nasty as he liked!

"Alright, have it your own way. But if you ever find yourself needing any help -"

"Thanks. But I think I can manage things well enough. Why don't you and I get out of this stuffy room and promenade the deck and get some of these kinks out of our brains?"

We paid and left. But it had suddenly grown very cold on deck and after a few minutes we returned each to his own cabin.

9

Next morning the window of our cabin was engulfed. The sea was in an uproar.

Neither Ada nor Alma showed up for breakfast or luncheon. All thought of going on deck was abandoned by everyone.

Three distinct card parties grew up in the saloon. One of English men and women. Another of engineers. And a third of Americans and Jews, which I joined.

There was at our table a little Canadian Jew called Zauber, en route to Galicia with funds for the starving, entrusted to him by their relatives in Montreal. He attracted to himself attention not at our table alone. Small, meager, of a sallow complexion, he talked rapidly and excitedly about everything and quarreled interminably at the drop of a card. His manners and mannerisms became the butt of the merriment of the ship.

Among other things Zauber was very keen on "exchange." You knew that the pound had risen to three dollars and eighty cents when he offered you three dollars and seventy five cents for it. He had two busy vest coat pockets, one for American quarters, the other for Canadian ones.

When an American quarter fell on the table he would contrive to change it for one of his Canadian quarters. By this transaction he earned six cents. No one objected. He enjoyed the liberty afforded a pet monkey.

I might have been able to bear the Canadian Yiddle if it weren't for the prize fighter O'Brien at our table. O'Brien—a burly raucous fellow with a coarse infectious laugh—addressed Zauber as "kike." If Zauber was hurt he didn't show it. On the contrary. It appeared to please him so much, I half suspected he realized how deeply it annoyed me.

After calling Zauber 'kike' O'Brien's biggest pleasure came from slapping Zauber's hand every time it fell innocently on the table, of digging him in the ribs and kicking his shins on the slenderest pretenses. He laughed uproariously every time he sounded the word "kike," and every time he slapped and kicked the Jew. The table joined him without prejudice. The Jew was good game.

Once, when the uproar following one of O'Brien's particularly hilarious pranks on the Jew had attracted some of the unattached passengers to our table, I caught sight of Solomon towering over the rest. There was a scowl in the face with which he regarded O'Brien's, but when he saw me staring at him he made a sour grimace and walked off.

I was glad when dinner time came and put a temporary end to Zauber and O'Brien's tricks. The table was even barer than it had been for luncheon. But in the midst of the meal a steward brought me a note. It was from Alma, and it asked me to step into her cabin after dinner.

"Come in," said Alma. I found her, when I entered her cabin, seated at her little writing table, a pen poised in her hand over some letter paper. "Please sit down," she murmured, pointing to a chair opposite her. "And because I've not come to the table today please do not treat me like an invalid. It's just a touch of seasickness, and I wouldn't be surprised to find myself coming up for breakfast tomorrow."

"And Ada?"

"Ada's gone visiting—so that we might have this conversation. She was sure, though, you wouldn't come. She offered me odds on it."

"And you didn't take her up?"

Alma leaned back magnificently and looked at me with tremendous intentness. "I don't bet on a sure thing. I knew that you'd come because you're in love with me."

"And how, pray, do you know that?"

She looked defiant. "I know."

"You know only that I'm in the habit of staring at you. Don't other men stare at you?"

"Of course. Many of them. But don't you see, the staring of other men means nothing to me."

"And mine does?"

"Yes," she said quietly. "I love you, too."

I looked at her. It was as if a picture I admired had found voice and returned me the compliment. I felt absolutely incapable of continuing the conversation from that point. I thought of the nearest subterfuge. "And Stewart?" I asked.

"I'm going to tell him tomorrow."

"What will you tell him?"

"That I don't love him and will never marry him. It wouldn't make any difference now what is to be the outcome of you and me. I simply don't love him anymore, and I won't have him annoying us."

I shook my head. "How do you think he'll take it?"

"I don't know," she snapped. "And I don't think I care. He'll be much more sensitive about what the boys think of it than of how it affects him with me. I'm ready to forget that I've ever known Stewart." She paused. "You're not afraid of him, darling?"

"Not exactly. But I would not think of underrating the force of his displeasure. Stewart's not a child, although he is quite as uncivilized as one. There's sure to be a mess. But let's say no more about it."

She put down her pen and drew her chair closer to mine. "We've two and a half days more at sea," she whispered. "They're going to be terribly long, aren't they, darling?"

I nodded. I couldn't speak. I had never found my energies so completely tied up before.

She leaned forward so that I could feel her sweet breath on my face. "Why don't you kiss me?" she said. "Your eyes have been pleading for it since the first time they looked at me."

I took her head in both of my hands gently and touched her curved lips with my mouth.

She gave me a little pleasure of her own and drew her mouth back, laughing. "You kiss like—like a virgin," she cried.

"I do adore you," I pleaded.

"Your eyes adore me," she said with assumed severity. "But your mouth treats me entirely too respectfully. Have you never kissed before?"

"I used to kiss my prayer-book," I said to her.

"Your prayer-book!" she exclaimed.

"Yes." And I explained to her, like every other Jewish child, I had been taught to kiss the covers of a book on opening and closing it, as a token of my affection for my studies."

"But you must have kissed living people. Your mother -"

"I never kissed my mother and I do not remember that she ever kissed me."

"But surely -"

"Surely I've kissed women, yes. But I have never given myself over to the business with great enthusiasm."

"Well, then," she said, "I have at last found myself the occupation of a lifetime. I shall teach you how to kiss. But you know, you are terribly wistful when you speak of your Jewishness. It sounds like the beginning of a story. Some day you must tell it to me. But in the meantime you must kiss me."

I now lifted her bodily out of her chair and drew her to me so that I clasped her wholly in my arms.

"You are learning already," she cried, drawing away her warm face. "Tell me are you married?"

I nodded.

"Children?"

"Yes, darling. Two."

"And your wife?"

"Very beautiful and relentlessly intelligent. I assure you I am not at all worthy of her."

"Of course, or you would not throw yourself into my arms. And the children?"

"Don't ask. They're both born into the courts of the Sun."

She caught her breath swiftly. "And how could it be otherwise! But tell me: what are you going to do with me?"

I looked at her a moment. "I don't know," I said. "I don't see how I can have anything to say about disposing of you."

"I don't understand you, darling."

"I feel like a beggar who has been invited to the office of a banker, and the first thing the banker asks him is how he expects to dispose of all the money in the bank. I can't believe that you are mine to dispose of."

She got off my lap and resumed her place opposite me. "Maybe I'm not for you to dispose of," she said, and a moment later was kneeling before me. "Don't believe me when I say things like that, darling," she pleaded. "I do love you. We'll find a way out, too, in time."

I just about managed to kiss her once more, hurriedly, before Ada, in a majestic black cape, swept in. "I'm glad you're still here, Roth," she said breezily.

"I've got some good advice for you. Alma's little boy friend's found out about your coming here, and if you want to sleep soundly tonight I suggest that you ask your steward for another cabin. The boy's at the bar now, with the rest of the engineers in his party, all stewed to the gills."

"I should have changed my cabin before," I replied. "But I'm afraid it's too late now. Stewart'll think I'm running away from him."

"Aren't you?" asked Ada archly.

Why did everyone take it for granted that because that worm was angry, I had to be afraid! Was I afraid! I'd find out soon enough.

"No," I replied to Ada, and added: "Good night." It was all I could do to restrain myself from banging the door as I went out.

10

In the blind rush for my cabin, I could only think of two people. It would probably upset me completely to meet Cohen—of that I was certain. As for the other, I did want to encounter him. The cabin which he shared with me seemed the logical place to seek him out. And yet, deep in my heart, I loathed the prospect of looking at him. Maybe, I said to myself, you've reached the point where the sight of a Jew has become obnoxious to you; but you are still far from being at ease with the rest of the world . . . Then whom was I looking for?

I felt a distinct sense of mystery enveloping me as I opened wide the cabin door and shut it slowly behind me. The cabin seemed quite bare.

The Scotchman was out—probably drinking again. Yet for all of the cabin's bareness I did not feel alone. I felt cornered, shadowed as though my destiny had suddenly become embodied and was haunting me. I stepped forward hesitantly, paused at the water basin, and caught sight of the mysterious presence.

Something so familiar and yet so strange! Either I had never been quite so near him before, or I had never glimpsed him in the proper moment of space. The whole man before me seemed to blaze like a torch, as I tried to make up my mind why so much more of me feared him than had ever feared anything else before in a lonely universe.

His brow darkened so that it was like a shadow cast by his fierce shock of black hair. His eyes stared with startling intelligence out of their deep sockets.

They seemed more afraid of being seen than of what they might see if they dared to receive vision. His full thick lips were pressed together with the contemptuous despair of an animal which is cornered, but knows that it will be allowed to escape. Without apparently opening his mouth he made distinct mouthless speech.

JUDAS: What do you want with me?

I: I want you to order the pride to die out in your eyes. I want you to be ashamed and confess your guilt.

JUDAS: But I am guilty of nothing. So what is there to be ashamed of?

I: Perhaps you can explain what you happen to be doing here. Spying on me, aren't you? But what is spying to you that it should worry your conscience? And whom do you think you serve by imposing your unpleasant presence on me?

JUDAS: You yourself.

I: Perfect. It's what I expected you to say. It wouldn't properly be you if you didn't interpret your easy meanness as an act of unselfish philanthropy. That's the most damnable thing about you. You must lie and cheat because it's second nature with you.

But you must always be doing it in the name of some worthy cause. You put your ill-smelling hands on a man, and proceed to carefully, painstakingly choke the life out of him.

But that is not enough. Not for you. You must explain to the world that you are really doing a good thing, that you are choking the man out of sheer love of him.[37]

---

[37] "The difference," says Boris Abramovitch in Skolom Ash's *Three Cities*, "between the Russians and the Jews consists rather in this: that the Russian loves to confess the evil that he does to his fellow-men, while the Jew prefers to confess only his good deeds. He conceals the evil within him, or forces himself to express it. The reason at the back of this is that the Russian likes to have something on his conscience; without a few pecks of sin, as it were, he doesn't like to show himself in the street, and if he shouldn't happen to have committed any he thinks up a few sins simply that he may be able to promenade with the mark of Cain on his brow. The Jew, on the other hand, likes always to have a clean conscience so as to be on the sure side. The slyness for which Jews are so famed consists in keeping their 'account' in the spiritual ledger perpetually balanced, as if an inspector might come along at any minute. A Jew may commit the meanest offenses, but he will always find some way of putting them in such a pure light in his own mind that they are changed into little virtues. If nothing else will serve, then he will make the good Lord his accomplice, as Jacob did. If a Christian had tricked Laban like*

JUDAS: I do love you.

I: Of course. I do not doubt it. You love me, just as you love your mother, your wife, your sons or your daughters. For you are not content with being merely good: you are respectable, too. You have made of your house a very fortress of respectability. No one loves a mother more than you love a mother.

No one adores a sister more tenderly than you adore a sister. But you have built a fence about your home and about those you fancy to love. You have drawn an ominous line under your life and under the lives of those related to you by the more obvious blood-ties.

Do you remember what they taught you in school about a line? That it's really imaginary, that it has no existence in the physical world? Such a line you have drawn to separate yourself from the world you rob, choke and murder.

You think it is the essence of virtue to feed your own mother and starve the mothers of others. You think it an irreproachable thing to build a tender shelter about your sister and expose the sisters of others to shame and hunger. Well, you have fooled yourself.

There is no difference between your mother and other mothers, between your sister and other sisters, between your daughter and the daughters of the people you hold aloof from as strangers. And so, without knowing it, you have consigned your own precious mothers, sisters and daughters to your own loathsome brothels.

JUDAS: I cannot understand this passion of yours. I have done nothing wrong, nothing unlawful.

I: I do not accuse you of being unlawful, but of being inhuman. Why, pray tell me, do you praise only what you sell, and invariably scowl at what you buy? Is that not against all sense of decency and humanity?

You purchase what seems fair in your eyes, and certainly it must be precious to the one who parts with it. Yet when you are making the fatal exchange—money for beauty—you have not a smile or a kind

---

Jacob - even if only in a small fraud like the peeled wands - he certainly would have felt guilty; but Jacob actually made a good deed out of it, on the excuse that it was necessary for his wife and children. The Jew is always prepared to transform his dirty, brutally egotistic interests into holy virtues. That's the kernel, if you'll excuse my saying so, of Jewish cunning."

word for the man who is about to enrich you by yielding something of a reluctant order to your grasping faculties.

Have you ever seen yourself when you offer something for sale? What you sell may have usefulness. If it ever had beauty the beauty died in it the moment you touched it.

Yet as you offer your awful offal your face lights up with animation, your lips curve with joyous anticipation, and only words of praise tinkle from your tongue.

JUDAS: That's *handel,* business.

I: Maybe. *Handel* seems to justify you in almost every one of your monstrous acts. But if I were you I would try to change about a bit. I would be a little critical of what I sell, and a bit appreciative of what I buy.

If only as a first exercise in elementary honesty. And I have another major recommendation to make. You have already got yourself into the habit of wearing glasses. Why not wear smoked glasses?

JUDAS: Why?

I: So that you will see less and find what you do see a little less desirable. Nothing in the world seems to me to be quite as extensive and as destructive as your vision. You seem to see everything. And whatever you see you want.

JUDAS: But my wants have never been immoderate.

I: You mean you never thought your wants were immoderate. How could you consider any want of yours immoderate when in your black heart you feel that as a son of that old thief Jacob you are the true owner of everything lovely and desirable on earth?

Maybe if you will see less your heart will lust less and your arms and your hands will not always be reaching out for the property of others. If I were you I would lose no time finding densely smoked glasses to cover the eyes. Otherwise hands might be extended to pluck them out.

JUDAS: One or two eloquent gestures in that direction have already been made.

I: Yes, I know. And you are not frightened. Not because you are unafraid. Because you know that always, at the last moment, the world is softened by your pleas, and withholds its hands. You have learned thoroughly the trick of falling on your knees before it and

246

imploring mercy in the names of all your sacred devils. So frequently have you given this performance that the world has almost come to regard those sacred devils as its own.

The grand result may be that instead of the world plucking out your terrible eyes, it will be you who, with your filthy fingers, will nail out the eyes of the world. For you have succeeded in teaching the world mercy without ever seriously entertaining the idea yourself.

JUDAS: So you even fear for the world on account of me?

I: And with good reason. In the struggle for civilization the issue has always been between the world and you: the world striving upward, you pulling down, down. It will be a wonderful thing for the world when you are quite completely gone.

JUDAS: You hate me, don't you?

I: Yes, I hate, I loathe you.

JUDAS: I can't understand why?

I: I don't fully understand it myself. But I do know that I hate you. I particularly hate your face, face of a Judas, of a *Satzkin*. The revengeful heels left their tracks on that horrible face of yours. It is a face which has absorbed an ocean of outraged spit, and it is drooping with a dark greenness out of the mean corners of your mouth.

JUDAS: And that you think is a good enough reason for your hatred?

I: Look at you. You have no bank, yet your are represented at all bank counsels. You have no army of your own, yet you dictate wars in which armies of the young of the world are destroyed. You have no honor, no decency, and yet you talk continually of your pride. You have no real possessions of your own, yet you are always prepared to advise other people how to divide what is their own.

All the things in the world which are hateful are hateful in you. And the things which in the rest of the world are lovely and lovable in you are hateful and contemptible. If it is a beautiful thing in a brother to love a sister it is a mean thing when it is a Jewish brother loving a Jewish sister.

If it is a beautiful thing for a man to stand up for his country, when it is a Jew who stands up for his country the act is corroded with hatefulness. I know that the whole arrangement of the universe, as I am living in it, is a sort of benevolent democracy in which the smaller as well as the more monstrous reptiles, the insects which attack one's blood from within and those planetary powers which shape us from without, each has a function, a usefulness, a justification. So have you, I suppose.

But I abhor you even more than I abhor lice, spiders, diseased orifices of the body, roaches, the germs of syphilis and gonorrhea, and those rebellious little aristocrats who compose cancer. You seem to me to be some un-healable disease in the blood of the race. Without you, life for humanity might be as free, joyous, happy-go-lucky and adventurously fatal as it must be for the rest of animal creation, as it probably was for those lucky races who spermed into a world that had not yet fallen under the shadow of your dominion.

I do not know when I hate you most: by day or by night, when you are victorious or when you have lost, old or young, stout or lean, drunk or sober, just or unjust, when you are most happy or when you are most miserable.

I only know that I hate you with a hatred so steady and deadly that it consumes in me all sense of time and place.

What can I do to you to prove to you how fearfully I detest you? Abuse you with speech as I am doing now?

Futile gesture!

About whom have nastier or more terrible things been said? Spit on you? The whole world has spit in your face and ground its heel into the spittle. I know.

This solid drinking glass may well do something a whole world has failed to do. See me hold it up? In another moment it will go crashing through your horrible skull. . . .

The mirror fell in a thousand shattered fragments at my feet.

APPENDIX

Donna Blanca

XVII APPENDIX

DO JEWS EMIT A PECULIAR ODOR?

I have treated the Jews in every important phase of the life of the world about them. I have traced them back to their origins as described (but how mistakenly understood!) by the author of *Genesis*. I have described them as workers, or rather as a race of fortune-hunters, people instinctively reluctant to submit themselves to the less glamorous labors of mankind.

I have surveyed them, through dark unfriendly lenses, pursuing vain, greedy careers as lawyers, physicians, moneylenders, merchants, gangsters; as citizens of a country and of the world; as actors and theatrical managers; as conductors of brothels, licensed and unlicensed; as social climbers confusing and belittling all fine social standards; also as Zionists following a hastily dyed banner.

There is still another matter which I cannot allow to become a part of the regular body of my book. It is a matter on which I do not think I care to venture either an opinion or a guess. I refer to the peculiar bad odor which attaches to the name Jew. The word odor is here to be understood as physical, not moral.

From time immemorial people have believed that, aside from religious considerations, there is in the flesh and the make up of the Jew a mysterious odorous canker that renders association with him uncomfortable in the extreme. *Genesis* records that the Egyptians shrank from physical contact with the Jews. The chronicles of other nations and other times, though not as eloquent, yield similar testimony.

What is the truth in all this? Unable to undertake the role of an impartial witness, I am here summoning the testimony of three men, each the greatest intellect and the most representative personality of hiscentury: Sir Thomas Browne for the seventeenth century, Voltaire for the eighteenth, and Heinrich Heine for the nineteenth:

Sir Thomas Browne:

"That *Jews* stink naturally, that is, that in their race and nation there is an evil savour, is a received opinion we know not how to admit; although concede many questionable points, and dispute not the verity of sundry opinions which are of affinity hereto. We will acknowledge that certain odours attend on animals, no less than certain colors; that pleasant smells are not confined unto vegetables, but found in divers animals, and some more richly than in plants. And though the Problem of *Aristotle* inquire why no animal smells sweet beside the Parde? yet later discoveries add divers sorts of *Monkeys,* the *Civet Cat, and Gazela,* from which our Musk proceedeth. We confess that beside the smell of the species, there may be individual odours, and every Man may have a proper and peculiar savour; which although not perceptible unto Man, who hath this sense, but weak, yet sensible unto *Dogs,* who hereby can single out their masters in the dark. We will not deny that particular Men have sent forth a pleasant savour, as *Theophrastus* and *Plutarch* report of *Alexander* the great, and *Tzetzes* and *Cardan* do testify of themselves. That some may also emit an unsavory odour, we have no reason to deny; for this may happen from the quality of what they have taken; the factor whereof may discover itself by sweat and urine as being unmasterable by the natural heat of Man, not to be dulcified by concoction beyond an unsavory condition: the like may come to pass from putrid tumours, as is often discoverable in putrid and malignant fervors. And sometime also in gross and humid bodies even in the latitude of sanity; the natural heat of the parts being insufficient for a perfect and thorough digestion, and the errors of one concoction not rectifiable by another. But that an unsavory odour is gentilities or national unto the *Jews,* if rightly understood, we cannot well concede; nor will the information of reason or fancy induce it.

"For first, upon consult of Reason, there will be found no easy assurance to fasten a material or temperamental propriety upon any nation; there being scarce any condition (but what depends upon clime) which is not exhausted or obscured from the commixture of intervenient nations either by commerce or conquest; much more will it be difficult to make out this affection in the *Jews;* whose race however pretended to be pure, must needs have suffered inseparable commixtures with nations of all sorts; not only in regard of their proselytes, but their universal dispersion; some being posted from several parts of the earth, others quite lost, and swallowed up in those nations where they planted. For the tribes of *Reuben, Gad,* part of *Manasseh* and *Naphthali,* which were taken by *Assur,* and the rest at the sacking of *Samaria,*which were led away by *Salmanasser* into *Assyria,* and after a year and a half arrived at *Arsereth,* as is delivered in *Esdras;* these I say never returned, and are by the *Jews* as vainly expected as their*Messiahs.* Of those of the tribe of *Judah* and *Benjamin,* which were led captive into *Babylon* by *Nebuchadnezzar,* many returned under *Zorobabel;* the rest remained, and from thence long after upon invasion of the *Saracens,* fled as far as *India;* where yet they are said to remain, but with little difference from the *Gentiles.*

"The Tribes that returned to *Judea,* were afterward widely dispersed; for beside sixteen thousand which *Titus* sent to *Rome* unto the triumph of his father *Vespasian,* he sold no less than an hundred thousand for slaves. Not many years after, *Adrian* the Emperor, who ruined the whole Country, transplanted many thousands into *Spain,* from whence they dispersed into divers Countries, as into *France* and*England,* but were banished after from both. From *Spain* they dispersed into *Africa, Italy, Constantinople,* and the Dominions of the *Turk,* where they remain as yet in very great numbers. And if (according to good relations) where they may freely speak it, they forbear not to boast that there are at present many thousand *Jews* in *Spain, France,* and *England,* and some dispensed withal even to the degree of Priesthood; it is a matter very considerable, and could they be smelled out, would much advantage, not only the Church of Christ, but also the coffers of Princes.

"Now having thus lived in several Countries, and always, in subjection, they must needs have suffered many commixtures; and we are sure they are not exempted from the common contagion of Venery contracted first from Christians. Nor as fornications infrequent between them both; there commonly passing opinions of incitement, that their Women desire copulation with them rather then their own Nation, and affect Christian carnality above circumcised venery. It being therefore acknowledged, that some are lost, evident that others are mixed, and not sure that any are distinct, it will be hard to establish this quality upon the Jews, unless we also transfer the same unto those whose generations are mixed, whose genealogies are *Jewish,* and naturally derived from them.

"Again, if we concede a National unsavouriness in any people, yet shall we find the *Jews* less subject hereto than any, and that in those regards which most powerfully concur to such effects, that is, their diet and generation. As for their diet whether in obedience unto the precepts of reason, or the injunctions of parsimony, therein they are very temperate; seldom offending in ebriosity or excess of drink, nor erring in gulosity or superfluity of meats; whereby they prevent indigestion and crudities, and consequently putrescence of humors. They have in abomination all flesh maimed, or the inwards any way vitiated; and therefore eat no meat but of their own killing. They observe not only fasts at certain times, but are restrained unto very few dishes at all times; so few that whereas St. *Peters* sheet will hardly cover our Tables, their Law doth scarce permit them to set forth a Lordly feast; nor any way to answer the luxury of our times, or those of our forefathers. For of flesh their Law restrains them many sorts, and such that complete our feasts: That Animal, *Propter conviva natum,* they touch not, nor any of its preparations, or parts so much in respect at *Roman* Tables, nor admit they unto their board, *Hares, Conies, Herons, Plovers*or *Swans.* Of *Fishes* they only taste of such as have both fins and scales; which are comparatively few in numbers, such only, saith *Aristotle,* whose Egg or spawn is arenaceous; whereby are excluded all cetaceous and cartilaginous *Fishes;* many pectinal, whose ribs are rectilineal; many costal, which have their ribs embowed; all spinal, or such as have no ribs, but only a backbone, or somewhat analagous thereto, as *Eels, Congers, Lampries;* all that are testaceous, as *Oysters, Cocles, Wilks, Scollops, Muscles;* and likewise all crustaceous, as *Crabs, Shrimps* and *Lobsters.* So that observing a spare and simple diet, whereby they prevent the generation of crudities; and fasting often whereby they might also digest them; they must be less inclinable unto this infirmity then any other Nation, whose proceedings are not so reasonable to avoid it.

"As for their generations and conceptions (which are the purer from good diet), they become more pure and perfect by the strict observation of their Law; upon their injunctions whereof, they severely observe the times of Purification, and avoid all copulation, either in the uncleanness of themselves or impurity of their Women. A Rule, I fear, not so well observed by Christians; whereby not only conceptions are prevented, but if they proceed, so vitiated and defiled, that durable inquinations remain upon the birth. Which, when the conception meets with these impurities, must needs be very potent; since in the purest and most fair conceptions, learned men derive the cause of Pox and *Meazels,* from principals of that nature; that is, the menstruous impurities in the mother's blood, and virulent tinctures contracted by the Infant, in the nutriment of the womb.

"Lastly, Experience will convict it; for this offensive odor is no way discoverable in their Synagogues where many are, and by reason of their number could not be concealed: nor is the same discernable in commerce or conversation with such as are cleanly in Apparel, and decent in their Houses. Surely the Vilziars and *Turkish* Basha's are not of this opinion; who as Sir *Henry Blunt* informeth, do generally keep a *Jew* of their private Counsel. And were this true, the *Jews* themselves do not strictly make out the intention of their Law, for in vain do they scruple to approach the dead, who livingly are cadaverous, or fear any outward pollution, whose temper pollutes themselves. And lastly, were this true, yet our opinion is not impartial; for unto converted *Jews* who are of the same seed, no Man imputeth this unsavoury odor; as though Aromatized by their conversion, they lost their scent with their religion, and smelt no longer then they savoured of the *Jew.*

"Now the ground that begat or propagated this assertion, might be the distasteful aversness of the Christian from the *Jew,* upon the villainy of that fact, which made them abominable and stink in the nostrils of all Men. Which real practise and metaphorical expression, did after proceed into a literal construction; but was a fraudulent illation; for such an evil savour their father *Jacob* acknowledged in himself, when he said, his sons had made him stink in the land, that is, to be abominable unto the inhabitants thereof. Now how dangerous it is in sensible things to use metaphorical expressions unto the people, and what absurd conceits they will swallow in their literals; an impatient example we have in our profession; who having called an eaten *ulcer* by the name of a Wolf, common apprehensive conceives a reality therein; and against ourselves ocular affirmations are pretended to confirm it.

"The nastiness of that Nation, and sluttish course of life hath much promoted the opinion, occasioned by their servile condition at first, and inferiour ways of parsimony ever since; as is delivered by *Mr. Sandys.* They are generally fat, saith he, and rank of the savours which attend upon sluttish corpulency. The *Epithetes* assigned them by ancient times, have also advanced the same; for *Ammianus Marcellinus* describeth them in such language; and *Martial* more ancient, in such a relative expression sets fourth unsavoury *Bassa*.

Quod jejunia Sabbatoriorum.

Mallem, quam quod oles, olere Bassa.

"From whence notwithstanding we cannot infer an inward imperfection in the temper of that Nation; it being but an effect in the breath from the outward observation, in their strict and tedious fasting; and was a common effect in the breaths of other Nations, became a Proverb among the *Greeks,* and the reason thereof begot a Problem in *Aristotle*.

"Lastly, if all were true, and were this savour conceded, yet are the reasons alleadged for it no way satisfactory. *Hucherius,* and after him *Alsarius Crucius,* imputes this effect unto their abstinence from salt or salt meats; which how to make good in the present diet of the *Jews,* we know not; nor shall we conceive it was observed of old, if we consider they seasoned every Sacrifice, and all oblations whatsoever; whereof we cannot deny a great part was eaten by the Priests. And if the offering were of flesh, it was salted no less than thrice, that is, once in the common chamber of salt, at the foot-step of the Altar, and upon the top thereof, as is at large delivered by Maimonides.

"Nor if they refrained all salt, is the illation very urgent; for many there are, not noted for ill odours, which eat no salt at all; as all carnivorous Animals, most Children, many whole Nations, and probably our Fathers after Creation; there being indeed in every thing we eat, a natural and concealed salt, which is separated by digestion, as doth appear in our tears, sweat and urines, although we refrain all salt, or what doth seem to contain it.

"Another cause is urged by *Compegius,* and much received by Christians; that this ill savour is a curse derived upon them by Christ, and stands as a badge or a brand of a generation that crucified their*Salvator.* But this is a conceit without all warrant; and an easie way to take off dispute in what point of obscurity soever. A method of many Writers, which much depreciates the esteem and value of miracles; that is, therewith to salve not only real verities, but also non-existencies. Thus have elder times not only ascribed the immunity of *Ireland* from any venomous beast, unto the staff or rod of *Patrick;* but the long tails of Kent, unto the malediction of *Austin.*

"Thus therefore, although we concede that many opinions are true which hold some conformity to this, yet in assenting hereto, many difficulties must arise: it being a dangerous point to annex a constant property unto any Nation, and much more this unto the *Jew;* since this quality is not verifiable by observation, since the grounds are feeble that should establish it; and lastly, since if all were true, yet are the reasons alleged for it, of no sufficiency to maintain it."

Marie Francois Auret de Voltaire:

"You order me to draw you a faithful picture of the spirit of the Jews, and of their history, and—without entering into the ineffable ways of Providence, which are not our ways—you seek in the manners of this people the source of the events which that Providence prepared.

"It is certain that the Jewish nation is the most singular that the world has ever seen; and although, in a political view, the most contemptible of all, yet in the eyes of a philosopher, it is, on various accounts, worthy of consideration.

"The Guebers, the Banins, and the Jews, are the only nations which exist dispersed, having no alliance with any people, are perpetuated among foreign nations, and continue apart from the rest of the world.

"The Guebers were once infinitely more considerable than the Jews, for they are castes of the Persians, who had the Jews under their dominion; but they are now scattered over but one part of the East.

"The Banians, who are descended from the ancient people among whom Pythagoras acquired his philosophy, exists only in India and Persia; but the Jews are dispersed over the whole face of the earth, and if they are assembled, would compose a nation much more numerous than it ever was in the short time that they were masters of Palestine. Almost every people who have written the history of their origin, have chosen to set it off by prodigies; with them all has been miracle; their oracles have predicted nothing but conquest; and such of them as have really become conquerors have had no difficulty in believing these ancient oracles which were verified by the event. The Jews are distinguished among the nations by this—that their oracles are the only true ones, of which we are not permitted to doubt. These oracles, which they understand only in the literal sense, have a hundred times foretold to them that they should be masters of the world; yet they have never possessed anything more than a small corner of land, and that only for a small number of years, and they have not now so much as a village of their own. They must, then, believe, and they do believe, that their predictions will one day be fulfilled, and that they shall have the empire of the earth.

"Among the Mussulmans and the Christians they are the lowest of all nations, but they think themselves the highest. This pride in their abasement is justified by an unanswerable reason—viz., that they are in reality the fathers of both Christians and Mussulmans. The Christian and the Mussulman religions acknowledged the Jewish as their parent; and, hold this parent in reverance and in abhorrence.

"It were foreign to our present purpose to repeat that continued succession of prodigies, which astonishes the imagination and exercises the faith. We have here to do only with events purely historical, wholly apart from the divine concurrence and the miracles which God, for so long a time, vouchsafed to work in this people's favor.

"First, we find in Egypt, a family of seventy persons producing, at the end of two hundred and fifteen years, a nation counting six hundred thousand fighting men; which makes, with the women, the children and the old men, upward of two millions of souls. There is no example upon earth of so prodigious an increase of population; this people, having come out of Egypt, stayed forty years in the deserts of Stony Arabia, and in that frightful country the people much diminished.

"What remained of this nation advanced a little northward in those deserts. It appears that they had the same principles which the tribes of Stony and Desert Arabia have since had, of butchering without mercy the inhabitants of little towns over whom they had the advantage, and reserving only the young women. The interests of population have ever been the principal object of both. We find that when the Arabs had conquered Spain, they imposed tributes of marriageable girls; and at this day the Arabs of the desert make no treaty without stipulating for some girls and a few presents.

"The learned have agitated the question whether the Jews, like so many other nations, really sacrificed men to the Divinity. This is a dispute on words; those whom the people consecrated to the anathema were not put to death on an altar, with religious rites; but they were not the less immolated, without its being permitted to pardon any one of them.

"Leviticus (xxxvii., 29) expressly forbids the redeeming of those who shall have been devoted. Its words are, "They shall surely be put to death." By virtue of this law it was that Jephthah devoted and killed his daughter, that Saul would have killed his son, and that the prophet Samuel cut in pieces Ding Agag, Saul's prisoner. It is quite certain that God is the master of the lives of men, and that it is not for us to examine His laws. We ought to limit ourselves to believing these things and reverencing in silence the designs of God, who permitted them.

"It is also asked what right had strangers like the Jews to the land of Canaan? The answer is, that they had what God gave them.

"No sooner had they taken Jericho and Lais than they had a civil war among themselves, in which the tribes of Benjamin was almost wholly exterminated—men, women, and children; leaving only six hundred males. The people, unwilling that one of the tribes should be annihilated, bethought themselves of sacking the whole city of the tribe of Manasseh, killing all the men, old and young, all the children, all the married women, all the widows, and taking six hundred virgins, whom they gave to the six hundred survivors of the tribe of Benjamin, to restore that tribe, in order that the number of their twelve tribes might still be complete.

"Meanwhile, the Phoenicians, a powerful people, settled in the coasts from time immemorial, being alarmed at the depredations and cruelties of these newcomers, frequently chastised them; the neighboring princes united against them; and they were seven times reduced to slavery, for more than two hundred years.

"At last they made themselves a king, whom they elected by lot. This king could not be very mighty, for in the first battle which the Jews fought under him, against their masters, the Philistines, they had, in the whole army, but one sword and one lance, and not one weapon of steel. But David, their second king, made war with advantage. He took the city of Salem, afterwards so celebrated under the name of Jerusalem, and then the Jews began to make some figure on the borders of Syria. Their government and their religion took a more august form. Hitherto they had not means of rising a temple, though every neighboring nation had one or more. Solomon built a superb one, and reigned over this people about forty years.

"Not only were the days of Solomon the most flourishing days of the Jews, but all the kings upon earth could not exhibit a treasure of approaching Solomon's. His father, David, whose predecessor had not even iron, left to Solomon twenty five thousand six hundred and forty eight millions of French livres in ready money. His fleets, which went to Ophir, brought him sixty eight millions per annum in pure gold, without reckoning the silver and jewels. He had forty thousand stables, and the same number of coach-houses, twenty thousand stables for his cavalry, seven hundred wives, and three hundred concubines. Yet he had neither wood nor workmen for building his palace and the temple; he borrowed them of Hiram, King of Tyre, who also furnished gold; and Solomon gave Hiram twenty towns in payment. The commentators have acknowledged that these things need explanation, and have suspected some literal error in the copyist, who alone can have been mistaken.

"On the death of Solomon, a division took place among the twelve tribes composing the nation. The kingdom was torn asunder, and separated into two small provinces, one of which was called Judah, the other Israel—nine tribes and a half composing the Israelitish province, and only two and a half that of Judah. Then there was between these two small peoples a hatred, the more implacable as they were kinsman and neighbors, and as they had different religions; for at Sichem and at Samaria they worshipped "Baal"—giving to God a Sidonian name; while at Jerusalem, they worshipped "Adonai." At

Sichem were consecrated two calves; at Jerusalem, two cherubim—which were two winged animals with double heads, placed in the sanctuary. So, each faction having its kings, its gods, its worship, and its prophets, they made a bloody war upon each other.

"While this war was carried on, the kings of Assyria, who conquered the greater part of Asia, fell upon the Jews; as an eagle pounces upon two lizards while they are fighting. The nine and a half tribes of Samaria and Siches were carried off and dispersed forever; nor has it been precisely known to what places they were led into slavery.

"It is but twenty leagues from the town of Samaria to Jerusalem, and their territories joined each other; so that when one of these towns was enslaved by powerful conquerors, the other could not long hold out. Jerusalem was sacked several times; it was tributary to kings Hazael and Razin, enslaved under Tiglah-Pilser, three times taken by Nebuchodonosor, or Nebuchadnezzar, and at last destroyed. Zedekiah, who had been set up as king or governor by this conqueror, was led, with his whole people, into captivity in Babylonia; so that the only Jews left in Palistine were a few enslaved peasants, to sow the ground.

"As for the little country of Samaria and Sichem, more fertile than that of Jerusalem, it was re-peopled by foreign colonies, sent there by Assyrian kings, who took the name of Samaritans.

"The two and a half tribes that were slaves in Babylonia and the neighboring towns for seventy years, had time to adopt the usages of their masters, and enriched their own tongue by mixing with it the Chaldaean; this is incontestable.

"The historian Josephus tells us that he wrote first in Chaldaean, which is the language of his country. It appears that the Jews acquired but little of the science of the Magi; they turned brokers, money changers, and old clothes men; by which they made themselves necessary, as they still do, and grew rich.

"Their gains enabled them to obtain, under Cyrus, the liberty of rebuilding Jerusalem; but when they were to return into their own country, and those who had grown rich at Babylon, would not quit so fine a country for the mountains of Corlesyria, nor the fruitful banks of Euphrates and the Tigris, for the torrent of Kedron. Only the meanest part of the nation returned with Zerobabel. The Jews of Babylon contributed only their alms to the rebuilding of the city and the temple; nor was the collection a large one; for Esdras relates that no more than seventy thousand crowns could be raised for the erection of this temple, which was to be that of all the earth.

"The Jews still remained subject to Alexander; and when that great man, the excusable of all conquerors, had, in the early years of his victorious career, began to raise Alexandria, and make it the center of the commerce of the world, the Jews flocked there to exercise their trade of brokers; and there it was that their rabbis at length learned something of the sciences of the Greeks. The Greek tongue became absolutely necessary to all trading Jews.

"After Alexander's death, this people continued subject in Jerusalem to the kings of Syria, and in Alexandria to kings of Egypt; and when these kings were at war, this people always shared the fate of their subjects, and belonged to the conqueror.

"From the time of their captivity at Babylon the Jew never had particular governors taking the title of king. The pontiffs had the internal administration, and these pontiffs were appointed by their masters; they sometimes paid very high for this dignity, as the Greek patriarch at Constantinople pays for his at present.

"Under Antiochus Epiphanes they revolted; the city was once more pillaged, and the walls demolished. After a succession of similar disasters, they at length obtained for the first time, about a hundred and fifty years before the Christian era, permission to coin money, which permission was granted them by Antiochus Sidetes. They then had chiefs, who took the name of kings, and ever wore a diadem. Antigonus was the first who was decorated with this ornament, which without the power, confers but little honor.

"At that time the Romans were beginning to become formidable to the kings of Syria, masters of the Jews; and the latter gained over the Roman senate by presents and acts of submission. It seemed that the wars in Asia Minor would, for a time at least, give some relief to this unfortunate people; but Jerusalem no sooner enjoyed some shadow of liberty than it was torn by civil wars, which rendered its condition under its phantoms of kings much more pitiable than it had ever been in so long and various a succession of bondages.

"In their internecine troubles, they made the Romans their judges. Already most of the kingdoms of Asia Minor, Southern Africa, and three-fourths of Europe, acknowledged the Romans as their arbiters and masters. "Pompey came into Syria to judge the nation and to depose several petty tyrants. Being deceived by Aristobulus, who disputed the royalty of Jerusalem, he avenged himself upon him and his party. He took the city; had some of the seditious, either priests or Pharisees, crucified; and not long after, condemned Aristobulus, King of the Jews, to execution.

"The Jews, ever unfortunate, ever enslaved, and ever revolting, again brought upon them the Roman arms. Crassus and Cassius punished them; and Metellus Scipio had a son of King Aristobulus, named Alexander, the author of all the troubles, crucified.

"Under the great Caesar, they were entirely subject and peaceable. Herod, famed among them and among us, for a long time was merely tetrarch, but obtained from Antony the crown of Judaea, for which he paid dearly; but Jerusalem would not recognize this new king, because he was descended from Esau, and not from Jacob, and was merely an Idumaean. The very circumstance of his being a foreigner caused him to be chosen by the Romans, the better to keep this people in check. The Romans protected the king of their nomination with an army; and Jerusalem was again taken by assault, sacked, and pillaged.

"Herod, afterwards protected by Augustus, became one of the most powerful sovereigns among the petty kings of Arabia. He restored Jerusalem, repaired the fortifications that surrounded the temple, so dear to the Jews, and rebuilt the temple, itself; but he could not finish it, for he wanted money and workmen. This proves that, after all, Herod was not rich; and the Jews, though fond of their temple, were still fonder of their money.

"The name of king was nothing more than a favor granted by the Romans; it was not a title of succession. Soon after Herod's death, Judaea was governed as a subordinate Roman, by the proconsul of Syria, although from time to time the title of king was granted, sometime to one Jew sometimes to another, for a considerable sum of money, as under the emperor Claudius, when it was granted to the Jew Agrippa.

"A daughter of Agrippa was that Berenice, celebrated for having been beloved by one of the best emperors Rome can boast. She it was who, by the injustice she experienced from her countrymen, drew down the vengeance of the Romans upon Jerusalem. She asked for justice, and the factions of the town refused it. The seditious spirit of the people impelled them to fresh excesses. Their character at all times was to be cruel; and their fate, to be punished.

"This memorable siege, which ended in the destruction of the city, was carried on by Vespasian and Titus. The exaggerating Josephus pretends that in this short war, more than a million of Jews were slaughtered. It is not to be wondered at that an author who puts fifteen thousand men in each village should slay a million. What remained were exposed in the public markets; and each Jew was sold at about the same price as the unclean animal of which they dare not eat.

"In this last dispersion they again hoped for a deliverer; and under Adrian, whom they curse in their prayers, there arose one Baroxhebas, who called himself a second Moses—a Shiloh—a Christ. Having assembled many of these wretched people under his banners, which they believed to be sacred, he perished with all his followers. It was the last struggle of this nation, which has never lifted its head again. Its constant opinion, that barrenness is a reproach, has preserved it; the Jews have ever considered as their two first duties, to get money and children.

"From this short summary it results that the Hebrews have ever been vagrants, or robbers, or slaves, or seditious. They are still vagabonds upon the earth, and abhorred by men, yet affirming that heaven and earth and all mankind were created for them alone.

"It is evident, from the situation of Judaea, and the genius of this people, that they could not but be continually subjugated. It was surrounded by powerful and warlike nations, for which it had an aversion; so that it could neither be in alliance with them, nor protected by them. It is impossible for it to maintain itself by its marine; for it soon lost the port which in Solomon's time it had on the Red Sea; and Solomon himself always employed Tyrians to build and to steer his vessels, as well as to erect his palace and his temple. It is then manifest that the Hebrews had neither trade nor manufactures, and that they could not compose a flourishing people. They never had an army always ready for the field, like the Assyrians, the Medes, the Persians, the Syrians, and the Romans. The laborers and artisans took up arms only as occasion required, and consequently could not form well disciplined troops. Their mountains, or rather their rocks, are neither high enough, not sufficiently contiguous, to have afforded an effectual barrier against invasion. The most numerous part of the nation, transported to Babylon, Persia, and to India, or settled in Alexandria, were too much occupied with their traffic and their brokerage to think of war. Their civil government, sometimes republican, sometimes pontifical, sometimes monarchial, and very often reduced to anarchy, seems to have been no better than their military discipline.

"You ask, what was the philosophy of the Hebrews? The answer will be a very short one—they had none. Their legislator himself does not anywhere speak expressly of the immortality of the soul, nor of the rewards of another life. Josephus and Philo believe the soul to be material; their doctors admitted corporeal angels; and when they sojourned at Babylon, they gave to these angels the names given them by the Chaldeans—Michael, Gabriel, Raphael, Uriel. The name of Satan is Babylonian, and is in some wise the Arimanes of Zoroaster. The dogma of the immortality of the soul was developed only in the course of ages, and among the Pharisees. The Sadducees always denied this spirituality, this immortality, and the existence of the angels. Nevertheless, the Sadducees communicated uninterruptedly with the Pharisees, and had even sovereign pontiffs of their own sect. The prodigious difference in opinion between these two great bodies did not cause any disturbance. The Jews, in the latter times of their sojourn at Jerusalem, were scrupulously attached to nothing but the ceremonials of their law. The man who had eaten pudding or rabbit would have been stoned; while he who denied the immortality of the soul might be high-priest.

"It is commonly said that the abhorrence in which the Jews held other nations proceeded from their horror of idolatry; but it is much more likely that the manner in which they at the first exterminated some of the tribes of Canaan, and the hatred which the neighboring nations conceived for them, were the cause of this invincible aversion. As they knew no nations but their neighbors, they thought that in abhorring them they detested the whole earth, and thus accustomed themselves to be the enemies of all men.

"One proof that this hatred was not caused by the idolatry of the nations is that we find in the history of the Jews that they were very often idolaters. Solomon himself sacrificed to strange gods. After him, we find scarcely any king in the little province of Judah that does not permit the worship of these gods and offer them incense.

"The province of Israel kept its two calves and its sacred groves, or adored other divinities.

"This idolatry, with which so many nations are reproached, is a subject on which but little light has been thrown. Perhaps it would not be difficult to efface this stain upon the theology of the ancients. All polished nations had the knowledge of a supreme God, the master of the inferior gods and of men. The Egyptians themselves recognized a first principle, which they called Knef, and to which all beside was subordinate. The ancient Persians adored the good principle, Orosmanes; and were very far from sacrificing to the bad principle, Arimanes, whom they regarded nearly as we regard the devil. Even to this day, the Guebers have retained the sacred dogma of the unity of God. The ancient Brahmins acknowledged only one Supreme Being; the Chinese associated no inferior being with the Divinity, nor had any idol until the times when the populace were led astray by the worship of Fo, and the superstitions of the honzes. The Greeks and the Romans, notwithstanding the multitude of their gods, acknowledge in Jupiter the absolute sovereign of heaven and earth. Homer, himself in the most absurd poetical fictions, has never lost sight of this truth. He constantly represents Jupiter as the only Almighty, sending good and evil upon earth, and with a motion of his brow, striking gods and men with awe. Altars were raised, and sacrifices offered to inferior gods, dependent on the one supreme. There is not a single monument of antiquity in which the title of sovereign of heaven is given to any secondary deity—to Mercury, to Apollo, to Mars. The thunderbolt was ever the attribute of the master of all, and of him only.

"The idea of a sovereign being, of his providence, of his eternal decrees, is to be found among all philosophers and all poets. In short, it is perhaps as unjust to think that the ancients equaled the heroes,

266

the genii, the inferior gods, to him whom they called the father and master of the gods, as it would be ridiculous to imagine that we associate with God the blesses and the angels.

"You then ask whether the ancient philosophers and law-givers borrowed from the Jews, or the Jews from them? We must refer the question to Philo; he owns that before the translation of the Septuagint the books of his nation were unknown to strangers. So great people cannot have received their laws and their knowledge from a little people, obscure and enslaved. In the time of Osis, indeed, the Jews had no books; in his reign was accidentally found the only copy of law then in existence. This people, after their captivity at Babylon, had no other alphabet than the Chaldaean; they were not famed for any art, any manufacture whatsoever; and even in the time of Solomon they were obliged to pay dear for foreign artisans. To say that the Egyptians, the Persians, the Greeks, were instructed by the Jews, were to say that the Romans learned the arts from the people of Brittany. The Jews never were natural philosophers, nor geometricians, nor astronomers. So far were they from having public schools for the instruction of youth, that they had not even a term in their language to express such an institution.

"The people of Peru and Mexico measured their year much better than the Jews. Their stay in Babylon and in Alexandria, during which individuals might instruct themselves formed the people to no art save that of usury. They never knew how to stamp money; and when Antiochus Sidetes permitted them to have a coinage of their own, they were almost incapable of profiting by this permission for four or five years. Indeed, this coin is said to have been struck at Samaria. Hence, it is, that Jewish medals are so rare, and nearly all false. In short, we find in them only an ignorant and barbarous people, who have long united the most sordid avarice with the most detestable superstition and the most invincible hatred for every people by whom they are tolerated and enriched. Still, we ought not to burn them."

From Voltaire to Heinrich Heine is a long step only in time. The natures of the men were very similar, in spite of the difference between the two worlds into which they were both injected. Heine began as a Jew, the career which was to make him the pre-eminent man of letters of his century. He began on the lowest rung of the ladder: I feel safe in letting the case rest where he leaves it in his famous ballad entitled *Disputation.*

To make it readable in English, I have had to take some important liberties, both of rhyme and rhythm:

In the aula at Toledo
all the trumpeters are blowing.
From the city to the tourney
merrily the mass is flowing.

This is not to be a combat
wherein steel on steel advances.
Finely edged and deft scholastic
words will be the only lances.

Gallant Paladins whose thoughts are
only for the sex that fires
have surrendered the arena
to the rabbis and the friars.

For the iron helmets wherein
All high matters are disputed
scapula and *arbei-confuss*
this day will be substituted.

Which God is the true and only
God? The one whose brawny story
Rabbi Judah of Navarre says
is the fabric of man's glory?

Or the Christian God the Friar
Jose the Franciscan swears is
Father, Holy Ghost and Saviour
as the crucifix he wears is?

Out of a profound conviction
backed by logic learned at college
and quotations from authorities
one cannot but acknowledge,

they will argue out the matter;
each will set a little faster
the procession of the facts that
will decide which God is master.

They have both agreed beforehand
that, no matter how contrary,
he who loses shall embrace the
godhead of his adversary.

For the Jew, should he be vanquished,
baptism is the grim provision.
And the Christian, if he lose, must
undergo a circumcision.

Each one had eleven followers,
brave as only champions could be,
pledged to share his fate no matter
what the outcome of it would be.

So that while the Friar's backers
with unflinching faith and steady
hold the sacred water vessels
for a lively Christening ready,

swinging sprinkling brooms and censers
wherefrom incense smoke is rising,
briskly do the rabbi's followers
whet their knives for circumcising.

In the hall, prepared for battle,
rest, relentless, both the forces,
and the crowd awaits the signal,
eager for the brave discourses.

Underneath the golden canopy,
with their courtiers gathered round them,
beam the king and queen. The queen is
such a child, it does confound them.

Pert French nose, small chin, and tiny
white teeth roguishly, beguiling:
bright, bewitching are the rubies
of her mouth when she is smiling.

What a change is this from Paris!
What a horror to befall her!
Known at home as Blanche de Bourbon,
Donna Blanca here they call her!

And the king's name is Don Pedro,
with the nickname of *The Cruel*.
But this day he looks a little
less the brute and more the fool.

If the smile he gives the friars
to the Jews is no less sunny,
it's because they lead his troops and,
more important, lend him money.

Now the sound of drum and trumpet
blare the signal. Soon the battle
of religions is to break out,
and the wordy sabers rattle.

The Franciscan friar opened
with a burst of sacred passion,
and his voice now harsh, now growling,
crowed up in a curious fashion:

"In the name of God the Father
and the Son and Ghost," he cried out,
"Let me first make sure that every
Devilish sprite in you has died out."

(He had learnt that in such combats
little devils oft have hidden
In the insides of the Jews, and
prompted them when they were chidden.)

Having thus yanked out the devil
with his loudest exorcism,
the Franciscan flared with dogmas
quoted from the catechism.

Firstly, he explained, the godhead,
wherein three are comprehended,
may be one God, when convenient,
or the three in one God blended.

Then he told how in a stable,
with its beasts of burden laden,
God was born, and how his mother
bore Him yet remained a maiden.

How they recognized His presence
in the Bethlehem stable manger,
with a calf and heifer lowing
meekly round the lighted stranger.

How the Saviour, now grown older,
from king Herod's minions flying,
went to Egypt and, still later,
bowed to Pilate, still defying,

and was crucified. How Pilate
really wanted to release him,
but the cursed Jew cried only
crucifixion would appease him.

How the Lord, albeit buried
in a dark and bowldered prison,
on the third day into heaven
had in princely triumph risen.

And when as the proper time comes
he'll return to earth in splendor
at Jerosophat to judge them,
every jewborn proud offendor.

"Tremble Jews!" the friar thundered.
"It is he whom you tormented
cruelly, with thorns and scourges,
and your lying unrepented!

"It is plain that the vindictive,
foul and conscienceless behaviour
that resulted in the murder
of our precious one the Saviour,

"still is strong in you, O demons,
spewed out by the lower regions;
that your bodies are the barracks
of the Devil's scary legions.

"Is not this the grave opinion
of Aquinas famed in story
as the Mighty Ox of Learning
by the monks of pious glory?

"O you Jews! you are hyenas,
wolves and jackals foul and hateful,
graveyard prowlers who think only
those who lick the great are grateful.

"Not content with being monkeys,
gallows-birds and bate perfidious,
you must emulate the mud-born
crocodile and vampire hideous.

"You are owls and you are ravens,
rattlesnakes, disgusting adders,
cockatrices, screech-owls, Christ will
trample out like empty bladders.

"Toads and blindworms vipers! must you
really burn? Or would you rather
save your souls? Then flee the rabbi
to the bosom of the Father.

"Seek the church of love, the bright one,
where the well of mercy bubbles.
Bow your head into the hallowed
basin and wash off your troubles.

"Wash away the ancient Adam
and the vices that efface it.
From your heart the stain of rancor
wash, that God's love might replace it.

"You can surely hear the Saviour.
And how well your new names suit you!
On his bosom shed the Cohens
and the Levys that pollute you.

"For our God is love incarnate,
like a little lamb that's cherished.
To atone your sins he let you
nail him on the cross, and perished.

"Therefore we are mild and human,
slow to get into a passion,
fond of peace and charitable,
in the Saviour's gentle fashion.

"And hereafter up in heaven,
into seraphim converted,
we shall wander, blest forever,
lilies in our hands inserted.

"We shall walk in spotless raiment
(Not the stupid gray we're wearing!)
Made of silk, brocade and muslin,
Ribbons brightening to daring.

"On our tonsures golden tresses
where the bald spots now distress them!
Charming virgins deft of finger
into pretty knots will dress them.

"In those higher spheres the goblets
in circumference so spacious
will, for holding golden wine, be
infinitely more capacious.

"On the other hand, much smaller
than the mouths of earthly ladies
will the mouths be of the darlings
of whose joy our rapture made is.

"So in drinking, laughing, kissing
we shall pass the ages proudly,
singing happy hallelujahs,
singing sacredly and loudly."

Here the friar ceased. His followers,
sensing an illumination,
hastened forward with their vessels,
for the baptism-operation.

But the water-hating Hebrews
seemed obsessed with sickly grinning;
and the rabbi of Navarre rose,
cleared his throat, and made beginning:

"For the sake of my salvation,
I suppose, you have be-howled me,
and with dung-carts of abuse and
barrows full of insults fouled me.

"Each man follows but the method
 to his wants best calculated.
So, instead of being angry,
thank you, I'm propitiated.

"First, your Trinitarian doctrine
Jews will never learn to swallow.
You might teach them how to see it,
but you cannot make them follow.

"That three persons in your godhead
and no more are comprehended
is most moderate. The ancients
on six thousand gods depended.

"I am ignorant entirely
of this God of yours, my brother.
Nor have I the precious honor
to have met his virgin mother.

"I regret that some twelve hundred
Years back (your church professes)
he should have encountered with us
grievous disagreeablenesses.

"That the Jews in truth destroyed him
rests upon your say-so solely,
the *delicta corpus* having
on the third day vanished wholly.

"It is equally uncertain
whether he is a connection
of our God who never married
to the best of our recollection.

"Our God like a bleeding lambkin
for his people perish? Never.
He is not so philanthropic,
and, besides, too precious clever.

"He is far from love incarnate.
Rarely to affection yields he.
God of thunder, God of vengeance,
thunders not caresses wields he.

"Yes, our God is great and living.
In his heavenly hall is glory,
and compared with him eternal
ages are but transitory.

"He is living. He is lusty.
Not a priestly myth to fright us,
Like your consecrated wafer,
or the shadow of Cocytus.

"He is strong and He is daring.
Sun and moon and constellation
in his hands, like people, vanish
when he frowns his indignation.

"Ah that terrifying greatness,
sings King David, none can measure!
Heaven his throne and earth his footstool
are but playthings of his pleasure!

"He is fond of pleasing music.
Festal hymns to Him are grateful.
But like grunts of suckling pigs He
finds the chimes of churches hateful.

"Where Leviathan the mighty
swims the awful floorless ocean,
now and then the Lord will tease him
and the waves into commotion,

"(save, of course, upon the ninth day
of the month of Ab, the morrow
when they burnt his holy temple –
that is still his day of sorrow!),

"more than a hundred miles Leviathan
measures, and the sea's his feeder,
Bigger than Og King of Bashan,
with a tail thick as a cedar.

"But his flesh is very dainty,
and its flavor is perfection,
as God's favorites will find out
on the day of resurrection.

"God will choose among the pious
only those whose faith was stable,
and for them, and for them only,
will he set his golden table.

"With a little garlic whitely
dressed, and browned in wine, and toasted,
pieces of Leviathan will
look like Matelotes roasted.

"Can you see white garlic gravy
that horseradish bits embellish?
Such a dainty even our friar
Jose and his friends would relish.

"And the raisin sauce about it
makes a most delicious jelly.
You have but to taste it and it's
practically in your belly.

"What the Lord has cooked is for you,
fish and meat. If you are able
to withstand a circumcision,
you're assured a place at table."

Smirking, smiling, spoke the rabbi,
words enticing and insulting;
and the sound the other Jews made
with their carvers was exulting,

as though it were but a matter
of arranging for the friar
to give up the precious foreskin,
forfeit to the rabbi's ire.

But the monks remained unshaken
by the rabbi's sour derision,
and were far from being ready
to submit to circumcision.

And the Friar Jose hotly
cried: "The Jew has disregarded
reason, and the laws of logic
most ignobly has discarded.

"What has fish to do with wafer?
Raisin sauce with Christ's salvation?
Shall a touch of garlic banish
the bad odor of a nation?

"From the rabbi's shameless bragging
one cannot determine whether
This Jew-God of his is fiddler,
lawyer, cook or toreador.

"Is my garb that of a jester?
Do I look as if I'd fool them?
I advise baptismal water
though it might no more than cool him".

To this speech the cautious rabbi
with a fawning answer followed.
He was boiling over. But a
Hebrew's gall is better swallowed.

He recited from the Mishna
treatises and commentaries,
quoted from the Tausvus-Yontoff
where it delicately varies.

And the angry friar mourning
arguments he was in want of,
raged: "I hope the devil takes you
with your graceless Tausvus-Yontoff."

"Can profanity go further!"
Up the rabbi leaps and screeches,
and the patient years forgotten,
like a maniac's now his speech is.

"If the Tausvus-Yontoff's nothing,
What remains O vile detractor!
Lord, you cannot overlook this!
Punish, God, this malefactor!

"Is not Tausvus-Yontoff really
your own very self? And can he
go on living who has used your
name more wretchedly than any?

"Bid the earth consume him like the
wicked followers of Korah
whose misdeeds were not against you
but against your holy Torah?

"Punish, Lord, this wicked baseness
with your loudest thunder's thunder;
with the pith and brimstone with which
you laid Sodom's sinners under.

"Show this old capuchin what you
did to Pharaoh to assure him
that you really meant to free us.
Smite him, but you need not cure him.

"With a hundred thousand warriors
marched Mizzrayim's lord and master,
all in armor shining, but you
marched before us, stronger, faster.

"You but raised your arm to drown them.
Pharaoh and his host were smitten
with less effort than this friar
needs to drown a common kitten.

"Strike, Jehovah, at this baldhead
that the wicked may see clearly
that the lightnings of your anger
are not smoke and bluster merely.

"Then I'll sing your praise and glory,
evermore and O so proudly.
I will dance and sing like Miriam.
I will even sing more loudly."

At this point the outraged friar
interrupted in a fury:
"God Almighty, if you heard him,
Slay him and his lousy Jewry.

"Before Ashtoreth and Belial,
Lucifer whose vain ambition
blindly led him with the rebel
angels down into perdition,

"I defy and mock you, rabbi,
with your devilfish unsavory.
I have eaten Jesus Christ and
I am proof against your knavery.

"O instead of talking to you
I would sooner roast and bake you,
You and all your race, upon a
Funeral pyre, devil take you!"

So the rabbi and the friar
merge the fight in chaos utter.
Plainly it is pointless for them
to go on to rail and stutter.

Twelve long hours this thing has lasted,
neither showing signs of tiring,
though the ladies stifle half yawns
and their gallants are perspiring.

Even the court has grown impatient.
So the king, to end their snarling,
holds his hands up, and to Donna
Blanca turns, and asks that darling:

"Tell me, frankly, your opinion.
Who is right here, who is liar?
To whom would you give the verdict,
to the rabbi or the friar?"

Donna Blanca's eyes are thoughtful
that before had shone so gladly.
Donna Blanca's childlike mouth is
wistful as she answers sadly:

"How can I say who is right here?
Whose the precious truth is solely?
But I fear me both the rabbi
and the friar smell most foully!"

CPSIA information can be obtained
at www.ICGtesting.com
Printed in the USA
BVHW082307021019
560015BV00009B/188/P